# CONVOYS TO RUSSIA 1941-1945

*HMS SCORPION accompanies Russia bound merchant ships through the surface fog so prevalent in Arctic waters.*

# CONVOYS TO RUSSIA

## Allied Convoys and Naval Surface Operations in Arctic Waters 1941-1945

"The whole thing is a most unsound operation
with the dice loaded against us in every direction"

(First Sea Lord, Admiral of the Fleet Sir Dudley Pound to Chief of Naval Operations,
Fleet Admiral Ernest King, 18 May 1942)

**by**

**Bob Ruegg and Arnold Hague**

# CONTENTS



*Front cover: Convoy PQ18 under air attack*
*Rear cover: The Russian Icebreaker FEDOR LITKE, 23rd February 1942*




**First published in 1992 by the World Ship Society**
**28 Natland Road, Kendal, LA9 7LT England,**
**Revised and augmented edition published 1993**

**ISBN 0 905617 66 5**

## INTRODUCTION

This book stems from research commenced in 1988 following the decision to extend the period of application for the Soviet Arctic Commemorative Medal. It rapidly became apparent that no listing existed of ships which participated in events in the North 1941-45 , neither were the available records at the Public Record Office complete. This text is the result of two years' research aimed at producing a complete list of all vessels, naval and mercantile, that took part in operations connected with North Russia in the period 21 June 1941 to the end of 1945.

It is stressed that ALL ships that participated have been included except submarines, the researchers having felt that it would be invidious to exclude vessels that played any part in a convoy passage or operation, yet did not arrive in a Russian port. Therefore, warships which provided cover for Arctic convoys, or which participated in operations that had no merchant content, are included. The Home Fleet, which provided massive cover for many of the Arctic operations, quite often had to have the destroyer screen in three distinct parts as endurance dictated that destroyers had to leave to refuel. Specifically excluded are submarines that operated off North Norway, except where they did so as part of an individual convoy: it proved too complex to assess whether or not at some time in a particular patrol there was a connection with a specific operation.

While the material in the book has been derived from official sources, the work should not be used as authority for claims of any sort, including requests for medals.

Also included in the general text are lists of the independent passages made by merchant ships, principally Russian. Unfortunately, lack of records in Britain has prevented the listing of voyages undertaken in Russian waters, save for a brief account of the movements of the tanker HOPEMOUNT, which serves as an example of less common duties.


## ACKNOWLEDGEMENTS

In a work of this complexity, the assistance of many people is vital, and the authors are grateful for the way in which their task has been eased by willing co-operation. In some cases, the sheer volume of assistance, or the importance of sources or information made available, demands individual recognition. Therefore the authors wish to thank Rodney Agutter, Roy Leach, Alan Niven and Steve Pearson for their long and tedious work checking multiple lists; Ken Macpherson and Paul Kemp for assistance with photographs; Miss Jenny Wraight for her unfailing ability to produce source material at the Guildhall Library; David Brown and his colleagues at Naval Historical Branch, Alan Francis and Mike McAloon, for help and encouragement, and Michael Crowdy who undertook the unenviable task of editing an unwieldy manuscript. There has also been help from overseas (in addition to Ken Macpherson already mentioned), here W R Hultgren has been of particular value as his percipient questions have caused extra information to be searched out, and errors to be exposed. Colonel Danilov of Moscow was also a welcome source of photographs, and an additional contact in Russia. To all who have encouraged us over the past two years, whether mentioned individually or not, go our thanks and our hope that the end result will be of value to all.

## PHOTOGRAPHIC ACKNOWLEDGEMENTS

With the exception of those illustrations listed shortly, all photographs are drawn from the authors private collections and consist largely of Admiralty or other official views. The panorama of Murmansk, and photographs of Soviet warships were made available by Professor Danilov of Moscow; photographs of Polyarnoe, HMS SOMALI and onboard HMS ONSLAUGHT are the property of World Ship Society member Mr Swanson, who served onboard during the ship's first commission in Northern waters. Some photographs illustrating the early convoys come from a collection of prints by the late Captain Youngs, O.B.E., R.N.R., an Officer of HMS SPEEDWELL, then based in North Russia, the sinking of HMS LEDA was contributed by Ken Macpherson.

Without exception, all photographs were taken during preparation for, or in the course of, operations or convoys to or from North Russia; in the majority of cases specific dates or convoys can be attributed to the illustrations.

The former Admiralty archive no longer exists, however some parts of it, and many of the official wartime photographs, are now held by the Imperial War Museum, as is also the "Speedwell" collection, itself of fascinating content. Readers are recommended to consult Mr Paul Kemp of the Photographic Department of the I.W.M., himself the author of the pictorial "Russian Convoys" in the Warship Illustrated series, and the excellent visual presentation on supplies to Russia which has been prepared and is available to visitors by appointment.

# Supplies to Russia

Upon the invasion by Germany of the USSR, a nation which had, at best, been a dubious neutral became one of the Allies, however dissimilar the political views of Britain and the USSR might have been. The situation is best summed up by a remark attributed to Winston Churchill that "If Hitler invaded Hell, I would at least make a favourable reference to the Devil."

Supplies to Russia came, initially, solely from British sources with a greatly increasing quantity from America from January 1942 onwards. There were three routes for supply, via the North Russian ports of Archangel and Murmansk with which this book is concerned, via the Persian Gulf and rail links to the USSR, and in Russian ships from the West Coast USA to Vladivostok via the north Pacific, Russia and Japan not then being at war. Not surprisingly, this last was little used, if only because of the scarcity of Russian tonnage outside Russian waters; some 2% of supplies went by this route. The Persian Gulf route, almost entirely used for supplies from the USA, accounted for just over 75% of all supplies to Russia, while the North Russian convoy route lifted the balance of 23%.

Cargo inward was entirely war material, or directly connected with the war effort. In the case of supplies via Murmansk etc, the cargoes can be divided between those for immediate use in the Northern theatre of operations and which therefore had an immediate effect on the land fighting there, and those for use by Russian industry or general use in the USSR.

Items for reuse were, for example, explosives in bulk (taking PQ 18 as an example, cargo included over 11,000 tons of TNT), and motor transport for local and nationwide use (PQ 18 lifted 4,400 motor vehicles of all sorts) while "local use" included aircraft (in the early days Hurricanes shipped from the UK comprised the major fighter component in the Murmansk area), and fuel oil for the Northern Fleet and British ships needing to refuel in Russian ports.

Once again using PQ 18 as a reasonably typical convoy, the 39 ships which sailed carried 4,400 vehicles, 835 tanks, 566 aircraft, over 11,000 tons of high explosive, over 157,000 tons of general cargo, and 9,541 tons of fuel oil (this last item excluding that carried in the escort oilers).

Passengers were also carried: Service drafts for the parties based at Archangel and Murmansk, diplomatic and industrial personnel for Moscow, relief crews for merchant ships, repatriated survivors, and Russians proceeding abroad on duty. Most ships outward bound from Russia were, for obvious reasons, in ballast but, where circumstances permitted, the Russians loaded cargo to obtain desperately needed currency. Such cargo included large quantities of lumber, some ores (principally chrome), apatite, cotton, tobacco etc. Sometimes somewhat unusual items appear: 17 tons of badger hair, over 50 tons of caviar, and a quantity of rags figure in one ship's manifest!

### Cargo shipped to North Russia in a typical convoy (PQ 18)

| Ships from UK | Vehicles | Tanks | Aircraft | Explosives | Other cargo |
|---|---|---|---|---|---|
| 11 | 312 | 230 | 271 | 1,601 tons | 37,799 tons |
| Ships from USA | | | | | |
| 16 | 2,588 | 384 | 175 | 7,297 tons | 72,288 |
| Total | **2,900** | **614** | **446** | **8,898 tons** | **110,087 tons** |
| PLUS LOSSES | | | | | |
| Ships ex UK | | | | | |
| 4 | 123 | 89 | 38 | 134 tons | 10,862 tons |
| Ships ex USA | | | | | |
| 8 | 1,385 | 132 | 82 | 2,249 tons | 36,554 tons |
| Total shipped | **4,408** | **835** | **566** | **11,281 tons** | **157,503 tons** |

**PLUS 9,541 tons of fuel oil, lost in the tanker ATHELTEMPLAR**

# The Threat

At all times, the German threat based in northern Norway contained two elements, either air and surface combined or air and submarine.

The surface threat was posed by the presence in the far North of major units of the surface fleet, headed by TIRPITZ. This modern battleship armed with 8 15in guns, arrived in Norway in January 1942 and, despite being damaged in varying degrees between September 1943 and July 1944 required the constant presence in British waters of at least two battleships and one fleet carrier operational at all times. Furthermore, these ships of the Home Fleet had to be constantly available in support of the Russian convoys lest a sortie be made.

## NORTH RUSSIAN TERMINALS AND LIKELY AREAS OF ATTACK

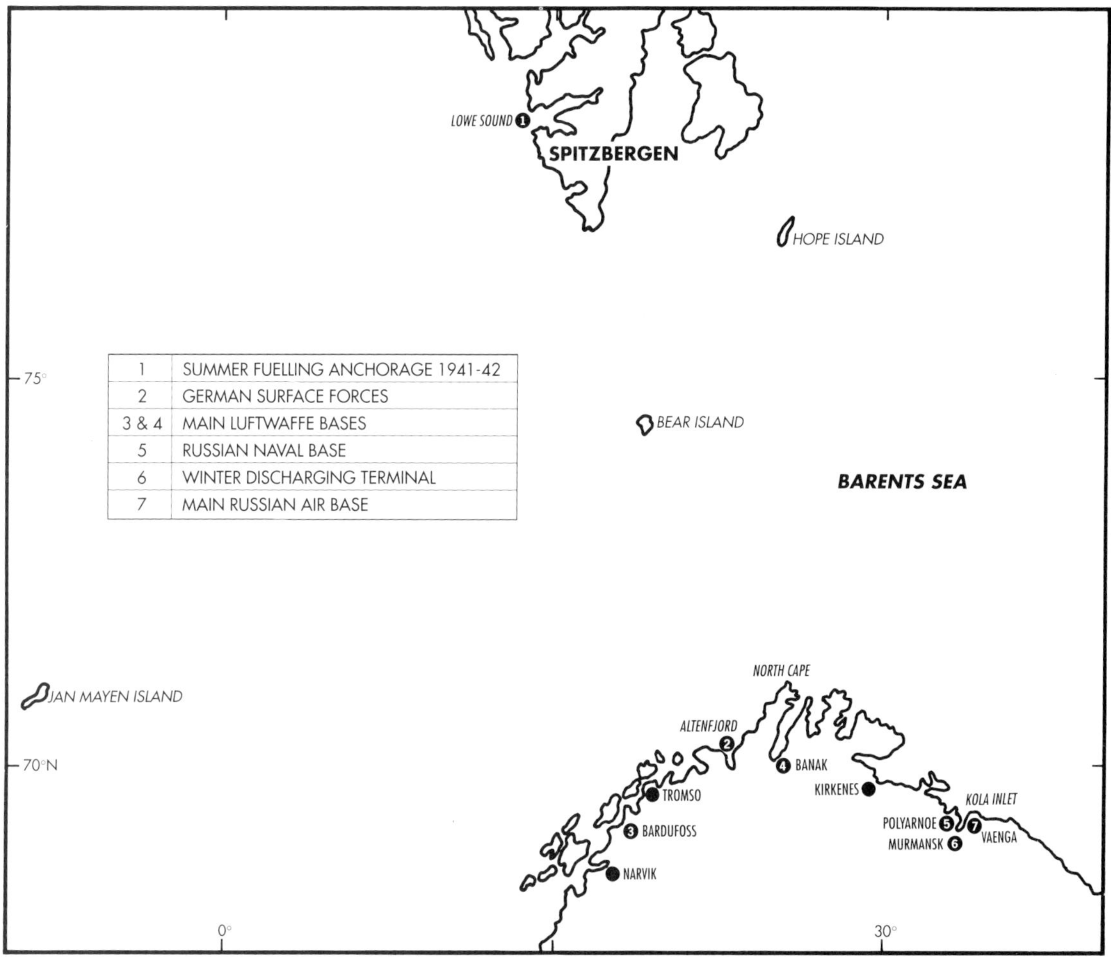


TIRPITZ was supported in 1943 by the battlecruiser SCHARNHORST, armed with 9 11in guns, and in 1942 and 1943 by one or other of the two armoured ships ADMIRAL SCHEER and LUTZOW (6 11in guns), the cruisers ADMIRAL HIPPER and PRINZ EUGEN (8 8in guns), and cruisers KOLN and NURNBERG (9 5.9in guns). German destroyers based in Norway were also heavily armed either with five 5.9 or five 5in guns.

All of these ships enjoyed the advantage that they could sortie at will, choosing the time and position for attack, whereas the escorts had to be on the alert at all times.

Surface ships, by sheer threat, posed major problems for the convoys; actual performance as measured by the Barentz Sea and North Cape actions was most disappointing for the Germans. Indeed, the complete failure of the attack on JW 51B led to the dismissal of the German Commander-in-Chief and the virtual disbandment of the surface fleet.

German submarine strength in Norway generally varied greatly, rising from 4 in January 1942 to around 40 in 1943, declining to 20 in 1944/45. Not all of these were allocated to the convoy route and the height of submarine operations on the Russian route was in late 1944 and early 1945 when about 20 boats were available and deployed. These were greatly assisted by the deplorable Asdic conditions created by thermal layers in the cold northern waters, and in the end the only effective means of attack was by carrier borne aircraft on submarines caught on the surface when endeavouring to close convoys. The submarines remained the major threat to the convoys to the end.

Air strength available for attacks on convoys varied greatly; in early 1942 the Luftwaffe disposed of some 60 bombers and 30 dive bombers able to intercept the convoys. By June of that year (the time of PQ 17 and PQ 18), numbers had risen to over 100 Ju 88 bombers, 30 dive bombers, about 50 torpedo bombers and 30 long range reconnaissance aircraft. The Kriegsmarine also controlled a substantial number of reconnaissance aircraft.

The numbers of aircraft, particularly torpedo carriers, declined sharply after PQ 18, partly due to heavy casualties and also to the more pressing need for the squadrons in the Mediterranean where they were to remain until the winter of 1944 when they returned to northern Norway. The success of the attacks on PQ 18 was, however, not repeated, and the air threat declined thereafter.

# The Senior British Naval Officer, North Russia (SBNONR)

With the entry of the USSR into the war, and the commencement of naval operations and convoys to and off North Russia, it became necessary to establish a Royal Navy presence in the area. Accordingly, the appointment of SBNONR was made, a Rear Admiral, with a small shore staff originally located in Murmansk, later moving to Polyarnoe the headquarters of the Commander-in-Chief, Russian Northern Fleet. A SBNO with staff was also

*HMS MATCHLESS alongside the Polyarnoe Naval Base in December 1943.*

based at Archangel, and after the move to Polyarnoe in 1943 there was a similar appointment at Murmansk to handle affairs there. The original organisation at Murmansk was known as Naval Party 100 and they, plus the ships' companies of the submarines based there in 1941 and the 1st and 6th Minesweeper Flotillas and other attached ships which served there for many months at a time in 1941 to 1943, were the basis for the formation in the 1980s of the North Russian Club, all of whose members had both served in Russian Convoys AND been operationally employed in Russian waters or ashore in Russia.

Relations at Murmansk with the Soviet Navy were, generally, good, and with the port under the operational control of the Northern Fleet, the needlessly obstructive attitude of civilian and political officials was of lesser consequence than at Archangel where such authorities wielded much greater power in the absence of a senior naval commander on the Russian side.

Communications at Murmansk were a major problem, the town and harbour and the naval HQ being on opposite sides of the Inlet, while the anchorage for escorts lay even further away. Communications, whether by road, telephone or W/T were very difficult and it was normal for a minesweeper to be held alongside at Murmansk to provide a W/T link between shore staff and the anchorage, while the provision of adequate boats to serve the shipping anchored off was never properly resolved. Open boats were unsuitable in winter weather, and the 72 foot Motor Launch shipped out for use finally arrived in July 1945! A trawler (HMS CHILTERN) was retained for winter use as a despatch boat, although even she could be immobilised by poor coal.

Almost all stores used by the base party and attached ships, and by convoys forming in Russia, had to be shipped in, including fuel. It was to be 1943 before adequate reserves could be built up and ammunition dumps prepared; prior to that a number of special trips had to be made to Russia by HM Ships to freight ammunition to escorts who had severely depleted their stocks on the way to North Russia.

Medical facilities were poor, and Russian resources ( and practices ) were totally inadequate by British standards; unfortunately political interference for some reason prevented the provision of British facilities ashore until the end of 1942, and even then the position was not good.

Relations locally varied greatly, apparently dictated by events far away in Moscow. Obscure and infinitely varying rules greatly affected the provision of stores, mail and individuals even though intended for RN ships and use. Even personnel arriving for duty had to have passports and visas, which were at the mercy of Customs and Immigration officials, not Russian naval authorities. There was a constant litany of complaint, indeed despair, at the problems so created.

The SBNONR had one further problem: by virtue of his rank he was the senior British Officer present in North Russia, and as such the authorities appear to have regarded him as responsible for all Britons in the area, regardless of Service or civilian status. In consequence, the unfortunate incumbent found himself embroiled in disputes of discipline onboard merchant ships, between Merchant Navy personnel and the Soviet authorities, and between members of other Services and the Russians. One problem, regarding an Army DEMS gunner, signed on Ship's Articles of course, who had upset the Russians by his comments (whilst drunk) on Communism as seen in a North Russian wartime winter, took the Rear Admiral many months to sort out, his principal efforts being to extract the sergeant from Russian hands and return him to Britain.

The following text is part of a report compiled by the Senior British Naval Officer, North Russia, dated June 1944, and forwarded to the Admiralty for information and guidance. This is an abridged version of the original text which is contained in file ADM199/1104 in the Public Record Office at Kew.

# MURMANSK

The following notes have been compiled for the information of those in Britain who have to work with us here in Murmansk, and for those who may be appointed to work out here.

## The Kola Inlet

The Kola Inlet runs roughly North and South from 69.18N to the town (village) of Kola in 68.53N where the River Kola runs in, thereafter the Inlet is known as the River Tuloma.

On the western shore and about five and a half miles inside the mouth of the Inlet lies Polyarnoe where the Commander-in-Chief of the Russian Northern Fleet has his administration and where the Senior British Naval Officer, North Russia is also placed. The latter is a Rear Admiral, and administers Archangel, Murmansk, Polyarnoe and Vaenga and has the operational control of our warships and the JW and RA convoys to and from these waters. Eight miles by water and on the opposite shore lies Vaenga where we have an Auxiliary Hospital with beds for 74 patients and the necessary staff. A large Russian operational aerodrome is there, and a pier, at which destroyers and smaller craft can berth, serves the village from the water. There is no power of any kind on this pier but water is laid on — not fit for drinking. Vaenga is the Northern terminus of the railroad, a single track from Murmansk which only appears to be used for goods traffic for war stores; the road from Murmansk also stops there. Twelve miles down this road is Rosta, a naval repair yard with two dry-docks, the larger capable of holding a 9,000 ton cruiser, the smaller a Fleet destroyer, there are also an oil and a coaling jetty. Four miles further south comes Murmansk.

From the above it will be seen that our administrative centre and Murmansk are 16 miles by road plus 8 miles by water apart, or 21 miles by water. During many months of the year, for perhaps 3 days at a stretch, ice, snow and blizzards will render the road impassable; fog and gales in the Inlet will render the same disservice for boat traffic and a highly temperamental telephone is all that remains. Therefore it is in the highest degree important that the correct address for stores and correspondence should be used. SBNO North Russia is at Polyarnoe, SBNO Murmansk is in that delectable city and has to do with the merchant ships from convoys: many Authorities still appear to believe that these two posts are the same.

## Murmansk

Murmansk lies along the Eastern shore of the Inlet from 69N to 68.57N and from 33.03E to 33.05E. Further expansion to the East is problematical as the country is hilly and very rocky in that direction. Up till 1928 it was a small town of wooden buildings with some coastal traffic and fairly extensive fisheries. Then it was decided to expand it as the Soviet's ice-free Northern port and an ambitious building programme in brick and cement was embarked on, while the quays were added to and an adequate system of lines was laid to serve these quays by rail. The outbreak of war stopped this scheme and, in 1942, it was subjected to the most severe bombing attack then inflicted on any European city, Valetta perhaps excepted. The wooden construction of so many buildings and almost all the quays rendered large areas of the town only too susceptible to incendiary attack, while the unreliability of cement under Arctic conditions produced unhappy results in the larger buildings. Throughout the summer of 1942 the town continued to smoulder and by the end, almost all the Northern half of the town had gone, while a considerable part of the remainder was heavily damaged: at a rough estimate in June 1944, one third has been entirely demolished, one third is not fit for habitation and not one single building has a half of its full complement of glass. Repairs and a little new building have been started recently.

Quite recently two provision shops have blossomed out into most appetising windows displaying hams, sausages and fish, made of wood. They avoid the charge of acquiring one's roubles under false pretences by having nothing on sale within whatever. Later on the individual citizen may dispose of his surplus vegetables there, otherwise they are merely two of the food centres where the Comrades may draw their daily rations. Otherwise the only things to draw one's eye are crude war posters. The social life appears to be confined to Clubs, in Murmansk there are four, one army, two navy and an International sailor's club. Only the latter has made the slightest attempt at extending hospitality to the British and American Missions here and, during convoys, it is rather a place to be avoided. We lend films for showing there and that is the only evening amusement except, that at times, the films are followed by a dance.

Recreations are very few. In winter there is ski-ing and it is good fun from February until the middle of April, but the country does not lend itself to real running, the Russians chiefly confine themselves to cross country work and, at the beginning of April, held a Northern Winter Sports meeting at which 5, 7 and 10 kilometre races for men and women were held.

Occasional travelling concert parties of the ENSA type, and equally mediocre, visit a hall in one of the clubs and charge one an extortionate number of roubles for a very hard seat. Once the snow is off the low lying land,

*The ruined town of Murmansk in 1942, showing the extent of the devastation. Sunken ships and a huge fire in the docks area in the background.*

about the first half of June, football starts. Our own experience has been that the games are well-conducted, the men are fit but not very expert, though that may only be so at the start of the season, and the crowd is friendly to British sides.

Sporadic gardening, strictly utilitarian, is also in evidence, but its outward appearance would shame any Village Allotment Committee out of business in Britain. It appears that the State provides the seeds or seedlings and demands a third or less of the crop, depending on the type of seed provided ie potatoes or seedlings—one third, but seeds—less. For the information of ships visiting here, it should be noted that the Russian audiences at any entertainment — football, concert or films, are very well behaved, enthusiastic and critical, though the small-boy element at football matches can be excluded from the first category.

## General conditions

From 3rd December until 19th January the sun does not rise above the horizon, so from 3 to 5 hours twilight around midday are little help to working conditions. The opposite obtains from 3rd June to 19th July and print can be read in the open at any hour of the day from the end of April until late in August.

In the winter the snow and Northern Lights prevent absolute darkness except during blizzards, which have been rare in the winter of 1943/44 and snow squalls. The lowest observed day temperature was minus 10F, with the night temperature 15 degrees or more lower. In still weather this temperature is not really troublesome to those who are well nourished and adequately clothed, with wind accompanying these temperatures one feels it on ears and face, though walking will keep the rest of one's body quite warm. Snow continues to fall until some time in June and will start again at the end of August or early in September. A general thaw set in about mid April 1944, low lying snow had gone by the end of May, but patches still lie on the hills at the time of writing, the end of June. The main Inlet remains ice-free though bays and spaces between quays become frozen over, however the rise and fall of the tide and the constant movements of shipping prevent this ice becoming thick enough to be troublesome.

In trying to picture the working of this Port by British eyes, the above conditions must constantly be borne in mind, other factors which materially affect a true estimate are that the artificial light necessary to work cargoes for 4 months of the year must obviously be kept at a minimum with the Front a bare 30 miles away and are subject to constant interruptions for Air Alerts.

Steam machinery must be constantly watched and warmed through or it will become frozen up and the same applies to all mechanical vehicles. Roads become filled with powdery snow, constantly churned up, which yet acquires sufficient solidity between the wheel tracks to suspend a vehicle from its under-carriage, leaving its wheels air-borne. Constant snow falls bury items of cargo feet deep on the quays and these can quite easily disappear until the thaw. Gloves can only be discarded for short spells, so that such simple operations as screwing a shackle through a cargo sling or passing a wire strop will take a vast time and will probably be inefficiently done.

Interpreters. of whom there are never enough, are girls from the Technical College in Moscow, and the simplest nautical terms are a sealed book to them. Russia possesses no race of seamen. Authorities in the docks are usually drawn from civil engineers. As an example, the Chief Dock Pilot wearing the uniform of a Lieutenant Commander of the Reserve asked the writer whether the DUKE OF YORK, then in the Inlet, was a destroyer!.

## Authorities (a) Town

The military side of life in Murmansk, which means nine tenths of its existence, is administered by an Engineer Rear Admiral who is also Admiral Superintendent to the Northern Fleet based on Polyarnoe. In the last resort he can galvanise any department into activity though his Staff is prone to ''pass the baby''.

The Diplomatic Representative is the link between the Foreign Missions and the Russian Departments and can be most helpful, or the reverse. Entry and exit visas on passports, many types of local permits and similar snags are, or can be, dealt with by him.

The Commissar of Militzia—relative rank of Major General — is in charge of that Force, i.e. Police, this latter name having been changed owing to its unhappy associations in the peoples' minds. He can be of real help in connection with obstreperous seamen ashore, driving offences and so on.

The Mayor has to do with town accommodation, though the majority now comes under one or other of the services.

Intourist — Manager. Hotel for travellers, victualling of Foreign Missions, railway tickets and seat reservations, domestic staffs for the Missions and can provide an excellent meal if a dinner-party becomes necessary.

## (b) Port

The general work of discharging cargoes and the supply of return cargoes is under the control of the Representative of the Department of Foreign Trade. Our Shipping Officers have maintained a close liaison with this official and that is an absolute essential requirement to efficient work.

The Manager of the Port is the executive in the Port and is assisted by despatchers who berth ships and arrange rail movements and dock pilots.

Customs are much the same as in other ports, though a quite amazing number of permits are needed to bring one box of bacon from a ship to the Mission or to a railway wagon for onward despatch. A close liaison and much patience with the determination not to attempt to smuggle or bounce them, have produced reasonably happy relations and satisfactory results.

''Inflot'' are the Ships' Representatives and carry out all the domestic necessities for ships in foreign ports.

The Frontier Guard supply sentries on the dock gates for the control of personnel and cargo entering and leaving the Port and at the ships' gangways. Either they, or the Northern Fleet, or the Army, depending on the locality, also supply the guards at the road barriers which exist in considerable profusion on Murmansk's two roads, to the North and the South.

The Convoy Captain arranges ships' anchor berths in the Inlet on arrival and before sailing in convoy and provides Pilots for movements in the Inlet, this is done by officers from the Northern Fleet. Except when convoys are moving he works from Polyarnoe.

*A general view of Polyarnoe in December 1943.*

*Part of the older section of the port of Murmansk, probably early in 1942; it illustrates the problems of handling cargo at Russian terminals.*

## The Port of Murmansk

The port consists of a number of wooden quays along most of the water frontage of the town.

**SUDNO VERF** (Ship wharf). This quay is situated at the Southern extremity of the Port area. Mainly used for repairing small Naval vessels and submarines. The quay is of wood and in a very dilapidated condition. Wooden bollards (in number 12) are used for securing vessels. The quay is served by a single track line of rails, from which 3 loop lines run to connect up with Repair shops situated close by.

No facilities for storage of cargo. No cranes on this quay. Fresh water is laid on.

Approach to the quay is bad owing to the close proximity of a Reef, and great care has to be taken when berthing. There are 6 slips suitable for Trawlers and ''Coastal'' type submarines in the area of which the Sudno Verf forms the quay wall. The area is completely fenced off and is served by a single track railway line.

Used for the first time by merchant ships other than of Soviet nationality during the Convoy Season of 1943/44, for ballasting (sand and timber supplied direct from trucks). Two merchant ships, one Liberty type and one Empire have been berthed at the one time at the quay, occupying the extreme Southern end. The Crane ships *EMPIRE BARD, EMPIRE ELGAR* and *LAPLAND* have also used this berth for discharging.

To date it has not been found possible to obtain entrance to any of the Repair shops in this area, and repair facilities can therefore only be guessed at, but judging from the dismantled state of Submarines seen at various times alongside the jetty, it can be assumed that considerable facilities exist for almost all types of regular work. This area has suffered very little from bomb damage.

**FISH QUAY** This quay is situated between the SUDNO VERF and CABOTAJNEE QUAY. Wooden construction throughout. Berths for two vessels. No bollards; mooring chains and rings. Two lines of rails serve the quay. On part of the North side of the quay the flooring slopes upward and permits cargo being easily handled into Trucks or Flat cars, which are cleared by a single track railway. One large warehouse, in a good state of repair, is situated alongside the shore end berth. There is a Coal Elevator built on to the end of this warehouse, but it is in a very dilapidated condition. The elevator has been used once or twice this season for bunkering Russian trawlers. Fresh water is available from the quay. There is a coaling berth suitable for small coastal type vessels of shallow draft situated at the extreme shore end of the quay.

**CABOTAJNEE QUAY** (Coasting Quay) This quay is situated between the FISH QUAY and the WAR PORT. Of wooden construction throughout with five wooden bollards; permits of berthing one vessel of LIBERTY, OCEAN or EMPIRE type. No railway lines serve the quay, there are no cranes and no warehouses for storage of cargo. The area surrounding the quay has been badly damaged by bombing, but it is very suitable for dumping cargo. Clearance from this area can be effected in Winter by use of sledges, and this method was successfully used in the 1943/44 Convoy Season. So far as is known, the Season just ended saw the use of this quay for the first time by British and U.S.A. merchant vessels.

## Commercial Port

Railway lines serving this area:

*5 lines from the Main Port
1 line from the Timber Quay
1 line from the War Port area.

*It should be noted that all Railway lines serving the various quays in the Commercial Port area, eventually merge into the five lines referred to above, and these lines then pass through a narrow bottle neck at the entrance to the Port. Clearance of cargo by rail from this area is therefore easily disrupted.

## War Port

Although this area is included under the heading COMMERCIAL PORT no merchant vessels are able to discharge at the quay, which can only accommodate one medium size tug or similar craft, and various small motor boats used by the Russian Northern Fleet.

The Commercial Port of Murmansk has suffered heavy damage as the result of bombing, with the result that little in the way of warehouse storage now exists. There is one large Shed (referred to as Shed 47) situated alongside Berths 10 and 11, a small shed situated at Berth 7, and a medium size shed situated in the angle formed by berths 3 and 4. All cargo which cannot be accommodated in the Sheds mentioned above, must of necessity be dumped on the quays, and when possible covered with tarpaulins as sole protection against weather.

## Berths 1 & 2

Rails serving the quay, 3 in number, plus 2 outer lines. This area is timbered and in good repair (result of work by the Port Authority during Summer of 1943). No iron bollards; vessels moor with wire strops. No cranes. Fresh water laid on. It should be noted that the area lying between Berths 1,2,3,4 & 5 is the largest "timber floored" area in the Port.

## Berth 3

This is only used as a "lightening" berth. It is not served by rail; no cranes available; fresh water is laid on. This quay is in a bad state of repair.

## Berths 4 & 5

Rails serving quay, 4 in number. Ring-bolts for mooring, plus 4 wooden bollards faced with iron. Despatchers Office situated opposite Berth 4, and the Shed (medium sized) referred to in the Port notes is also adjacent. Fresh water is laid on. No cranes. Air Raid shelter opposite Berth 4.

Length of quays about 900 feet.

## Berths 6 & 7

Rails serving quays, 3 in number. No bollards. 7 or 8 mooring rings. No cranes. Fresh water laid on. Shed opposite Berth 7, in a fair state of repair. Large Air Raid shelter opposite Berth 6.

Length of quays about 900 feet.

## Berth 8

This quay is very badly damaged. Chiefly used for bunkering; a Conveyor is fitted for this purpose. No rails or cranes serve this berth. Fresh water is not available. There is considerable storage available for coal in the area of this quay, but in the Convoy Season it is chiefly occupied by cargo awaiting removal from the docks.

## Berths 9, 10 & 11

Rails serving quays, 2 in number plus 3 outer lines serving berths 9 and 10. Berths 10 and 11 faced with concrete. Bollards 10 (iron), 3 (wood—iron faced). Quays are timber floored, in a fair state of repair. 1 Electric travelling "Luffing" crane, believed capable of lifting up to 11 tons. Fresh water is laid on. 1 large Shed (concrete) No 47, opposite berths 10 and 11. Air Raid Shelter adjacent to Berth 11.

Note. Berth 9, which was previously known to be a foul berth (cement faced quay wall blown into water by bombing) may now be clear. Divers have been working at this berth recently and a large block of concrete was noted being raised. This may well have caused the damage sustained by *EMPIRE CELIA* to her bilge keel. The entrance to these berths is bad, being served by a narrow channel in which vessels find it impossible to turn round.

## TIMBER QUAY. Berths 12, 13 & 14

Accommodates two Merchant ships. Can also accommodate, at shore end of quays, several small tugs and motor boats. Quays constructed of timber, covered in some places with sand and stone. Condition of quay "good". Fresh water laid on. One main railway line serves this area. No bollards, 9 mooring rings. There are 6 lines of rails inside this area, of which three directly serve the quays. No storage sheds. Length of quays about 1,000 feet.

Cranes. Dockside: 3, 3, 6 and 5 tons
Shoreside: 2, 5 and 8 tons

Note: Cranes are of English construction and were brought to Murmansk from Archangel in the Summer of 1943 by *EMPIRE BARD* and *EMPIRE ELGAR*.

Shore end of quay dries out at low water. Reef in close proximity to Berth 12.

Considerable quantities of cargo can be stowed on the quays, and can easily be handled by the Cranes which run on rails. Despatchers Office on quay.

Large Air Raid Shelter serving these berths.

Note: The Chief Despatchers Office for the Port of Murmansk is situated close to the entrance to the Timber Quay.

It is believed that a connection for an Oil Pipeline is in existence at the shore end of this quay. A Pipeline runs from underground storage tanks situated on the shore road from Murmansk to Rosta, and appears to terminate at the shore end of the Timber Quay. There have been no signs to date of the coastal tankers *UKAGIR* and *JELIABOV* either discharging or loading at this quay.

## ROSTA

Comprised of the following, Bunkering quays, Berth 15, Artillery Quay, Oil Jetty, Drydocks and Repair Shops.

**All this area is controlled by the Northern Fleet, with the exception of Berth 15 which is under jurisdiction of Murmansk Port Authority**

### Bunkering Quays

Capable of taking two vessels at one time for bunkering. viz, *FORT VERCHERES* and *EMPIRE PROWESS.* Several small electrically driven conveyor belts are available. The quay side is not served by railway lines. Ample storage accommodation for coal available. No cranes on quay.

Fresh water is not available at this quay, but if necessary can be obtained by water boat.

Signal tower on south end of quay.

Coal is conveyed to this area by a single track line from the Marshalling Yards at Murmansk, and thence to the ships side by conveyor belting or small tubs running on rails.

### Berth 15

Used originally for discharging ammunition and explosives from Merchant ships, prior to them proceeding to Murmansk to discharge remainder of cargo. It was also used for loading Apatite. Offers berthage for one vessel. Fresh water is not available from quay. Quay is served by two railway lines.

Last season a shed existed at this quay for storage of Apatit, but this has now been removed and workmen have been busy in this area, but purpose of work is unknown.

During the 1943/44 Convoy Season this quay was used for ballasting with sand.

### Artillery Quay, Rosta

A small jetty used exclusively by the Red Army for loading small vessels with ammunition etc for transfer to the MISHUKOV shore en route for the Northern Front. Does not offer suitable berthage for a Merchant ship. No cranes on quay when last visited (1943), and no opportunity has occurred this season to note if any changes have taken place.

Field guns in considerable numbers are often stored in the area adjacent to this jetty which is patrolled by Red Army sentries and not by the usual Frontier Guard.

### Oil Jetty, Rosta

Used solely for discharging Fuel Oil. (No "Spirit" tanker has used this quay since December 1942). Offers berthage for one 10,000 ton tanker. Fresh water is laid on at quay.

### Drydocks and Repair Shops, Rosta

A map of this area and detailed report of all machinery installed in the shops, sizes of drydocks etc, was forwarded to M.W.T in 1943, a copy of which was made available for N.I.D at the same time.

## Section B

The Inlet has 45 numbered anchor berths, and though the great depths found in most of it preclude many more from being used, 121 ships were berthed between the arrival of JW 57 and the departure of RA 59. Thirteen destroyers were berthed alongside at Polyarnoe and Vaenga, 12 dry cargo ships were berthed at Murmansk, 28 laden and 40 light dry cargo ships and 2 light and 3 laden tankers were in anchor berths with the rest of the escorting war-vessels, mostly in Vaenga Bay, though a few of these smaller craft were secured alongside cruisers and escort carriers.

*HMS SHEFFIELD lies in Kola Inlet with the minesweeper HMS SEAGULL alongside. The larger ships frequently hosted the smaller escorts in this manner, supplying such comforts and facilities as they could, particularly to ships based at Murmansk such as the Halcyon class minesweepers.*

During the Convoy Season 4 signal stations alongside the Inlet are manned by our Signalmen, at Polyarnoe, Vaenga, Manukov Point and Murmansk. Communication with Merchant ships at anchor is not rapid but can usually be effected in course of time. In the 6 winter months navigation into and within the Inlet is frequently handicapped by a local and low-lying fog. Severe gales are not frequent, only two of sufficient severity to cause ships to drag their anchors being recalled in the winter of 1943/44.

*One of the four signal stations beside the Inlet in December 1943.*

# Minesweepers in North Russia

While from time to time various escorts remained in North Russia either due to damage, the need for detached duty or the advent of summer making passage dangerous, it was the practice from the earliest convoys to base ships of the HALCYON class at Murmansk to provide a minesweeping capability. Surprisingly, in view of their long-standing penchant for mine warfare, the Russian Fleet appears at that time to have lacked such a basic skill.

The pattern of service was for the individual minesweepers to take passage to Russia as escorts of an eastbound convoy, and to remain on station throughout the next winter, returning home in one of the spring convoys after

*Halcyon class minesweepers lead a convoy through pack ice off the Russian coast during the winter of 1941/42, with two elderly freighters astern.*

relief. While in Russian waters they were responsible for sweeping out the westbound convoys, and meeting the inward eastbound ones, usually some 48 hours away from Murmansk. Anti-submarine escort was also required of them, and they were called upon to operate as far East and North as the ice edge in the Kara Sea whenever movements took place there. There was, of course, the usual preventive sweeping to be undertaken in the Murmansk approaches, bearing in mind that the front line was under fifty miles away for much of the period of their service.

The escort of convoys could assume major proportions, and it was minesweepers that were present when the cruiser EDINBURGH endeavoured to return after damage, while BRAMBLE was lost engaging a force led by the cruiser ADMIRAL HIPPER. The duties of the ships in harbour were also manifold, for apart from sweeping they provided the communications link, operated as AA guardships, controlled shipping in the anchorages, provided advice and training to the Russians and carried out multifarious local duties.

All this was performed by small ships with very limited facilities, which had certainly not been built for Arctic conditions. Recreational facilities ashore were almost nonexistent and self-help was the order of the day. Some assistance could be given by larger ships of the Fleet which called between convoys, and the SBNONR was constantly pressing for canteen stores, mails etc to be specifically embarked for his ships and shore party.

As minesweepers became available to the Russians, either by transfer from the RN of suitable small craft or by provision of US built craft, the need for the HALCYONs diminished, but throughout their stay the British Flag Officers were universal in their praise for the efficiency, enthusiasm and cheerful acceptance of conditions by all members of their ships' companies.

A few other small ships, principally trawlers, shared similar duties to the minesweepers, and one deserves mention above all. The trawler CHILTERN, having escorted a convoy to Murmansk, was retained for local duty responsible directly to SBNONR. Serving in Russia for the remainder of the war, her crew's conditions can best be summed up by the Admiral's comment at the end of a period of refit by the Russians at Murmansk that "he had sent the ship to Archangel, which at least would be a change of scenery for the crew". Conditions must have been poor if Archangel was regarded as a rest camp billet!

# Merchant ships in North Russia

As already stated, the primary purpose of this book is to record those ships which took part in what are known, most commonly, as the "Russian convoys", not to detail the history or present opinions about them. However, there are some little known aspects of the operations that deserve attention in this work.

During each year of the operations, it was inevitable that some ships would remain in Russian waters over the summer months, either because they had not been unloaded when the last convoy of the season sailed, or due to damage. Merchant ships in this position usually proceeded to Archangel where they were at least further away from air attack than at Murmansk, some traded between Murmansk and Archangel (usually with timber) and a few in the White Sea.

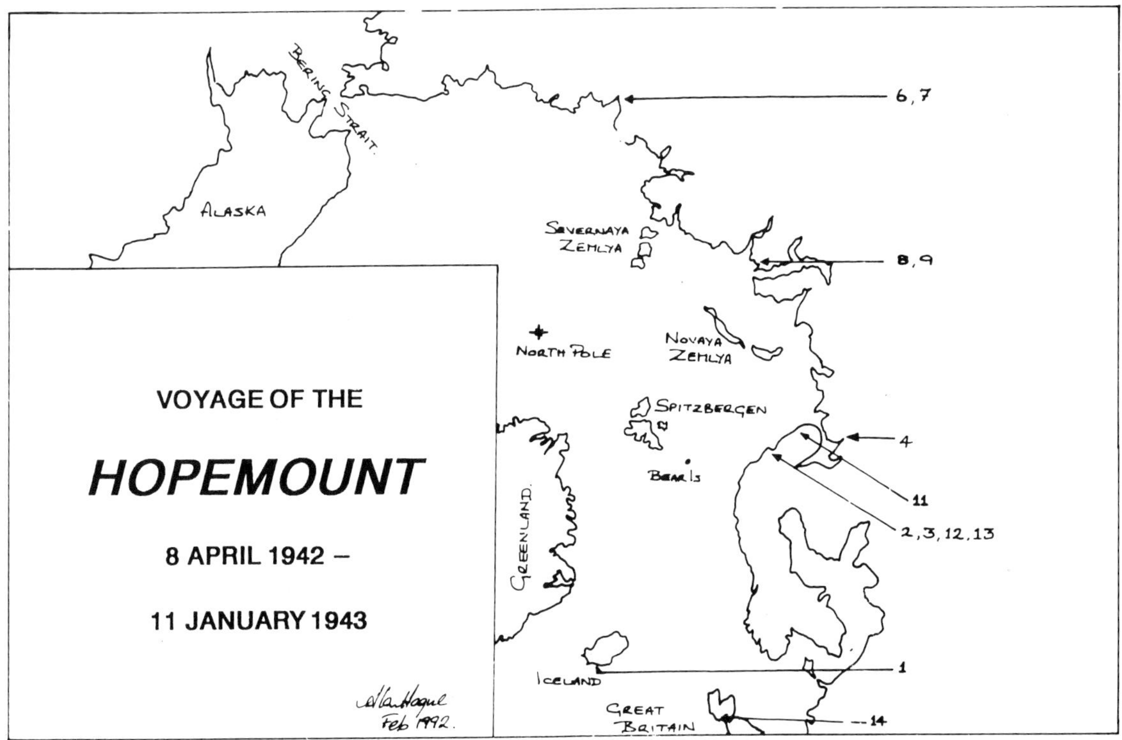


| KEY | MOVEMENTS AT KEY POINTS |
|---|---|
| 1 | Sailed from Reykjavik 8 April 1942 in PQ 14 |
| 2 | Arrived at Murmansk 19 April 1942 in PQ 14 |
| 3 | Sailed from Murmansk 29 June 1942 to Archangel |
| 4 | Sailed from Archangel 29 July 1942 eastwards |
| 5 | Arrived Hansen Island 25 August 1942, warning of German surface raider |
| 6 | Arrived at Tiksi 31 August 1942, loading oil and water |
| 7 | Met Russian warships from Vladivostok on 18 September 1942 and fuelled them |
| 8 | Arrived Dikson on return passage 26 September 1942, again fuelling Russian destroyers |
| 9 | Sailed Dikson 6 October 1942 westwards |
| 10 | Arrived Yugorski Shar 11 October 1942. Remained until 20 November 1942 |
| 11 | Met British minesweepers at Iokanka 29 November 1942 and obtained medical aid and food |
| 12 | Arrived at Murmansk for repairs |
| 13 | Sailed Murmansk in RA 51 30 December 1942 for Britain |
| 14 | Arrived Loch Ewe 11 January 1943 in RA 51 en route to repairs |

The following notes are culled from a brief and very restrained report made by the Master of the British tanker *HOPEMOUNT,* and give some slight impression of circumstances that could face ships.

*HOPEMOUNT* had gone out in convoy PQ 14, and although attacked she was fortunately undamaged, and duly delivered her cargo of fuel oil and gas oil. She then lay in the river at Murmansk from April to June 1942, during which time she went to action stations on 132 separate occasions, indicative of the scale of attack mounted against that port.

In June 1942 *HOPEMOUNT* was ordered to support Russian operations in the White Sea, and went initially to Archangel on 29 June escorted by HAZARD and LEDA, remaining there for three weeks. On 29 July, escorted by BRAMBLE, HAZARD and SEAGULL, corvettes DIANELLA, LA MALOUINE and LOTUS, 2 Russian destroyers and 3 icebreakers , she sailed for Dickson Harbour, all save the icebreakers leaving the convoy at the ice edge. The purpose of the voyage was to support the annual Arctic convoy from the West to rendezvous in the far North with ships from Vladivostok.

By 18 August *HOPEMOUNT* was at Cape Chelyuskin, and she got as far as Hansen Island by 25 August. Here there was considerable alarm as it was reported that a German auxiliary cruiser was following the convoy, and indeed on 26 August such a ship was reported in sight. Fortunately, for the convoy was proceeding with icebreakers in heavy ice, the alarm proved false, the suspect ship being a Russian. However, those aboard *HOPEMOUNT* would have been less than happy to realise that the reported ''auxiliary cruiser'' was, in fact, the armoured ship ADMIRAL SCHEER which had entered the Kara Sea, staying south of the ice, six days earlier. She eventually withdrew, after very poor results, on 28 August.

On 31 August *HOPEMOUNT,* by now with a damaged propeller, arrived at Tiksi where she loaded a further 3,000 tons of oil and obtained some fresh water. Here she remained until 18 September, on the 16th meeting three Russian destroyers which had come through from Vladivostok to reinforce the Northern Fleet. Reportedly there had been ten such, the remainder having turned back due to ice. Post war information indicates that the return of seven ships may have referred to the entire west bound convoy, for only four destroyers are named, BAKU, RAZUMNY, RAZYARENNY and REVNOSTNY which had left Vladivostok on 15 July. REVNOSTNY was in collision on 18 July and was left behind, the remainder duly arriving at Tiksi.

*The Russian destroyer RAZYARENNY lying in Kola Inlet. She was one of the Vladivostok based ships met by the tanker HOPEMOUNT during the trans Arctic convoy of the summer of 1942.*

Starting back westward, *HOPEMOUNT* was left behind by the faster Russian ships, finally arriving after a solitary passage at Dickson on 26 September where she fuelled the Russian destroyers. The remainder of her convoy joined her on 1 October and the intervening period was spent trying to extract desperately needed supplies from the Russians. By this time, the crew were subsisting on dried peas, flour, corned beef and tea. The cook was able to supply flapjacks as there was cooking oil onboard, but not bread, while water was at best brackish rather than fresh.

Sailing west again on 6 October *HOPEMOUNT* got in to Yugorski Shar on 11 October, remaining there until 19 October when the minesweepers HALCYON, HAZARD and SHARPSHOOTER arrived to sweep the area, detonating a number of air laid mines. The sweepers, and two corvettes that also arrived, departed on 21 October and it was left to Russian icebreakers to break *HOPEMOUNT* out through thickening ice to clear water, which was reached on 20 November. By now the damaged propeller meant that the ship could not keep the convoy speed, so once again she proceeded alone, finally being collected at Iokanka by British minesweepers on 29 November.

On fuelling the minesweepers, the Master obtained fresh water and medical aid, the doctor from HMS HARRIER finding the whole crew to be suffering from scurvy due to their diet over the past months. On 8 December, the first mail to be received since leaving Britain in March arrived; *HOPEMOUNT* then went to Murmansk where she was docked and the propeller repaired. She sailed for home in convoy RA 51, arriving finally in Methil on 16 January 1943.

The entire voyage was something of an epic, *HOPEMOUNT* reached 134E and 83N during her passage, probably a record for a British merchant ship even in 1992. Her Master, Captain W D Shields, wrote a very low key report, one of his few comments being that "we proceeded to Methil and on 16th, just to complete the voyage, we collided with another ship". His further comment on his crew is also a classic understatement "All.......... behaved extremely well, but nobody was outstanding—it was a case of all pulling together...". He must have been a remarkable Master with a first class crew and DEMS detachment.

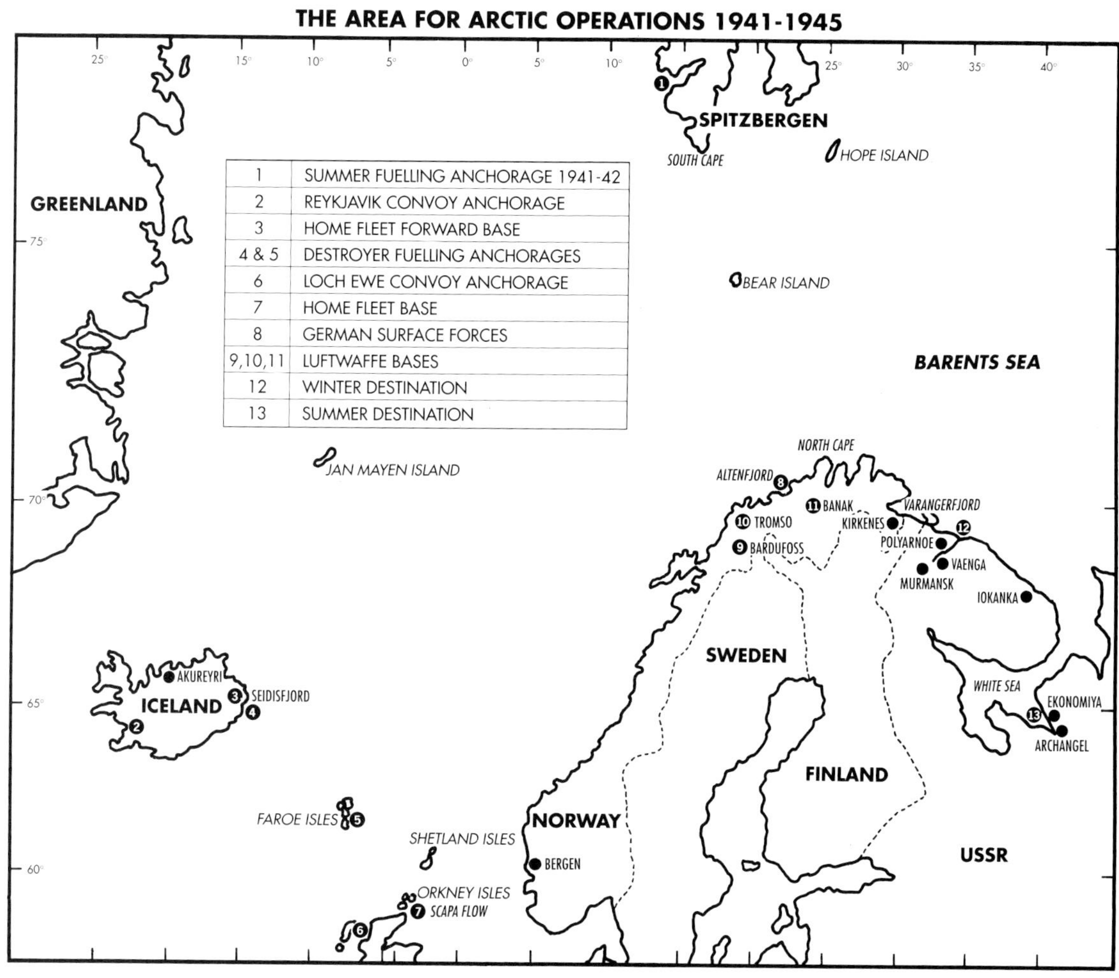

# Operation EF

Operation EF was the code title for a Fleet Air Arm attack on Tromso and Kirkenes, during the course of which the minelayer ADVENTURE was passed through to Archangel with special stores, including mines, for Russian use. During the initial part of her passage, ADVENTURE accompanied the forces for Operation EF, and she was then further covered by the cruiser SHROPSHIRE and destroyer ANTHONY before proceeding independently. She arrived at Archangel on 1 August and sailed on 4 August to return home unescorted.

# Submarines based at Murmansk

In order to support Russian forces during the initial German advance in the far North, it was decided to base British submarines at Polyarnoe and accordingly TIGRIS sailed from Scapa Flow on 26 July followed by TRIDENT on 1 August. Both boats were received at Polyarnoe where quarters were provided for spare crew, and arrangements made for stowage of stores, spares etc, the fullest possible co-operation being given by the Russian authorities.

These two boats were followed in November by the smaller S class SEALION and SEAWOLF which arrived on 6 and 10 November respectively in relief of the T boats which had returned to Britain. Both boats returned to Home waters in December, relieved in their turn by STURGEON which arrived at Polyarnoe 11 January 1942. She however remained only briefly on station.

The patrols conducted by the first four boats were successful both in sinkings, and in the problems they caused to the German command in north Norway with its dependence upon seaborne supplies imposed by the local geography. Their success was a source of some irritation to the Russians, who had yet to develop their full potential and who lacked the war experience of the British crews. Nevertheless, it also served as an example for the future, and the Northern Fleet submarines were certainly not lacking in offensive spirit in subsequent years

# The Convoys

## Operation DERVISH

This, the first convoy to North Russia, sailed from Liverpool on 12 August 1941 for Hvalfjord via Scapa Flow, arriving in Iceland 20 August to commence the passage to Russia on 21 August. The following ships sailed for Archangel:

| | | | | | |
|---|---|---|---|---|---|
| *ALCHIBA* | 23 Du | 4427/20 | *ESNEH* | 22 Br | 1931/19 |
| *LANCASTRIAN PRINCE* | 12 Br | 1914/40 | *LLANSTEPHAN CASTLE* | 21 Br | 11348/14 |
| *NEW WESTMINSTER CITY* | 11 Br | 4747/29 | *TREHATA* | 13 Br | 4817/28 |
| *ALDERSDALE* | Br | 8402/37 | | | |

The position of RFA *ALDERSDALE* in the convoy is unknown; convoy Commodore was in *LLANSTEPHAN CASTLE.*

A number of warships escorted the convoy for varying periods of time; the trawlers HAMLET and MACBETH were present from 12 to 31 August, the auxiliary AA ship POZARICA and trawlers CELIA, ST CATHAN and LE TIGER from 12 to 21 August. Trawler OPHELIA joined from 19 to 31 August. The destroyer escort comprised ELECTRA, 12 to 29 August, and ACTIVE and IMPULSIVE from 16 to 29. From 20 to 31 August the minesweepers HALCYON, HARRIER and SALAMANDER also provided close A/S escort. The cruiser AURORA provided cover 16 to 18 August, while the aircraft carrier VICTORIOUS, cruisers DEVONSHIRE and SUFFOLK, and destroyers ECLIPSE, ESCAPADE and INGLEFIELD provided distant cover from 24 to 30 August. There was no overt enemy activity, and the convoy reached Archangel 31 August.

## Operation GAUNTLET

Between 19 August and 10 September a force comprising the cruisers AURORA and NIGERIA, and destroyers ANTELOPE, ANTHONY, ECLIPSE, ICARUS and TARTAR, escorting the liner *EMPRESS OF CANADA*, 21,517/22 and the RFA tanker *OLIGARCH*, 6894/18, conducted operations at Spitzbergen involving the landing of a garrison, the conveyance of some 1800 Russian miners to Archangel, and the evacuation of the civilian Norwegian population. This was carried out without interference from the enemy.

During the return of the ships from Spitzbergen, AURORA and NIGERIA were detached from the remainder and ordered to investigate the Norwegian coast off Porsanger Fjord, probably as a result of decryption of German signals. Here the two ships encountered a small convoy escorted by the training ship BREMSE and trawlers, and a spirited action ensued at close quarters in appalling visibility.

At times, the range closed so much that main armament turrets could not train fast enough to maintain bearing on BREMSE; nevertheless, after a gallant action, she was sunk although her convoy escaped unscathed.

*HMS NIGERIA after the action in which the German BREMSE was sunk, showing the damage forward received from an unknown source.*

During this action NIGERIA suffered severe damage for'ard to the bow below the waterline, damage usually attributed to collision with the wreck of BREMSE. However, post war analysis shows that BREMSE was still afloat and in action when the damage occurred, and the true cause remains a mystery which is unlikely to be resolved in view of the lack of contemporary investigation. The most probable cause is a floating mine, possibly from a Russian submarine lay in the vicinity. Whatever the cause, there was anxiety in NIGERIA during her passage home owing to heavy weather and consequent strain on the remaining forward bulkhead; the ship however arrived safely and was duly repaired.

## Operation STRENGTH

Between 30 August and 14 September the aircraft carrier ARGUS, cruiser SHROPSHIRE and destroyers MATABELE, PUNJABI and SOMALI conveyed Hurricane aircraft and associated Royal Air Force personnel to Archangel. The covering force comprised the aircraft carrier VICTORIOUS, cruisers DEVONSHIRE and SUFFOLK and destroyers ECLIPSE, ESCAPADE and INGLEFIELD.

## Passage of missions to Russia

Between 22 and 27 September the cruiser LONDON conveyed a British and American mission to Archangel returning, as shown below, with QP 1.

## Convoy QP 1

Sailing from Archangel on 28 September, the convoy consisted of the returning "DERVISH" ships plus Russian vessels:

| | | | | | |
|---|---|---|---|---|---|
| *ALCHIBA* | 21 Du | 4427/20 | *ALMA ATA* | 32 Russ | 3611/20 |
| *BLACK RANGER* | 22 Br | 3417/41 | *BUDENNI* | 43 Russ | 2482/23 |
| *ESNEH* | 12 Br | 1931/19 | *LANCASTRIAN PRINCE* | 11 Br | 1914/40 |
| *LLANSTEPHAN CASTLE* | 31 Br | 11348/14 | *MOSSOVET* | 24 Russ | 2981/35 |
| *NEW WESTMINSTER CITY* | 42 Br | 4747/29 | *RODINA* | 13 Russ | 4441/22 |
| *SEVZAPLES* | 33 Russ | 3974/32 | *STARY BOLSHEVIK* | 23 Russ | 3974/33 |
| *SUKHONA* | 25 Russ | 3124/18 | *TREHATA* | 41 Br | 4817/28 |

The Commodore ship was, again, *LLANSTEPHAN CASTLE* and the Vice Commodore *TREHATA.*

The cruisers LONDON and SHROPSHIRE accompanied the convoy from 28 September to 2 October and 2 to 10 October respectively. Destroyers ELECTRA (28 September to 9 October), ACTIVE (28 September to 5 October) and ANTHONY (4 to 9 October) also sailed. The trawlers MACBETH and HAMLET escorted from 28 September to 9 October with OPHELIA from 28 September to 5 October. The minesweepers HALCYON, HARRIER and SALAMANDER (now based in North Russia) provided local eastern escort from 28 to 30 September.

The destroyer ANTHONY , escorting the escort oiler *BLACK RANGER,* joined the convoy on 4 October from convoy PQ 1.

OPHELIA developed defects, and had to be towed by ACTIVE to Akureyri where she arrived 10 October, while the merchantmen *MOSSOVET* and *SUKHONA* straggled from the convoy but arrived safely.

There was no enemy activity, and the convoy arrived at the Orkneys on 10 October.

## Convoy PQ 1

This convoy, the first in the normal coded sequence from the UK, sailed from Hvalfjord on 29 September, consisting of:

| | | | | | |
|---|---|---|---|---|---|
| *ATLANTIC* | 21 Br | 5414/39 | *BLACK RANGER* | 43 Br | 3417/41 |
| *BLAIRNEVIS* | 12 Br | 4155/30 | *CAPIRA* | 11 Pan | 5565/20 |
| *ELNA II* | 41 Br | 3221/03 | *GEMSTONE* | 33 Br | 4986/38 |
| *HARMONIC* | 42 Br | 4558/30 | *LORCA* | 23 Br | 4875/31 |
| *NORTH KING* | 31 Pan | 4934/03 | *RIVER AFTON* | 32 Br | 5479/35 |
| *VILLE D'ANVERS* | 22 Bel | 7462/20 | | | |

Convoy Commodore in *ATLANTIC* and Vice Commodore in *NORTH KING.*

Escort throughout consisted of the cruiser SUFFOLK, destroyer IMPULSIVE and minesweepers BRITOMART, GOSSAMER, LEDA and HUSSAR. The destroyers ANTHONY and ANTELOPE were present from 29 September to 2 and 4 October respectively, and ESCAPADE from 2 to 11 October, while the minesweeper HARRIER provided local escort 10/11 October. On 4 October ANTHONY was detached, escorting *BLACK RANGER,* the escort oiler, to join the homeward bound convoy QP 1. There was no enemy action during the passage of the convoy, which arrived at Archangel 11 October.

## Passage of the TUC Delegation to Russia

Between 6 and 12 October the destroyer ANTELOPE took a Trade Union Delegation from Scapa to Seidisfjord where it transferred to the destroyer NORMAN for passage to Archangel.

## Convoy PQ 2

This convoy, unusually, sailed from Scapa Flow on 17 October, formed as follows:

| | | | | | |
|---|---|---|---|---|---|
| *EMPIRE BAFFIN* | 22 Br | 6978/41 | *HARPALION* | 21 Br | 5486/32 |
| *HARTLEBURY* | 32 Br | 5082/34 | *ORIENT CITY* | 11 Br | 5095/40 |
| *QUEEN CITY* | 31 Br | 4814/24 | *TEMPLE ARCH* | 12 Br | 5138/40 |

Commodore was in *ORIENT CITY* and Vice Commodore in *HARPALION.*

The cruiser NORFOLK escorted from 18 to 30 October together with the destroyers ICARUS and ECLIPSE and the minesweepers BRAMBLE, SEAGULL and SPEEDY. Eastern escort was provided by GOSSAMER, HUSSAR and LEDA 29/30 October from their base at Archangel, where the convoy arrived 30 October without being attacked.

## Return of the TUC Delegation

This delegation returned to the UK in the destroyer NORMAN sailing on 27 October and arriving at Scapa Flow on 2 November.

## Convoy QP 2

The convoy cleared Archangel 3 November composed of:

| | | | | | |
|---|---|---|---|---|---|
| *ATLANTIC* | 21 Br | 5414/39 | *BLAIRNEVIS* | 13 Br | 4155/30 |
| *CAPIRA* | 11 Pan | 5565/20 | *CHERNYSHEVSKI* | 23 Russ | 3588/19 |
| *GEMSTONE* | 31 Br | 4986/38 | *HARMONIC* | 41 Br | 4558/30 |
| *IJORA* | 12 Russ | 2815/21 | *LORCA* | 33 Br | 4875/31 |
| *NORTH KING* | 43 Pan | 4934/03 | *RIVER AFTON* | 32 Br | 5479/35 |
| *STEPAN KHALTURIN* | 42 Russ | 2498/21 | *VILLE D'ANVERS* | 22 Bel | 17462/20 |

Commodore was in *ATLANTIC* and Vice Commodore in *GEMSTONE*

The cruiser NORFOLK escorted from 3 to 11 November, with the destroyers ECLIPSE and ICARUS from 3 to 17 November. Local escorts 3 to 5 November were the minesweepers BRAMBLE, LEDA and SEAGULL, while the trawlers CELIA and WINDERMERE joined from 11 to 13 November. There was no enemy activity, and the convoy arrived at Scapa Flow 17 November.

## Convoy PQ 3

This convoy reverted to Hvalfjord as its departure point, sailing on 9 November composed as below:

| | | | | | |
|---|---|---|---|---|---|
| *BRIARWOOD* | Br | 4019/30 | *CAPE CORSO* | Br | 3807/29 |
| *CAPE RACE* | 32 Br | 3807/30 | *COCLE* | 31 Pan | 5630/20 |
| *EL CAPITAN* | 12 Pan | 5255/17 | *SAN AMBROSIO* | 22 Br | 7410/35 |
| *TREKIEVE* | 11 Br | 5244/19 | *WANSTEAD* | 21 Br | 5486/28 |

The trawlers MACBETH and HAMLET escorted from 9 November to 15 and 14 November respectively, handing over on 14 November to the cruiser KENYA and destroyers BEDOUIN and INTREPID.

*BRIARWOOD* suffered ice damage and returned escorted by HAMLET. The position of *CAPE CORSO* in the convoy is unknown, but her passage is confirmed by Lloyd's records.

The convoy arrived unmolested at Archangel 22 November, having been met by a local escort of BRAMBLE, SEAGULL and SPEEDY on the 20th.

## Convoy PQ 4

This convoy sailed from Hvalfjord 17 November, made up of the following ships:

| | | | | | |
|---|---|---|---|---|---|
| *ALMA ATA* | Russ | 3611/20 | *BUDENNI* | Russ | 2482/23 |
| *DAN-Y-BRYN* | Br | 5117/40 | *EMPIRE METEOR* | Br | 7457/40 |
| *EULIMA* | Br | 6207/37 | *MOSSOVET* | Russ | 2981/35 |
| *RODINA* | Russ | 4441/22 | *SUKHONA* | Russ | 3124/18 |

Escorts were the trawlers BUTE and STELLA CAPELLA from 17 to 27 November, and the cruiser BERWICK and destroyers OFFA and ONSLOW from 25 to 27 November. GOSSAMER, SEAGULL and SPEEDY met the convoy on 27 November, and it arrived at Archangel 28 November.

## Convoy QP 3

This convoy sailed from Archangel on 27 November, comprising:

| | | | | | |
|---|---|---|---|---|---|
| *ANDRE MARTI* | 33 Russ | 2352/18 | *ARCOS* | 32 Russ | 2343/18 |
| *EMPIRE BAFFIN* | 11 Br | 6978/41 | *HARPALION* | 42 Br | 5486/32 |
| *HARTLEBURY* | 12 Br | 5082/34 | *KUZBASS* | 23 Russ | 3109/14 |
| *ORIENT CITY* | 21 Br | 5095/40 | *QUEEN CITY* | 41 Br | 4814/24 |
| *REVOLUTSIONER* | 22 Russ | 2900/36 | *TEMPLE ARCH* | 31 Br | 5138/40 |

Commodore was in *ORIENT CITY* and Vice Commodore in *TEMPLE ARCH.*

The *ARCOS* and *KUZBASS* suffered defects and returned to Archangel; the remainder of the convoy dispersed on 3 December, Russian ships proceeding to Kirkwall and British to Seidisfjord. All British ships were loaded, principally with timber, and passengers were embarked in *HARPALION* (1), *ORIENT CITY* and *QUEEN CITY* with 3 each, and 6 in *REVOLUTSIONER.*

Destroyers BEDOUIN and INTREPID escorted from 28 November to 2 December, and the cruiser KENYA from 29 November to 3 December. The minesweepers GOSSAMER and HUSSAR were present from sailing until 10 and 9 December respectively, taking the Russian ships to Kirkwall upon dispersal of the convoy.

British ships were escorted from Seidisfjord to Kirkwall between 9 and 12 December by the trawlers MACBETH and HAMLET.

There was no enemy activity in connection with this convoy.

## Convoy PQ 5

The convoy, which left Hvalfjord on 27 November, consisted of:

| | | | | | |
|---|---|---|---|---|---|
| *BRIARWOOD* | 21 Br | 4019/30 | *CHULMLEIGH* | 31 Br | 5445/38 |
| *EMPIRE STEVENSON* | 22 Br | 6209/41 | *KOMILES* | 23 Russ | 3962/32 |
| *PETROVSKI* | 32 Russ | 3771/21 | *ST CLEARS* | 12 Br | 4312/36 |
| *TREHATA* | 11 Br | 4817/28 | | | |

The minesweeper SHARPSHOOTER accompanied the convoy to Archangel, while her sisters HAZARD and HEBE were present from sailing until relieved on 7 December by BRAMBLE and SEAGULL. The cruiser SHEFFIELD joined the convoy 1 December, detaching to Murmansk on 7 December with HAZARD and HEBE.

There was no enemy activity, and the convoy arrived at Archangel on 13 December.

## Return of Royal Air Force personnel

Having handed over their Hurricane aircraft to the Russians the RAF personnel, conveyed to Russia in Operation STRENGTH, returned in the cruisers BERWICK and KENYA and destroyers INTREPID, OFFA and ONSLOW between 1 and 7 December.

## Visit of the Foreign Secretary to Russia

A party consisting of the Foreign Secretary, the Russian Ambassador to London, and their staffs, took passage to Russia in the cruiser KENT between 8 and 12 December.

## Convoy PQ 6

The convoy, departing Hvalfjord 8 December, consisted of:

| | | | | | |
|---|---|---|---|---|---|
| *DEKABRIST* | 22 Russ | 7363/03 | *EL MIRLO* | 23 Br | 8092/30 |
| *EL OCEANO* | 13 Pan | 6767/25 | *ELONA* | 21 Br | 6192/36 |
| *EMPIRE MAVIS* | 11 Br | 5704/19 | *EXPLORER* | 24 Br | 6235/35 |
| *MOUNT EVANS* | 12 Pan | 5536/19 | *ZAMALEK* | 14 Br | 1567/21 |

Commodore was in *ELONA,* Vice Commodore in *EMPIRE MAVIS. ZAMALEK* was attached as a Rescue Ship, but returned to Iceland, date unknown.

The trawlers HUGH WALPOLE, CAPE ARGONA and STELLA CAPELLA provided local escort from 8 to 12 December, when the cruiser EDINBURGH and destroyers ECHO and ESCAPADE took over for the passage to Archangel.

The minesweepers HAZARD and SPEEDY were sailed to meet the convoy, but encountered the German destroyers Z 23, Z 24, Z 25 and Z 27 on 17 December. This was the first attempt by the enemy to intercept the traffic to and from North Russia, and was inconclusive. The German ships mistook the two small minesweepers for much larger Russian destroyers, and an indecisive action resulted only in four hits on SPEEDY, who returned damaged. LEDA was sailed as a replacement, and with HAZARD met the convoy on 19 December escorting it to Murmansk where it arrived 20 December. Here, delays in unloading resulted in five ships having to winter in Russian waters. One of these, the tanker *EL OCEANO,* operated for some time under Russian control and, when returning to Murmansk for a homeward convoy in February 1942, broke away from her escort at night and made an independent passage to Iceland, arriving there 18 February 1942, after a good deal of anxiety had been caused to the British command at Murmansk.

## Foreign Secretary returns to the U.K.

Between 25 and 29 December, the cruiser KENT conveyed the Foreign Secretary and his party on their return from the conference in Moscow.

## Convoy QP 4

This convoy sailed from Archangel 29 December 1941, comprising:

| | | | | | |
|---|---|---|---|---|---|
| *BRIARWOOD* | 11 Br | 4019/30 | *CAPE CORSO* | 22 Br | 3807/29 |
| *CAPE RACE* | 43 Br | 3807/30 | *COCLE* | 41 Pan | 5630/20 |
| *DAN-Y-BRYN* | 32 Br | 5117/40 | *EL CAPITAN* | 12 Pan | 5255/17 |
| *EL MIRLO* | 33 Br | 8092/30 | *EULIMA* | Br | 6207/37 |
| *SAN AMBROSIO* | Br | 7410/35 | *SUKHONA* | 23 Russ | 3124/18 |
| *TREHATA* | 42 Br | 4817/28 | *TREKIEVE* | 31 Br | 5244/19 |
| *WANSTEAD* | 21 Br | 5486/28 | | | |

Commodore in *WANSTEAD* and Vice Commodore in *TREKIEVE. EULIMA* and *SAN AMBROSIO* were obliged to return, hence absence of convoy numbers above.

The minesweepers LEDA, SEAGULL and SPEEDY and trawlers BUTE and STELLA CAPELLA sailed with the convoy until 9 January 1942. Sister minesweepers BRAMBLE and HEBE also escorted from sailing until 5 January 1942, while the cruiser EDINBURGH and destroyers ECHO and ESCAPADE were present 5 to 9 January, on which date the convoy dispersed after an uneventful passage.

## Convoy PQ 7A

This convoy comprised two ships only, sailing from Hvalfjord 26 December 1941 escorted by the trawlers HUGH WALPOLE and OPHELIA.

| | | | | | |
|---|---|---|---|---|---|
| *COLD HARBOR* | Pan | 5010/20 | *WAZIRISTAN* | Br | 5135/24 |

These ships should have made a rendezvous with an ocean escort of the minesweepers BRITOMART and SALAMANDER, themselves en route to Russia as relief escorts. In the event, the rendezvous was not made, and the two merchantmen proceeded in company on their passage when the trawlers left on 27 December. On 1 January 1942 bad weather separated the two ships; one day later *WAZIRISTAN* was attacked and sunk by U 134. *COLD HARBOR* arrived at Murmansk 12 January.

## Convoy PQ 7B

The remaining ships designated for PQ 7 now being ready, they sailed from Hvalfjord on 31 December 1942 as follows:

| | | | | | |
|---|---|---|---|---|---|
| *ANEROID* | Pan | 5074/17 | *BOTAVON* | Br | 5848/12 |
| *CHERNYSHEVSKI* | Russ | 3588/19 | *EMPIRE ACTIVITY* | Br | 5335/19 |
| *EMPIRE HALLEY* | Br | 7168/41 | *EMPIRE HOWARD* | Br | 6985/41 |
| *EMPIRE REDSHANK* | Br | 6615/19 | *JUTLAND* | Br | 6153/28 |
| *REIGH COUNT* | Pan | 4657/07 | | | |

No lists have yet been found for this convoy, hence the names given are a reconstruction from various voyage records and reports. *EMPIRE HALLEY* subsequently became the Dutch *PIETER DE HOOGH* between 10 and 27 March, 1942 at Hull.

Escort comprised the trawler CAPE ARGONA and whaler WASTWATER until 4 January when the destroyers ICARUS and TARTAR took over. The cruiser CUMBERLAND failed to meet the convoy at the rendezvous, and proceeded independently to Murmansk. No contact was made with the enemy, and the convoy arrived safely at Murmansk on 11 January 1942.

## Convoy PQ 8

The first convoy of 1942, PQ 8 left Hvalfjord on 8 January with the following ships:

| | | | | | |
|---|---|---|---|---|---|
| *BRITISH PRIDE* | 22 Br | 7106/31 | *BRITISH WORKMAN* | 32 Br | 6994/22 |
| *DARTFORD* | 12 Br | 4093/30 | *EL ALMIRANTE* | 11 Pan | 5248/17 |
| *HARMATRIS* | 31 Br | 5395/32 | *LARRANGA* | 21 Amer | 3804/17 |
| *SOUTHGATE* | 41 Br | 4862/26 | *STARY BOLSHEVIK* | 42 Russ | 3974/33 |

Commodore in *HARMATRIS* and Vice Commodore in *LARRANGA*.

The initial escort, until 17 January, were the minesweepers HARRIER and SPEEDWELL, from 11 January joined by the cruiser TRINIDAD and the destroyers MATABELE and SOMALI. The eastern escort of HAZARD and SHARPSHOOTER joined 16 January and took the convoy in to Murmansk arriving 17 January.

Located by the enemy, the convoy was attacked by U 454 on 17 January, *HARMATRIS* being damaged, although towed in to Murmansk on the 20th. MATABELE was less fortunate; torpedoed, she blew up almost immediately, only two men surviving to be picked up.

## Convoy QP 5

Probably a desperate effort to clear the port of Murmansk as winter closed in, this convoy of four ships sailed on 13 January, three of them being "returners" from previous sailings:

| | | | | | |
|---|---|---|---|---|---|
| *ARCOS* | Russ | 2343/18 | *DEKABRIST* | Russ | 7363/03 |
| *EULIMA* | Br | 6207/37 | *SAN AMBROSIO* | Br | 7410/35 |

The destroyers ICARUS and TARTAR escorted until 19 January, with the cruiser CUMBERLAND in company 13 to 16 January. There was no contact with the enemy and the convoy dispersed on 19 January.

## Convoy QP 6

Six further ships cleared Murmansk on 24 January:

| | | | | | |
|---|---|---|---|---|---|
| *ANEROID* | Pan | 5074/17 | *CHERNYSHEVSKI* | Russ | 3588/19 |
| *EMPIRE ACTIVITY* | Br | 5335/19 | *EMPIRE HOWARD* | Br | 6985/41 |
| *EMPIRE REDSHANK* | Br | 6615/19 | *REIGH COUNT* | Pan | 4657/07 |

The eastern local escort for this convoy comprised two Russian destroyers, GREMYASCHI and SOKRUSHITELNY from 24 to 27 January, and the British minesweepers HARRIER and SPEEDWELL from 24 to 25 January. On 25 January the cruiser TRINIDAD, destroyer SOMALI and minesweepers BRAMBLE and HEBE joined, remaining until 28 January when the convoy dispersed. Ships of the convoy had all arrived at Loch Ewe by 2 February, including *EMPIRE REDSHANK* which was attacked and damaged by aircraft on 31 January.

## Convoy PQ 9/10

The next outward convoy to Russia was, in fact, a combination of two sailings and therefore bore a double number, a unique feature. Comprising ten ships.

| | | | | | |
|---|---|---|---|---|---|
| *ATLANTIC* | Br | 5414/39 | *EL LAGO* | Pan | 4221/20 |
| *EMPIRE SELWYN* | Br | 7167/41 | *FRIEDRICH ENGELS* | Russ | 3972/30 |
| *IJORA* | Russ | 2815/21 | *NOREG* | Nor | 7605/31 |
| *REVOLUTSIONER* | Russ | 2900/36 | *TBILISI* | Russ | 7169/12 |
| *TREVORIAN* | Br | 4599/20 | *WEST NOHNO* | Amer | 5769/19 |

It sailed from Reykjavik (a change of terminal) on 1 February. The Russian *KIEV* may also have formed part of the convoy, but positive evidence on this point is lacking.

A local escort of three trawlers (names unknown) was provided until 5 February, while the Norwegian armed whalers HAV and SHIKA accompanied the convoy throughout. Between 5 and 8 February the cruiser NIGERIA escorted, with the destroyers FAULKNOR and INTREPID from 5 to 10 February. The minesweepers BRITOMART and SHARPSHOOTER joined on 7 February and took the combined convoy in to Murmansk on 10 February. The convoy was not located by the enemy, and no hostile action took place.

The names of merchant ships in this convoy are the result of reconstruction of Lloyd's records, and comparison with later outward sailings from Russia.

## Visit of British Trade Delegation to Russia

A British Trade Delegation was conveyed to Russia between 9 and 15 February in the cruiser CAIRO.

## Convoy QP 7

This convoy departed from Murmansk 12 February and dispersed on 15 February. It consisted of:

| | | | | | |
|---|---|---|---|---|---|
| *BOTAVON* | Br | 5848/12 | *DARTFORD* | Br | 4093/30 |
| *EL ALMIRANTE* | Pan | 5248/17 | *EMPIRE HALLEY* | Br | 7168/41 |
| *JUTLAND* | Br | 6153/28 | *SOUTHGATE* | Br | 4862/26 |
| *STALINGRAD* | Russ | 3559/31 | *STARY BOLSHEVIK* | Russ | 3974/33 |

The minesweepers HAZARD and SPEEDWELL provided local escort on 12/13 February, then being relieved by BRITOMART and SHARPSHOOTER until 15 February when they too returned to their Russian base. The destroyers FAULKNOR and INTREPID also escorted from 13 to 15 February while the cruiser NIGERIA provided "over the horizon" cover for the same period.

There was no enemy activity, and all ships had arrived at Seidisfjord by 22 February.

## Convoy PQ 11

The ships of this convoy assembled at Loch Ewe and then sailed to Kirkwall on 6 February, from whence they made their departure for Russia on the 14th. The ships were:

| | | | | | |
|---|---|---|---|---|---|
| *ASHKHABAD* | Russ | 5284/17 | *BARRWHIN* | Br | 4998/29 |
| *CITY OF FLINT* | Amer | 4963/20 | *DALDORCH* | Br | 5571/30 |
| *EMPIRE BAFFIN* | Br | 6978/41 | *EMPIRE MAGPIE* | Br | 6211/19 |
| *HARTLEBURY* | Br | 5082/34 | *KINGSWOOD* | Br | 5080/29 |
| *LOWTHER CASTLE* | Br | 5171/37 | *MAKAWAO* | Hon | 3253/21 |
| *MARYLYN* | Br | 4555/30 | *NORTH KING* | Pan | 4934/03 |
| *STEPAN KHALTURIN* | Russ | 2498/21 | | | |

Between 11 and 17 February an unknown cable vessel sailed with the convoy, probably en route to northern cable grounds. The American *CITY OF FLINT* had previously visited Murmansk, but in a somewhat different capacity for she had been taken in prize by the German armoured ship DEUTSCHLAND in 1939 and sailed by her prize crew to Murmansk en route to Germany. After US protests she was later released in Norwegian waters while on her way to Germany.

*HMS NIGERIA, arriving from escorting convoy PQ 11, at Kola Inlet on 22 February 1942; note the ice covered fo'c'sle.*

The initial escort from Loch Ewe is unknown, but two destroyers, AIREDALE and MIDDLETON and the trawlers BLACKFLY, CAPE ARGONA and CAPE MARIATO took the convoy from Kirkwall 14 to 17 February. Also present from Kirkwall were the minesweepers NIGER (Senior Officer, Escort) and HUSSAR and the corvette OXLIP, while her sister SWEETBRIAR joined on 17 February. On 22 February, the cruiser NIGERIA joined, accompanied by the Russian destroyers GROMKI and GROZNI and the minesweepers HARRIER, HAZARD and SALAMANDER. The convoy arrived at Murmansk 22 February after an uneventful passage.

This convoy was the first involving both Hunt class escort destroyers and Flower class corvettes, ships that were to be increasingly involved in future operations.

*Icebreaker FEDOR LITKE escorting the tanker ELONA leaving Archangel for Murmansk, where ELONA was to join convoy QP 8 for return to Britain.*

## Convoy QP 8

The convoy, which left Murmansk on 1 March, comprised the following:

| | | | | | |
|---|---|---|---|---|---|
| *ATLANTIC* | Br | 5414/39 | *BRITISH PRIDE* | Br | 7106/31 |
| *BRITISH WORKMAN* | Br | 6994/22 | *COLD HARBOR* | Pan | 5010/20 |
| *EL LAGO* | Pan | 4221/20 | *ELONA* | Br | 6192/36 |
| *EMPIRE SELWYN* | Br | 7167/41 | *EXPLORER* | Br | 6235/35 |
| *FRIEDRICH ENGELS* | Russ | 3972/30 | *JORA* | Russ | 2815/21 |
| *LARRANGA* | Amer | 3804/17 | *NOREG* | Nor | 7605/31 |
| *REVOLUTSIONER* | Russ | 2900/36 | *TBILISI* | Russ | 7169/12 |
| *WEST NOHNO* | Amer | 5769/19 | | | |

The local escort on sailing was provided by the minesweepers HARRIER and SHARPSHOOTER until dawn on 3 March, and the Russian destroyers GREMYASCHI (Commodore (D), Northern Fleet) and GROMKI until dusk the same day. The ocean escort, also present from sailing, were the minesweepers HAZARD (SOE) and SALAMANDER, and the corvettes OXLIP and SWEETBRIAR. From 2 to 7 March the cruiser NIGERIA (CS 10) provided distant cover.

Because of the threat posed by the presence of the battleship TIRPITZ, now in North Norway, the Commander-in-Chief, Home Fleet arranged submarine and air searches, and took the Fleet to sea in support, both for this convoy and the concurrent PQ 12. This was the first occasion that such strong support was needed, and it became a feature of succeeding convoys until the final demise of TIRPITZ.

*The Harrison Line EXPLORER, in Kola Inlet on 26 February 1942, prior to joining the homeward bound convoy QP 8.*

On 3 March thin ice was encountered and the following day a south westerly gale scattered the convoy. Later re-forming, it was found that *IJORA* and *LARRANGA* were missing; they did not rejoin although *LARRANGA* subsequently arrived in Iceland. Further Force 10 weather again scattered the convoy on 6 March, forty foot waves being met, but ships succeeded in maintaining contact and re-forming. On 7 March, at noon, in moderating weather, PQ 12 was met, the convoys passing through each other's columns. At this time QP 8 obtained its first navigational "fix" of the passage and shortly afterwards had again to alter course to avoid ice.

Later that afternoon, distress calls were received from *IJORA*, now some 100 miles astern, which revealed she was under attack by German destroyers. In fact, TIRPITZ was at sea with three destroyers searching for the eastbound PQ 12, fortunately with no success other than the unfortunate *IJORA* which had been sunk by the destroyer FRIEDRICH IHN; the battleship was subsequently attacked (unsuccessfully) by aircraft from the Home Fleet's aircraft carrier VICTORIOUS.

Subsequent close support for the convoy was provided briefly by the cruisers KENT and LONDON, and on 9 March the convoy split, five ships heading for Hvalfjord, arriving there escorted by OXLIP and SWEETBRIAR on 11 March, the remaining ships going to Akureyri.

## Convoy PQ 12

The convoy assembled at Loch Ewe and proceeded to Reykjavik, whence it sailed for Russia on 1 March, comprising:

| | | | | | |
|---|---|---|---|---|---|
| *ARTIGAS* | 12 Pan | 5613/20 | *BALLOT* | 41 Pan | 6131/22 |
| *BATEAU* | 23 Pan | 4687/26 | *BEACONSTREET* | 32 Br | 7467/27 |
| *BELOMORCANAL* | 43 Russ | 2900/36 | *CAPULIN* | 52 Pan | 4977/20 |
| *DNEPROSTROI* | 42 Russ | 4756/19 | *EARLSTON* | 53 Br | 7195/41 |
| *EL COSTON* | 33 Pan | 7286/24 | *EL OCCIDENTE* | 22 Pan | 6008/10 |
| *EMPIRE BYRON* | 51 Br | 6645/41 | *LANCASTER CASTLE* | 63 Br | 5172/37 |
| *LLANDAFF* | 31 Br | 4825/37 | *NAVARINO* | 21 Br | 4841/37 |
| *SEVZAPLES* | 62 Russ | 3974/32 | *STONE STREET* | 11 Pan | 6131/22 |
| *TEMPLE ARCH* | 61 Br | 5138/40 | | | |

Commodore was in *LLANDAFF*, Vice Commodore in *EMPIRE BYRON* and Rear Commodore in *NAVARINO*.

The local Iceland escorts were the trawlers ANGLE, CHILTERN, NOTTS COUNTY and STELLA CAPELLA. Of five whalers due to join, SHERA, SHUSA, STEFA, SULLA and SVEGA, only two did so on 4 March, staying with the convoy until arrival; two returned and the fifth proceeded to Russia accompanied by the minesweeper GOSSAMER. Of the two which did join one, SHERA, iced up and capsized in the Barentz Sea later in the passage.

The destroyers OFFA and ORIBI joined on 4 March, and remained until 12 and 10 respectively, while the cruiser KENYA was present from 6 to 12 March, being detached from the covering force. On 11 March the local escort from Russia, minesweepers HARRIER, HUSSAR and SPEEDWELL and destroyer GREMYASCHI joined.

Distant cover for this convoy, and its east bound counterpart QP 8, was provided by the Home Fleet, battleships KING GEORGE V, DUKE OF YORK, battlecruiser RENOWN, aircraft carrier VICTORIOUS, cruisers BERWICK and KENYA, destroyers ASHANTI, BEDOUIN, ECHO, ECLIPSE, FAULKNOR, FURY, GROVE, ICARUS, INCONSTANT, INTREPID, JAVELIN, LANCASTER, LEDBURY, LOOKOUT, ONSLOW, PUNJABI, TARTAR, VERDUN, WELLS and WOOLSTON.

PQ 12 was sighted by German aircraft on 5 March and, as already mentioned in the narrative for QP 8, TIRPITZ and her destroyer screen sortied to attack. Due to weather and inadequate position reporting, neither convoy was found and the only result was the sinking of the straggler *IJORA* and an abortive Fleet Air Arm attack on TIRPITZ.

The convoy, sailing unmolested, arrived at Murmansk on 12 March, having lost the whaler SHERA due to ice and weather on 9 March and with the destroyer ORIBI damaged by ice during 6/7 March. *EL OCCIDENTE* and *SEVZAPLES* straggled on 6 and 11 March respectively, but arrived safely, while the *BATEAU* was obliged to return to Iceland; she was to be lost in a subsequent convoy.

## Convoy PQ 13

Departing Loch Ewe on 10 March, the convoy arrived at Reykjavik a week later, and sailed from there for Russia on 20 March, as shown below:

| | | | | | | | |
|---|---|---|---|---|---|---|---|
| *BATEAU* | | Pan | 4687/26 | *DUNBOYNE* | 11 | Amer | 3515/19 |
| *EFFINGHAM* | 12 | Amer | 6421/19 | *EL ESTERO* | 53 | Pan | 4219/20 |
| *ELDENA* | 13 | Amer | 6900/19 | *EMPIRE COWPER* | 31 | Br | 7164/41 |
| *EMPIRE RANGER* | 32 | Br | 7008/42 | *EMPIRE STARLIGHT* | 22 | Br | 6850/41 |
| *GALLANT FOX* | 62 | Pan | 5473/18 | *HARPALION* | 21 | Br | 5486/32 |
| *INDUNA* | 41 | Br | 5086/25 | *LARS KRUSE* | 43 | Br | 1807/23 |
| *MANA* | 33 | Hon | 3283/20 | *MANO* | 63 | Br | 1418/25 |
| *MORMACMAR* | 23 | Amer | 5453/20 | *NEW WESTMINSTER CITY* | 52 | Br | 4747/29 |
| *RACELAND* | 42 | Pan | 4807/10 | *RIVER AFTON* | 51 | Br | 5479/35 |
| *SCOTTISH AMERICAN* | | Br | 6999/20 | *TOBRUK* | 61 | Pol | 7048/42 |

Commodore was in *EMPIRE COWPER,* Vice Commodore in *RIVER AFTON.*

*BATEAU* and *SCOTTISH AMERICAN* (escort oiler), joined off Iceland and their convoy positions are unknown. Sailing order shown is that from Loch Ewe to Iceland, and may have been amended for the onward passage.

Escorts from Loch Ewe were the destroyers SABRE (an old 1914/18 "S" class ship), and LAMERTON, both 10 to 16 March, Polish BLYSKAWICA 10 to 17 March, and SALADIN (a sister to SABRE) 11 to 17 March.

The initial local escort from Reykjavik, other than the whaler SULLA is unknown. On 23 March the trawlers BLACKFLY and PAYNTER, whalers SILJA and SUMBA and the destroyers ECLIPSE and FURY joined. The cruiser TRINIDAD and destroyer LAMERTON were present 23 to 25 March.

Eastern escorts 29 to 30 March were the destroyer ORIBI, Russian GREMYASCHI and SOKRUSHITELNY and minesweepers GOSSAMER, HUSSAR and SPEEDWELL.

The following ships of the Home Fleet provided distant cover: battleships KING GEORGE V, DUKE OF YORK, battlecruiser RENOWN, aircraft carrier VICTORIOUS, cruisers EDINBURGH, KENT, destroyers ASHANTI, BEDOUIN, ECHO, ESCAPADE, ESKIMO, FAULKNOR, FORESIGHT, ICARUS, INGLEFIELD, LEDBURY, MARNE, MIDDLETON, ONSLOW, PUNJABI, TARTAR, and WHEATLAND. This increased distant defence was necessitated by the accretion of strength to the enemy, who now had not only TIRPITZ but the armoured ship ADMIRAL SCHEER, and the 8 inch cruiser ADMIRAL HIPPER, all operational in northern waters.

On 24 March the convoy was progressing well, but by 27 March it had been much scattered by heavy weather so that ships were dispersed over an area 150 miles long south of Bear Island. German aircraft sighted and sank the stragglers *EMPIRE RANGER* and *RACELAND* on 28 March. Late on 28 March the German destroyers Z 24, Z 25 and Z 26, which had sailed after a sighting report, rescued 61 survivors from the *EMPIRE RANGER.* Some information about the convoy movements appears to have been obtained from these survivors, so that in the very early hours of 29 March *BATEAU* was found and sunk in a brief action by Z 26, 7 men being rescued.

Continuing the search for the convoy, the destroyers now encountered TRINIDAD who had been warned by intelligence reports to expect such an attack. A close range action then developed in very poor visibility resulting in Z 26 being badly damaged and abandoned after further damage received from ECLIPSE. Meantime, a malfunction in a torpedo fired by TRINIDAD to finish off the damaged Z 26 caused it to hit TRINIDAD herself causing damage that sent her limping in to Murmansk.

The convoy meantime had split into small groups. In one the *INDUNA* briefly towed SULLA (out of fuel), losing the tow during the night. *INDUNA* was then sunk by U 376 on 30 March; *EFFINGHAM* was sunk by U 435 later the same day. SULLA herself was probably sunk by U 436 on 1 April. Of the remaining ships, all reached Murmansk by 31 March, but unfortunately two, *NEW WESTMINSTER CITY* and *EMPIRE STARLIGHT,* were subsequently damaged by air raids on that port and lost, although *EMPIRE STARLIGHT* was salved post war and returned to service. To close the score, post-war analysis confirms that U 585 was lost by mining on 30 March during the operations against the convoy, not ( as originally thought ) sunk by FURY on 29 March.

*Ships awaiting the departure of convoy QP 9 in Kola Inlet on 13 March 1942.*

## Convoy QP 9

The convoy cleared Kola Inlet on 21 March, containing the following ships:

| | | | | | | |
|---|---|---|---|---|---|---|
| *ASHKHABAD* | 34 Russ | 5284/17 | *BARRWHIN* | 12 Br | 4998/29 |
| *CITY OF FLINT* | 51 Amer | 4963/20 | *DALDORCH* | 41 Br | 5571/30 |
| *EARLSTON* | 24 Br | 7195/41 | *EMPIRE BAFFIN* | 44 Br | 6978/41 |
| *EMPIRE MAGPIE* | 13 Br | 6211/19 | *HARTLEBURY* | 11 Br | 5082/34 |
| *KINGSWOOD* | 21 Br | 5080/29 | *LLANDAFF* | 14 Br | 4825/37 |
| *LOWTHER CASTLE* | 32 Br | 5171/37 | *MAKAWAO* | 53 Hon | 3253/21 |
| *MARYLYN* | 22 Br | 4555/30 | *NORTH KING* | 52 Pan | 4934/03 |
| *PRAVDA* | 23 Russ | 2513/28 | *SHELON* | 33 Russ | 2251/18 |
| *STEPAN KHALTURIN* | 43 Russ | 2498/21 | *TREVORIAN* | 31 Br | 4599/20 |

*HMS BRITOMART on 15 March 1942 off Polyarnoe in Kola Inlet.*

From sailing until 23 March the local escort was the minesweepers GOSSAMER, HARRIER, HUSSAR, NIGER and SPEEDWELL and the Russian destroyer GREMYASCHI. The ocean escort joining 21 March to 3 April comprised the destroyer OFFA and the minesweepers BRITOMART and SHARPSHOOTER. The cruiser KENYA, which had embarked ten tons of bullion, was to have been present 22 to 27 March, but did not meet the convoy. Distant cover was provided by the Home Fleet, which had earlier provided that defence for the inward bound convoy PQ 13—qv.

PQ 13 absorbed most of the enemy's attention; however U 655 attempted an attack on QP 9 and was rammed and sunk by SHARPSHOOTER as a result. The minesweeper was damaged, but was able to continue with the convoy. *PRAVDA* straggled on 23 March, otherwise the convoy remained intact and arrived at Reykjavik 3 April.

## Convoy PQ 14

The convoy assembled at Oban and sailed from there 26 March for Iceland escorted by the destroyers AMBUSCADE, BLYSKAWICA, BULLDOG and RICHMOND and the trawler TANGO. The following ships sailed from Reykjavik for Murmansk on 8 April:

| | | | | | |
|---|---|---|---|---|---|
| *ALDERSDALE* | Br | 8402/37 | *ANDRE MARTI* | Russ | 2352/18 |
| *ARCOS* | Russ | 2343/18 | *ATHELTEMPLAR* | Br | 8992/30 |
| *BRIARWOOD* | Br | 4019/30 | *BRITISH CORPORAL* | Br | 6972/22 |
| *CAPE CORSO* | Br | 3807/29 | *CITY OF JOLIET* | Amer | 6167/20 |
| *DAN-Y-BRYN* | Br | 5117/40 | *EL MIRLO* | Br | 8092/30 |
| *EMPIRE BARD* | Br | 3114/42 | *EMPIRE HOWARD* | Br | 6985/41 |
| *EXTERMINATOR* | Pan | 6115/24 | *FRANCIS SCOTT KEY* | Amer | 7191/41 |
| *HEGIRA* | Amer | 7588/19 | *HOPEMOUNT* | Br | 7434/29 |
| *IRONCLAD* | Amer | 5685/19 | *MINOTAUR* | Amer | 4553/18 |
| *MORMACRIO* | Amer | 5940/19 | *PIETER DE HOOGH* | Du | 7168/41 |
| *SEATTLE SPIRIT* | Amer | 5627/19 | *SUKHONA* | Russ | 3124/18 |
| *TREHATA* | Br | 4817/28 | *WEST CHESWALD* | Amer | 5711/19 |
| *WEST GOTOMSKA* | Amer | 5728/19 | *YAKA* | Amer | 5432/20 |

Commodore in *EMPIRE HOWARD,* Vice Commodore in *BRIARWOOD, ALDERSDALE* escort oiler.
The local escort from 8 to 12 April consisted of the trawlers CHILTERN and NORTHERN WAVE and the destroyer WILTON. The minesweepers HEBE and SPEEDY also joined on 8 April, but were forced to return with ice damage on 13 April. The ocean escort from 12 to 19 April comprised the destroyers AMAZON, BEAGLE, BEVERLEY and BULLDOG, corvettes CAMPANULA, OXLIP, SAXIFRAGE and SNOWFLAKE, and trawlers DUNCTON, LORD AUSTIN and LORD MIDDLETON. The last two named joined the convoy on 8 April, DUNCTON may have left (possibly due to defects) on 13 April as did LORD AUSTIN although this is not clear from available records. Over the horizon cover was provided by the cruiser NORFOLK in the Bear Island area.

Home Fleet distant cover was provided by the battleships KING GEORGE V, DUKE OF YORK, aircraft carrier VICTORIOUS, and cruisers NIGERIA and KENT with a screen of the destroyers BEDOUIN, BELVOIR, ESCAPADE, ESKIMO, FAULKNOR, LEDBURY, MATCHLESS, MIDDLETON, OFFA, ONSLOW, SOMALI and WHEATLAND. The cruiser EDINBURGH together with the destroyers FORESIGHT and FORESTER were designated for the cover, but did not join.

Dense fog for 30 hours and 12 hours of heavy pack ice forced the return of many ships to Iceland, some of them joining convoy QP 10 to do so. In the end, only *ATHELTEMPLAR, BRIARWOOD, DAN-Y-BRYN, EMPIRE HOWARD, HOPEMOUNT, TREHATA, WEST CHESWALD* and *YAKA* were able to continue the passage to Russia.

Intermittent air attacks were made on the remnant of the convoy on 15 April, more persistent air and submarine attacks followed throughout 16 April during which U 403 scored three hits (out of five torpedoes fired) on *EMPIRE HOWARD.* The Commodore's ship sank within a minute of the first hit, sixteen dying including the Commodore and two ship's Officers; nine of the dead were still alive when picked up.

Two Russian destroyers joined the escort on 17 April, and the minesweepers GOSSAMER, HARRIER, HUSSAR and NIGER may have done so on 18 April, the records are unclear on this point. The convoy arrived at Murmansk on 19 April to endure further persistent air attacks while in port, after one of the worst passages to date, due almost entirely to appalling weather conditions.

An attempt by the German destroyers SCHOEMANN, Z 24 and Z 25 to attack the convoy was frustrated by poor weather and, to a degree, by poor tactical handling which drew trenchant criticism from higher authority.

*The Russian freighter KIEV, which was lost in convoy QP 10.*

## Convoy QP 10

This convoy, which sailed from Kola Inlet on 10 April, consisted originally of the following ships:

| | | | | | |
|---|---|---|---|---|---|
| *ARTIGAS* | 32 Pan | 5163/20 | *BEACONSTREET* | 41 Br | 7467/27 |
| *BELOMORCANAL* | 12 Russ | 2900/36 | *CAPULIN* | 42 Pan | 4977/20 |
| *DNEPROSTROI* | 33 Russ | 4756/19 | *EL COSTON* | 52 Pan | 7286/24 |
| *EL OCCIDENTE* | 51 Pan | 6008/10 | *EMPIRE COWPER* | 34 Br | 7164/41 |
| *HARPALION* | 13 Br | 5486/32 | *KIEV* | 22 Russ | 5823/17 |
| *MANA* | 53 Hon | 3283/20 | *NAVARINO* | 21 Br | 4841/37 |
| *RIVER AFTON* | 23 Br | 5479/35 | *SEVZAPLES* | 11 Russ | 3974/32 |
| *STONE STREET* | 43 Pan | 6131/22 | *TEMPLE ARCH* | 31 Br | 5138/40 |

Additionally, during the voyage, six ships from convoy PQ 14 joined to return to Iceland with weather and ice damage. These took the following positions:

| | | | | | |
|---|---|---|---|---|---|
| *CITY OF JOLIET* | 35 Amer | 6167/20 | *FRANCIS SCOTT KEY* | 14 Amer | 7191/41 |
| *IRONCLAD* | 54 Amer | 5685/19 | *MINOTAUR* | 55 Amer | 4553/18 |
| *MORMACRIO* | 24 Amer | 5940/19 | *WEST GOTOMSKA* | 44 Amer | 5728/19 |

Commodore was in *TEMPLE ARCH,* Vice Commodore in *NAVARINO. STONE STREET* returned to Kola Inlet after sailing.

Local escorts on sailing were the minesweepers GOSSAMER, HARRIER and HUSSAR and two unknown Russian destroyers 10 to 12 April. The ocean escort also sailed on 10 April and comprised the destroyers FURY, MARNE, ORIBI and PUNJABI to 21 April, with ECLIPSE, the minesweeper SPEEDWELL and trawlers BLACKFLY and PAYNTER from 10 to 17 April. The cruiser LIVERPOOL accompanied the convoy from 12 to 18 April, and the Home Fleet, which had covered PQ 14, provided the same service for QP 10.

The convoy was heavily attacked between Kola Inlet and Bear Island for three days, both by aircraft and submarines; six aircraft are believed to have been destroyed. The *STONE STREET* was damaged and forced to return to Kola, *EMPIRE COWPER* and *HARPALION* were both sunk by aircraft on 11 April, and on 13 April U 435 sank the *EL OCCIDENTE* and the *KIEV,* the latter already damaged by air attack.

*HMS BLACKFLY, entering Seidisfjord on 20 April 1942 to fuel, after escorting convoy QP 10 from Murmansk. She was returning to the UK after duty in Russian waters.*

## Convoy PQ 15

The convoy assembled at Oban and sailed for Reykjavik on 10 April, departing from there for Russia on 26 April with the following ships:

| | | | | | |
|---|---|---|---|---|---|
| *ALCOA CADET* | Amer | 4823/19 | *ALCOA RAMBLER* | Amer | 5500/19 |
| *BAYOU CHICO* | Amer | 5401/20 | *BOTAVON* | Br | 5848/12 |
| *CAPE CORSO* | Br | 3807/29 | *CAPE RACE* | Br | 3807/30 |
| *CAPIRA* | Pan | 5565/20 | *DEER LODGE* | Amer | 6187/19 |
| *EMPIRE BARD* | Br | 3114/42 | *EMPIRE MORN* | Br | 7092/41 |
| *EXPOSITOR* | Amer | 4959/19 | *FRANCIS SCOTT KEY* | Amer | 7191/41 |
| *GRAY RANGER* | Br | 3313/41 | *HEGIRA* | Amer | 7588/19 |
| *JUTLAND* | Br | 6153/28 | *KRASSIN* | Russ | 4902/17 |
| *LANCASTER* | Amer | 7516/18 | *MONTCALM* | Br | 1432/04 |
| *MORMACREY* | Amer | 5946/19 | *MORMACRIO* | Amer | 5940/19 |
| *PAUL LUCKENBACH* | Amer | 6606/13 | *SEATTLE SPIRIT* | Amer | 5627/19 |
| *SOUTHGATE* | Br | 4862/26 | *TEXAS* | Amer | 5638/19 |
| *TOP TOPA* | Amer | 5356/20 | *ZEBULON B VANCE* | Amer | 7177/42 |

Commodore was in *BOTAVON*, Vice Commodore in *CAPE RACE*. This was the first Russian convoy in which a Catapult Aircraft Merchant (CAM) ship sailed, the *EMPIRE MORN*. Also included in the convoy were two icebreakers, the Russian *KRASSIN* returning home, and the Canadian *MONTCALM* on her delivery voyage after purchase by the Russians.

From 26 April to 5 May the trawlers CAPE PALLISER, CHILTERN, NORTHERN PRIDE and VIZALMA escorted; the destroyer LEDBURY joined escorting the oiler *GRAY RANGER* but detached to return to Lerwick during the passage, arriving there 8 May; the minesweepers BRAMBLE, LEDA and SEAGULL were present for the whole period. From 28 April the auxiliary AA ship ULSTER QUEEN and the destroyers BADSWORTH, BOADICEA, MATCHLESS, SOMALI, VENOMOUS and Norwegian ST ALBANS were present. The submarine STURGEON was in company as part of the escort from 28 April to 1 May, thereafter carrying out a covering patrol. The cruiser LONDON escorted 30 April to 1 May, and NIGERIA 28 April to 2 May.

*The American battleship WASHINGTON arriving at Iceland to cover the passage of convoy PQ 15, the first time that she reinforced the Home Fleet in these duties.*

The Home Fleet covering force comprised the battleships KING GEORGE V, relieved by DUKE OF YORK after the collision referred to later, USS WASHINGTON, aircraft carrier VICTORIOUS, cruisers KENYA, USS TUSCALOOSA

*The American cruiser TUSCALOOSA at sea off Iceland prior to covering the passage of convoy PQ 15, the first time that she had joined the Home Fleet to undertake these duties.*

and USS WICHITA and the US destroyers MADISON, PLUNKETT, WAINWRIGHT and WILSON and the British BELVOIR, ESCAPADE, FAULKNOR, HURSLEY, INGLEFIELD, LAMERTON, MARNE, MARTIN, MIDDLETON, ORIBI and PUNJABI. The submarines STURGEON, TRUANT and UNISON, Polish JASTRZAB, Norwegian UREDD, and Free French MINERVE also operated covering patrols.

On 1 May, in low visibility east of Iceland, the destroyer PUNJABI was in collision with KING GEORGE V and sunk, 206 survivors being picked up. The damaged battleship was replaced in the covering force by the DUKE OF YORK.

*Damage to the bows of HMS KING GEORGE V after the collision which sank HMS PUNJABI on 1 May 1942, while the Fleet was covering convoy PQ 15.*

From 2 May the convoy was constantly shadowed and subjected to attacks by both aircraft and submarine. *BOTAVON* was damaged by air attack on the first day, and had to be sunk by the destroyer BADSWORTH. Aircraft also sank *CAPE CORSO* and *JUTLAND*, the derelict hulk of the latter being finished off by U 251 the following day; from the three ships 137 survivors were rescued.

A second "own goal" sinking took place on 2 May when the Polish submarine JASTRZAB was detected by ST ALBANS and SEAGULL and, being many miles outside her allotted patrol area, was attacked as an enemy and sunk.

On 3 May CAPE PALLISER was damaged by bombs, one aircraft being shot down; this was the last casualty before the convoy arrived at Murmansk on 5 May.

In addition to the presence of icebreakers and a CAM ship, this convoy was notable for the increased number of American merchant ships(15) and the presence of strong USN representation in the Home Fleet covering force.

## Convoy QP 11

This convoy sailed from Murmansk on 28 April:

| | | | | | |
|---|---|---|---|---|---|
| *ATHELTEMPLAR* | Br | 8992/30 | *BALLOT* | Pan | 6131/22 |
| *BRIARWOOD* | Br | 4019/30 | *DAN-Y-BRYN* | Br | 5117/40 |
| *DUNBOYNE* | Amer | 3515/19 | *EL ESTERO* | Pan | 4219/20 |
| *ELDENA* | Amer | 6900/19 | *GALLANT FOX* | Pan | 5473/18 |
| *MORMACMAR* | Amer | 5453/20 | *STONE STREET* | Pan | 6131/22 |
| *TREHATA* | Br | 4817/28 | *TSIOLKOVSKY* | Russ | 2847/35 |
| *WEST CHESWALD* | Amer | 5711/19 | | | |

The eastern local escort on 28/29 April was the Russian destroyers KUIBYSHEV and SOKRUSHITELNY, and the minesweepers GOSSAMER, HARRIER, HUSSAR and NIGER. The ocean escort from 28 April to 7 May was the destroyers AMAZON, BEAGLE, BEVERLEY and BULLDOG (SOE), the corvettes CAMPANULA, OXLIP, SAXIFRAGE and SNOWFLAKE, and the trawler LORD MIDDLETON. The destroyers FORESIGHT and FORESTER joined from 28 to 30 April, and the cruiser EDINBURGH arrived on 30 April. Home Fleet distant cover was as follows: battleships KING GEORGE V, DUKE OF YORK, aircraft carrier VICTORIOUS, cruiser KENYA and destroyer screen BELVOIR, ESCAPADE, FAULKNOR, HURSLEY, INGLEFIELD, LAMERTON, MARNE, MARTIN, MIDDLETON and ORIBI.

*HMS EDINBURGH shortly before sinking. Note the battle ensigns at her foremast and the masthead of the minesweeper alongside to port, which is embarking survivors.*

The convoy was reported on 29 April by submarines and aircraft and, on 30 April, EDINBURGH (which had just joined after embarking a large quantity of gold at Murmansk) was torpedoed by U 456 while taking station ahead of the convoy. The cruiser's stern was blown off, although her port shafts remained intact, and she commenced a slow return to Murmansk escorted by FORESIGHT and FORESTER joined later by the Russian GREMYASCHI and SOKRUSHITELNY and patrol vessel RUBIN.

In consequence of this incident, the German destroyers SCHOEMANN, Z 24 and Z 25 were ordered to sea to attack the damaged cruiser; meantime air and submarine attacks on the convoy itself had been frustrated by an alert escort. The German destroyers' first contact was with the convoy, not EDINBURGH, and a series of six attacks were made throughout the afternoon of 1 May. Although the AMAZON was hit hard, she survived, and the total result of all attacks was the sinking of *TSIOLKOVSKY* by torpedoes fired by Z 24 and Z 25. The attackers then withdrew to search for EDINBURGH but it was not until 2 May that they received an accurate position report from a U boat.

Closing EDINBURGH, now in a poor state and almost unmanageable, the German destroyers commenced a torpedo attack to finish her off. In fact, EDINBURGH opened a very accurate fire and hit SCHOEMANN with her second salvo so heavily that she was eventually abandoned and sank. Most of her crew were taken off by the other destroyers, 56 men left on rafts were picked up by U 88.

EDINBURGH meanwhile had been hit by one of the destroyer's torpedoes, which in effect cut the ship in two, all the longitudinal strength being destroyed. Accordingly, orders were given to abandon her, and she was finally sunk by a torpedo from FORESIGHT. A spirited action had been fought by the British ships, who were lucky to escape with only the FORESTER badly hit, while the action also had the effect of distracting attention from the convoy, which arrived safely at Reykjavik on 7 May.

Two major salvage operations were conducted in the early 1980s on EDINBURGH, despite the presence in the wreck of 57 dead, and after much work at considerable depth, over 95% of the bullion was recovered for the benefit of the British and Soviet governments (and the salvors!).

## HMS TRINIDAD sails for home

On 13 May, following emergency repairs at Murmansk, the cruiser TRINIDAD sailed for home. She had been damaged on 29 March by her own torpedo during the action near convoy PQ 13; now she faced the journey to a British repair yard.

Escorted by the destroyers FORESIGHT and FORESTER, themselves returning with damage after the EDINBURGH action, and MATCHLESS and SOMALI, and with Home Fleet covering force of battleship DUKE OF YORK, aircraft carrier VICTORIOUS, cruisers KENT, LIVERPOOL, LONDON, NIGERIA and NORFOLK with a destroyer screen of BLANKNEY, ECLIPSE, ESCAPADE, FAULKNOR, FURY, ICARUS, INGLEFIELD, LAMERTON, MARNE, MIDDLETON, ONSLOW, ORIBI, and WHEATLAND, it fell to the Luftwaffe to try and prevent her return.

*HMS TRINIDAD shortly before being sunk by HMS MATCHLESS after aircraft damage earlier on 14 May 1942. The photographer's ship is coming alongside to embark survivors.*

Air attacks began in the evening of 14 May when a force of some 25 Ju 88s and 10 torpedo bombers made abortive attacks. However, at 2245 local time, just before dusk, a solitary Ju 88 breaking from low cloud succeeded in hitting her with one bomb causing an immediate outbreak of fire which rapidly spread. A further near miss also blew off the temporary patch fitted by the Russians and added to the ship's problems. By midnight the fire was out of control and, with the impossibility of towing the stricken ship and the certainty of continued attack at dawn the next day, the cruiser was abandoned, survivors being taken off by FORESIGHT, and the hulk sunk by torpedo from MATCHLESS.

*HMS LONDON passing through an Icelandic anchorage, with ships assembling for convoy PQ 16. Centrally is the EMPIRE ELGAR with her heavy lift derrick; she was to take passage to Murmansk and remain there to handle major cargo items in the port in the absence of shore cranes.*

## Convoy PQ 16

This, the largest Russian convoy to date, sailed from Reykjavik 21 May with the following ships:

| Ship | No. Flag | Tons/Year | Ship | No. Flag | Tons/Year |
|---|---|---|---|---|---|
| *ALAMAR* | 73 Amer | 5689/16 | *ALCOA BANNER* | 12 Amer | 5035/19 |
| *AMERICAN PRESS* | 54 Amer | 5131/20 | *AMERICAN ROBIN* | 64 Amer | 5172/19 |
| *ARCOS* | 63 Russ | 2343/18 | *ATLANTIC* | 61 Br | 5414/39 |
| *BLACK RANGER* | Br | 3417/41 | *CARLTON* | 14 Amer | 5127/20 |
| *CHERNYSHEVSKI* | 81 Russ | 3588/19 | *CITY OF JOLIET* | 62 Amer | 6167/20 |
| *CITY OF OMAHA* | 32 Amer | 6124/20 | *EMPIRE BAFFIN* | 21 Br | 6978/41 |
| *EMPIRE ELGAR* | 71 Br | 2847/42 | *EMPIRE LAWRENCE* | 11 Br | 7457/41 |
| *EMPIRE PURCELL* | 44 Br | 7049/42 | *EMPIRE SELWYN* | 41 Br | 7167/41 |
| *EXTERMINATOR* | 93 Pan | 6115/24 | *HEFFRON* | 52 Amer | 7611/19 |
| *HYBERT* | 34 Amer | 6120/20 | *JOHN RANDOLPH* | 24 Amer | 7191/42 |
| *LOWTHER CASTLE* | 31 Br | 5171/37 | *MASSMAR* | 53 Amer | 5828/20 |
| *MAUNA KEA* | 23 Amer | 6064/19 | *MICHIGAN* | 43 Amer | 5594/19 |
| *MINOTAUR* | 72 Amer | 4553/18 | *MORMACSUL* | 84 Amer | 5481/20 |
| *NEMAHA* | 42 Amer | 6501/20 | *OCEAN VOICE* | 51 Br | 7174/41 |
| *PIETER DE HOOGH* | 92 Du | 7168/41 | *REVOLUTSIONER* | 91 Russ | 2900/36 |
| *RICHARD HENRY LEE* | 22 Amer | 7191/41 | *SHCHORS* | 82 Russ | 3770/21 |
| *STARY BOLSHEVIK* | 83 Russ | 3974/33 | *STEEL WORKER* | 13 Amer | 5685/20 |
| *SYROS* | 74 Amer | 6191/20 | *WEST NILUS* | 33 Amer | 5495/20 |

Commodore was in *OCEAN VOICE*, Vice Commodore in *EMPIRE SELWYN*, *EMPIRE LAWRENCE* was the CAM ship, escort oiler was *BLACK RANGER*.

Local escort on 21 May was the minesweeper HAZARD (which remained until 30 May) and trawlers ST ELSTAN and LADY MADELEINE; from 21 to 24 May the Free French trawler RETRIEVER and the British NORTHERN SPRAY 21 to 25 May. On 23 May the destroyer LEDBURY was present with the oiler *BLACK RANGER*, and the submarines SEAWOLF and TRIDENT joined, together with the ocean escort which comprised the destroyers ACHATES, ASHANTI, MARTIN, VOLUNTEER and Polish GARLAND, corvettes HONEYSUCKLE, HYDERABAD, STARWORT and Free French ROSELYS, and the auxiliary AA ship ALYNBANK. The ocean escort remained until 30 May, 31 May in the case of ALYNBANK.

Between 23 and 26 May cruiser cover was provided by KENT, LIVERPOOL, NIGERIA and NORFOLK screened by the destroyers MARNE, ONSLOW and ORIBI, while the Home Fleet provided distant cover with the battleships DUKE OF YORK, USS WASHINGTON, aircraft carrier VICTORIOUS, and cruisers LONDON and USS WICHITA screened by the destroyers BLANKNEY, ECLIPSE, FAULKNOR, FURY, ICARUS, INTREPID, LAMERTON, MIDDLETON, WHEATLAND and the USS MAYRANT, RHIND, ROWAN and WAINWRIGHT.

*Thee Russian destroyer KUIBYSHEV, a frequent escort for convoys in Russian waters.*

From 28 to 30 May the local eastern escort comprised Russian destroyers GROZNI, KUIBYSHEV and SOKRUSHITELNY and minesweepers BRAMBLE, GOSSAMER and SEAGULL, with LEDA joining on 30 May.

While the Home Fleet was prepared to move on advice of any sortie by German heavy units, the cruiser cover sailed close to the convoy to the northward. From 25 May the convoy was shadowed constantly until the 30th and there were frequent air attacks. *EMPIRE LAWRENCE* launched her Hurricane which bagged one aircraft and damaged another; several aircraft were dealt with by AA fire from the escort and the cruiser force.

*The EMPIRE LAWRENCE on 21 May 1942 sailing for convoy PQ 16. She was a Catapult Aircraft Merchant ship, and on 25 May her Hurricane shot down one attacker and damaged a second. The ship herself was sunk by air attack on 27 May.*

The first loss occurred on 26 May when *SYROS* was sunk by U 703; shortly after this the cruiser force turned away to join convoy QP 12. There were further unsuccessful attacks that day by air, but no further U boat attacks then, nor later. On 27 May the convoy altered course south slightly due to ice and during that afternoon there were a series of attacks by large numbers of Ju 88s, up to 100 aircraft being involved. During this phase *EMPIRE PURCELL, EMPIRE LAWRENCE, LOWTHER CASTLE, ALAMAR* and *MORMACSUL* were sunk. Additionally, *CITY OF JOLIET* was damaged, and sank later on 28th. *CARLTON* (already damaged on 25 May) was again hit and was towed back to Iceland by NORTHERN SPRAY, while *OCEAN VOICE, STARY BOLSHEVIK* and *EMPIRE BAFFIN* were damaged but continued in the convoy. From the seven ships lost, escorts rescued 471 survivors. A final casualty was the Polish destroyer GARLAND; damaged, she had to leave the escort and proceed alone.

On 28 May the first local escort of GROZNI(SO), SOKRUSHITELNY and KUIBYSHEV joined and assisted in repelling air attacks on that day and on the 29th. The minesweepers BRAMBLE, GOSSAMER, LEDA and SEAGULL joined on the 30th, and with the MARNE and ALYNBANK took six merchant ships on to Archangel. The Archangel section was attacked after detachment, as was the main body, but with no casualties. The Murmansk convoy arrived there 30 May, and the Archangel section on 1 June; unfortunately after arrival in port the *STEEL WORKER* was lost in an air raid.

## Convoy QP 12

The convoy, which sailed out of Kola Inlet on 21 May, comprised the following ships:

| | | | | | |
|---|---|---|---|---|---|
| *ALCOA RAMBLER* | 52 Amer | 5500/19 | *BAYOU CHICO* | 53 Amer | 5401/20 |
| *CAPE RACE* | 41 Br | 3807/30 | *EMPIRE MORN* | 51 Br | 7092/41 |
| *EXPOSITOR* | 11 Amer | 4959/19 | *FRANCIS SCOTT KEY* | 42 Amer | 7191/42 |
| *HEGIRA* | 13 Amer | 7588/19 | *ILMEN* | 12 Russ | 2369/23 |
| *KUZBASS* | 23 Russ | 3109/14 | *MORMACRIO* | Amer | 5940/19 |
| *PAUL LUCKENBACH* | 43 Amer | 6606/13 | *SCOTTISH AMERICAN* | 32 Br | 6999/20 |
| *SEATTLE SPIRIT* | 22 Amer | 5627/19 | *SOUTHGATE* | 31 Br | 4862/26 |
| *TEXAS* | Amer | 5638/19 | *TOPA TOPA* | 21 Amer | 5356/20 |
| *ZEBULON B VANCE* | 33 Amer | 7177/42 | | | |

Commodore was in *SOUTHGATE,* Vice Commodore in *CAPE RACE. EMPIRE MORN* was CAM ship. The positions of *TEXAS* and *MORMACRIO* are unknown, but sailings are confirmed.

The eastern local escort to 23 May was the Russian destroyers GROZNI and SOKRUSHITELNY and the minesweepers BRAMBLE, GOSSAMER, LEDA and SEAGULL. Ocean escort 21 to 27 May were the destroyers BADSWORTH and VENOMOUS, and auxiliary AA ship ULSTER QUEEN; from 21 to 29 May destroyers BOADICEA, ESCAPADE, INGLEFIELD and Norwegian ST ALBANS, minesweeper HARRIER and trawlers CAPE PALLISER, NORTHERN PRIDE, NORTHERN WAVE and VIZALMA.

From 26 to 28 May cruiser cover was provided by KENT, LIVERPOOL, NIGERIA and NORFOLK with the destroyers ICARUS, MARNE and ONSLOW, all detached from PQ 16, while the Home Fleet provided distant cover for both convoys, see PQ 16 for a listing of ships concerned.

The merchant ships *KUZBASS* and *HEGIRA* returned. There were no attacks on the convoy as the enemy was fully occupied with the inward bound, loaded, PQ 16. *EMPIRE MORN* launched her Hurricane on 25 May which engaged and shot down a shadower; unfortunately the Hurricane pilot was killed when his parachute failed to open when he ditched alongside the convoy.

## Convoy PQ 17

This convoy, probably the most widely known of World War II, departed from Reykjavik on 27 June, and dispersed in the evening of 4 July. Ships involved were:

| | | | | | |
|---|---|---|---|---|---|
| *ALCOA RANGER* | 53 Amer | 5116/19 | *ALDERSDALE* | 74 Br | 8402/37 |
| *AZERBAIDJAN* | 64 Russ | 6114/32 | *BELLINGHAM* | 43 Amer | 5345/20 |
| *BENJAMIN HARRISON* | 72 Amer | 7191/42 | *BOLTON CASTLE* | 23 Br | 5203/39 |
| *CARLTON* | 92 Amer | 5127/20 | *CHRISTOPHER NEWPORT* | 81 Amer | 7191/42 |
| *DANIEL MORGAN* | 93 Amer | 7177/42 | *DONBASS* | 34 Russ | 7925/35 |
| *EARLSTON* | 62 Br | 7195/41 | *EL CAPITAN* | 22 Pan | 5255/17 |
| *EMPIRE BYRON* | 71 Br | 6645/41 | *EMPIRE TIDE* | 63 Br | 6978/41 |
| *FAIRFIELD CITY* | 82 Amer | 5686/21 | *GRAY RANGER* | 52 Br | 3313/41 |
| *HARTLEBURY* | 31 Br | 5082/34 | *HONOMU* | 83 Amer | 6977/19 |
| *HOOSIER* | 12 Amer | 5060/20 | *IRONCLAD* | 13 Amer | 5685/19 |
| *JOHN WITHERSPOON* | 84 Amer | 7191/42 | *NAVARINO* | 42 Br | 4841/37 |
| *OCEAN FREEDOM* | 73 Br | 7173/42 | *OLOPANA* | 33 Amer | 6069/20 |
| *PAN ATLANTIC* | 41 Amer | 5411/19 | *PAN KRAFT* | 32 Amer | 5644/19 |
| *PAULUS POTTER* | 11 Du | 7168/42 | *PETER KERR* | 61 Amer | 6476/20 |
| *RATHLIN* | 35 Br | 1600/36 | *RIVER AFTON* | 51 Br | 5479/35 |
| *SAMUEL CHASE* | 91 Amer | 7191/42 | *SILVER SWORD* | 44 Amer | 4937/19 |
| *TROUBADOR* | 24 Pan | 6428/20 | *WASHINGTON* | 21 Amer | 5564/19 |
| *WEST GOTOMSKA* | Amer | 5728/18 | *WILLIAM HOOPER* | 14 Amer | 7177/42 |
| *WINSTON-SALEM* | 54 Amer | 6223/20 | *ZAAFARAN* | 55 Br | 1559/21 |
| *ZAMALEK* | 94 Br | 1567/21 | | | |

Commodore was in *RIVER AFTON,* Vice Commodore in *HARTLEBURY,* Rear Commodore in *EMPIRE BYRON.* The position of *WEST GOTOMSKA* in the convoy is unknown, probably as she returned to Iceland early in the convoy's passage, leaving there 27 July for the Clyde after repairs.

The ocean escort from 27 June to 4 July comprised the minesweepers BRITOMART, HALCYON and SALAMANDER, trawlers AYRSHIRE, LORD AUSTIN, LORD MIDDLETON and NORTHERN GEM, destroyer MIDDLETON and auxiliary AA ships POZARICA and PALOMARES. On 30 June the destroyers FURY, KEPPEL (SOE), LEAMINGTON, LEDBURY, OFFA and WILTON and corvettes DIANELLA, LA MALOUINE, LOTUS and POPPY also joined. The destroyer DOUGLAS also sailed, detaching 2 July with the escort oiler *GRAY RANGER.* The submarines P 614 and P 615 also accompanied the convoy as escorts from 30 and 27 June respectively until dispersal.

**1942**

From 1 to 4 July the cruisers LONDON, NORFOLK , USS TUSCALOOSA and USS WICHITA screened by destroyers USS WAINWRIGHT and ROWAN provided close cover, while the Home Fleet was at sea as distant cover, comprising the battleships DUKE OF YORK, USS WASHINGTON, aircraft carrier VICTORIOUS, and cruisers CUMBERLAND and NIGERIA with a destroyer screen of ASHANTI, BLANKNEY, ESCAPADE, FAULKNOR, MARNE, MARTIN, MIDDLETON, ONSLAUGHT, ONSLOW and WHEATLAND plus the USS MAYRANT and RHIND.

When the convoy was detected, the enemy placed the battleship TIRPITZ, armoured ships ADMIRAL SCHEER and LUTZOW and cruiser ADMIRAL HIPPER on alert to sail, and also detailed U boats and the Luftwaffe to prepare for attacks, which commenced on 1 July and gradually escalated. On 4 July three merchant ships were lost to air attack, *NAVARINO, WILLIAM HOOPER* and *CHRISTOPHER NEWPORT,* the wreck of the last named being sunk by the submarine P 614 later in the day.

*The freighter NAVARINO as she is hit in convoy PQ 17, prior to the dispersal of the convoy on the afternoon of 4 July 1942. She sank shortly aftwards.*

The air attacks on 4 July having been repelled with relatively slight loss, the convoy was in good spirits and perfect order, so that the Admiralty order to scatter the convoy, based on faulty interpretation of intelligence on the movement of the enemy surface forces, came as a terrible shock. The destroyers of the escort closed on the cruiser force and prepared, as they thought, to engage heavy units, the convoy meantime scattered. What followed was undoubtedly a disaster as further merchant ships were sunk at leisure by aircraft and U boats who were enabled to roam the onward route of the convoy with impunity, seeking the near defenceless merchant ships, 21 of which were sunk between 5 and 10 July as follows:

**By U boats**

*ALCOA RANGER, ALDERSDALE, CARLTON, DANIEL MORGAN, EARLSTON, EL CAPITAN, EMPIRE BYRON, HARTLEBURY, HONOMU, HOOSIER, JOHN WITHERSPOON, OLOPANA, RIVER AFTON.*

**By aircraft**

*BOLTON CASTLE, FAIRFIELD CITY, PAN ATLANTIC, PAN KRAFT, PAULUS POTTER, PETER KERR, WASHINGTON, ZAAFARAN.*

The dates, and units responsible for the sinkings, can be found by reference to the alphabetical list of losses.

After the convoy had scattered and when it was realised that there were not, in fact, surface units at sea, the smaller escorts still in the area commenced collecting what ships they could find to proceed to Archangel. Initially six ships were formed into a small convoy, *BENJAMIN HARRISON, EL CAPITAN, HOOSIER, OCEAN FREEDOM, SAMUEL CHASE* and *ZAMALEK.* The escorts were the corvette LOTUS, with the Convoy Commodore on board, and LA MALOUINE and POPPY, AA ships PALOMARES and POZARICA, minesweepers BRITOMART, HALCYON and SALAMANDER and trawlers LORD AUSTIN, LORD MIDDLETON and NORTHERN GEM. Sailing south from Novaya Zemlya, the convoy picked up some survivors en route, and was then again attacked by some 40 aircraft, losing *EL CAPITAN* and *HOOSIER* prior to arriving in Archangel on 11 July.

The first arrival at Archangel had been the Rescue Ship *RATHLIN* on 9 July, who brought in *BELLINGHAM* and *DONBASS.* After the arrival of the second group, Commodore Dowding sailed in POPPY on 16 July together with LA MALOUINE and LOTUS to search for more survivors. By the time they returned to Archangel on 24 July, reinforced by BRAMBLE, HAZARD, DIANELLA, LEDA and POZARICA, plus two Russian destroyers, a number of survivors had been rescued and they had with them *EMPIRE TIDE, SILVER SWORD, TROUBADOR, IRONCLAD* and *AZERBAIDJAN* plus the Russian icebreaker *MURMAN* and trawler *KEROV,* and the trawler AYRSHIRE of the escort. The final arrival was the *WINSTON-SALEM* which had been aground and arrived 28 July after being refloated, partly through the efforts of the US Naval Attache in Moscow who had made his way to the scene.

In all twenty four ships were lost in the convoy, and the remaining ships and escorts perforce remained in Russian waters until the later convoys of the summer, some being employed in the Kara Sea area.

## Convoy QP 13

The Archangel section of this convoy sailed on 26 June, met the Murmansk section on 28 June and proceeded as a single convoy, the complete list of ships being:

| | | | | | |
|---|---|---|---|---|---|
| *ALMA ATA* | 54 Russ | 3611/20 | *AMERICAN PRESS* | 62 Amer | 5131/20 |
| *AMERICAN ROBIN* | 61 Amer | 5172/19 | *ARCHANGELSK* | 64 Russ | 2480/29 |
| *ATLANTIC* | 81 Br | 5414/39 | *BUDENNI* | 43 Russ | 2482/23 |
| *CAPIRA* | 93 Pan | 5565/20 | *CHULMLEIGH* | 94 Br | 5445/38 |
| *CITY OF OMAHA* | 72 Amer | 6124/20 | *EMPIRE BAFFIN* | 31 Br | 6978/41 |
| *EMPIRE MAVIS* | 84 Br | 5704/19 | *EMPIRE METEOR* | 24 Br | 7457/40 |
| *EMPIRE SELWYN* | 51 Br | 7167/41 | *EMPIRE STEVENSON* | 14 Br | 6209/41 |
| *EXTERMINATOR* | 23 Pan | 6115/24 | *HEFFRON* | 42 Amer | 7611/19 |
| *HEGIRA* | 22 Amer | 7588/19 | HMS ALYNBANK | 63 | |
| *HYBERT* | 92 Amer | 6120/20 | *JOHN RANDOLPH* | 13 Amer | 7191/42 |
| *KOMILES* | 53 Russ | 3962/32 | *KUZBASS* | 34 Russ | 3109/14 |
| *LANCASTER* | 71 Amer | 7516/18 | *MASSMAR* | 82 Amer | 6828/20 |
| *MAUNA KEA* | 91 Amer | 6064/19 | *MICHIGAN* | 41 Pan | 5594/19 |
| *MORMACREY* | 11 Amer | 5946/19 | *MOUNT EVANS* | 74 Pan | 5536/19 |
| *NEMAHA* | 21 Amer | 6501/20 | *PETROVSKI* | 44 Russ | 3771/21 |
| *PIETER DE HOOGH* | 12 Du | 7168/41 | *RICHARD HENRY LEE* | 32 Amer | 7191/41 |
| *RODINA* | 73 Russ | 4441/22 | *ST CLEARS* | 33 Br | 4312/36 |
| *STARY BOLSHEVIK* | 52 Russ | 3974/33 | *YAKA* | 83 Amer | 5432/20 |

Commodore was in *EMPIRE SELWYN;* passengers were embarked in *ALMA ATA, BUDENNI, CHULMLEIGH, EMPIRE BAFFIN, EMPIRE MAVIS, EMPIRE SELWYN, KOMILES, MOUNT EVANS* and *PETROVSKI.*

Eastern local escort 26 to 28 June was provided by the Russian destroyers GROZNI, GREMYASCHI and KUIBYSHEV and the minesweepers BRAMBLE, HAZARD, LEDA and SEAGULL. The ocean escort from 26 June was, to 1 July the submarine TRIDENT, to 3 July the destroyers INGLEFIELD and INTREPID, to 5 July the minesweeper NIGER, to 7 July the minesweeper HUSSAR, corvettes HONEYSUCKLE, HYDERABAD, ROSELYS and STARWORT, the AA ship ALYNBANK, and the destroyers ACHATES, VOLUNTEER and Polish GARLAND. The trawlers LADY MADELEINE and ST ELSTAN were also present until 7 July. Home Fleet distant cover was provided by the force also covering PQ 17- qv.

The destroyer DOUGLAS, with the escort oiler *GRAY RANGER* joined from convoy PQ 17.

Thick weather prevailed for the duration of the voyage and the convoy was not attacked, although reported on 30 June and 2 July. Off North East Iceland on 4 July the convoy divided into 16 ships for Loch Ewe and 19 for Reykjavik, this latter portion sailing in five columns escorted by NIGER (SOE), HUSSAR, ROSELYS, LADY MADELEINE and ST ELSTAN.

During the final passage of the Iceland portion, visibility reduced to one mile and the NE wind increased to force 8; no sights had been obtainable for 48 hours. At 1910 the convoy formation was reduced to two columns to pass through the gap inshore of the British minefield off Straumness, and course for this was altered on a DR basis supported by soundings. At about 2200 NIGER, who had gone ahead to make a landfall with HUSSAR as a visual link to the convoy astern, sighted what appeared to be North Cape and ordered a course alteration. In fact NIGER had sighted a large iceberg, and at 2240 she blew up and sank just after she had realised her mistake and signalled the Commodore in *AMERICAN ROBIN.* In the reduced visibility six merchantmen struck mines, *EXTERMINATOR, HEFFRON, HYBERT, MASSMAR* and *RODINA* sinking and *JOHN RANDOLPH* being damaged. The remaining escorts entered the minefield to rescue survivors; the rest of the convoy spent the night imagining U boat or a surface attack. ROSELYS remained in the field for over six hours while picking up 179 survivors. HUSSAR eventually obtained an accurate fix on the shore line and led the convoy to safety, arriving at Reykjavik on 7 July.

## Operation GEARBOX

This operation codename was used on several occasions, always in connection with Spitzbergen. In this instance, it was used for the summer relief of the garrison there, carried out between 25 June and 3 July by the cruiser MANCHESTER and destroyer ECLIPSE. There was no interference by the enemy during the operation.

## Ammunition and stores to Archangel

The supplies of the escorts from PQ 17 now at Archangel having been gravely depleted, the destroyers MARNE, MARTIN, MIDDLETON and BLANKNEY were despatched on 20 July with replacements, sailing from Scapa Flow via Seidisfjord. Although these ships were sighted by aircraft off Jan Mayen Island, there was no enemy reaction, and they arrived safely at Kola Inlet on 24 July, having been fuelled en route by the RFA *BLACK RANGER* escorted by the destroyer WILTON.

## Independent passages to North Russia

At the request of the Soviet government, two Russian merchant ships, the *BELOMORCANAL* and *FRIEDRICH ENGELS,* lying loaded in Iceland, were sailed on 12 and 11 August respectively as independents to Archangel. Both ships arrived safely.

## Royal Air Force personnel and stores to Russia

In preparation for the basing of Hampden aircraft in North Russia, ground crews and equipment, plus a hospital unit and medical stores for British and Allied wounded and sick, were embarked at Greenock in the cruiser USS TUSCALOOSA, destroyers USSs RODMAN and EMMONS and the British ONSLAUGHT at Greenock which all sailed on 13 August. The force was met 800 miles off Archangel by the destroyers MARNE and MARTIN and escorted in. The medical unit with the force was not allowed to land, and eventually returned in convoy QP 14.

## Operation EU

On completion of the stores delivery, the USSs TUSCALOOSA, RODMAN and EMMONS returned to Britain, covered also by MARNE, MARTIN and ONSLAUGHT, sailing on 24 August. During the passage the three British destroyers were detached, as a result of Enigma decrypts, for a sweep to the south and they intercepted and sank the German minelayer ULM on 24 July. As many survivors as possible from PQ 17 were embarked in the ships of the force for the return journey, arriving in the UK on 28 August.

## Convoy PQ 18

Obliged, for political reasons, to sail a further convoy to Russia during the summer months, the Commander-in-Chief Home Fleet was determined to prevent any possible repetition of the PQ 17 debacle. The plans for this convoy therefore included a strong "fighting escort" of destroyers that were rigorously trained as a unit, and the first deployment of an escort carrier with a Russian convoy.

*HMS FURY with HMS ASHANTI in the background, exercising prior to sailing as the Fighting Destroyer Escort for convoy PQ 18.*

Ships of the convoy assembled in Loch Ewe and sailed from there for Iceland on 2 September. Of those sailing, *BEAUREGARD* had to return, while *GATEWAY CITY, OREMAR* and *SAN ZOTICO* were for passage to Iceland only. On 8 September six ships from Hvalfjord *(ANDRE MARTI, ATHELTEMPLAR, EXFORD, STALINGRAD, SUKHONA* and *TBILISI)* joined and the convoy proceeded in the formation shown:

| | | | | | |
|---|---|---|---|---|---|
| *AFRICANDER* | 94 Pan | 5441/21 | *ANDRE MARTI* | 14 Russ | 2352/18 |
| *ATHELTEMPLAR* | 45 Br | 8992/30 | *BLACK RANGER* | 54 Br | 3417/41 |
| *CAMPFIRE* | 63 Amer | 5671/19 | *CHARLES R McCORMICK* | 13 Amer | 6027/20 |
| *COPELAND* | 15 Br | 1526/23 | *DAN-Y-BRYN* | 81 Br | 5117/40 |
| *EMPIRE BAFFIN* | 11 Br | 6978/41 | *EMPIRE BEAUMONT* | 41 Br | 7044/42 |
| *EMPIRE MORN* | 53 Br | 7092/41 | *EMPIRE SNOW* | 31 Br | 6327/41 |
| *EMPIRE STEVENSON* | 91 Br | 6209/41 | *EMPIRE TRISTRAM* | 51 Br | 7167/42 |
| *ESEK HOPKINS* | 43 Amer | 7191/42 | *EXFORD* | 33 Amer | 4969/19 |
| *GOOLISTAN* | 74 Br | 5851/29 | *GRAY RANGER* | 65 Br | 3313/41 |
| *HOLLYWOOD* | 34 Amer | 5498/20 | *JOHN PENN* | 73 Amer | 7177/42 |
| *KENTUCKY* | 12 Amer | 5446/21 | *KOMILES* | 21 Russ | 3962/32 |
| *LAFAYETTE* | 62 Amer | 5887/19 | *MACBETH* | 101 Pan | 4941/20 |
| *MARY LUCKENBACH* | 93 Amer | 5049/19 | *MEANTICUT* | 44 Amer | 6061/21 |
| *NATHANIEL GREENE* | 72 Amer | 7177/42 | *OCEAN FAITH* | 71 Br | 7173/42 |
| *OLIGARCH* | Br | 6894/18 | *OLIVER ELLSWORTH* | 105 Amer | 7191/42 |
| *OREGONIAN* | 101 Amer | 4862/17 | *PATRICK HENRY* | 42 Amer | 7191/41 |
| *PETROVSKI* | 22 Russ | 3771/21 | *SAHALE* | 52 Amer | 5028/19 |
| *SCHOHARIE* | 64 Amer | 4971/19 | *ST OLAF* | 32 Amer | 7191/42 |
| *STALINGRAD* | 103 Russ | 3559/31 | *SUKHONA* | 104 Russ | 3124/18 |
| *TBILISI* | 75 Russ | 7169/12 | *TEMPLE ARCH* | 61 Br | 5138/40 |
| *VIRGINIA DARE* | 82 Amer | 7176/42 | *WACOSTA* | 92 Amer | 5432/20 |
| *WHITE CLOVER* | 23 Pan | 5462/20 | *WILLIAM MOULTRIE* | 83 Amer | 7177/42 |

Additionally, three Motor Minesweepers, MMS 90, MMS 203 and MMS 212 were with the convoy on delivery passage to the Russian Northern Fleet. Their orders were to act as rescue ships, and they did not therefore have position numbers allocated to them.

Commodore was in *TEMPLE ARCH,* Vice Commodore in *DAN-Y-BRYN,* Rear Commodore in *EMPIRE SNOW. COPELAND* was the designated Rescue Ship. The oilers *ATHELTEMPLAR, BLACK RANGER, GRAY RANGER* remained with the convoy, *OLIGARCH* was detached to Lowe Sound, Spitzbergen, to join *BLUE RANGER* to provide a fuelling point for ships of the escort. *EMPIRE MORN* was CAM ship.

Escorts from Loch Ewe on 2 September until after the Iceland meeting point were the destroyers CAMPBELL, ESKDALE, FARNDALE and MALCOLM and trawlers ARAB, DUNCTON, HUGH WALPOLE, KING SOL and PAYNTER. The destroyers MONTROSE and WALPOLE joined on 6 September also.

The ocean escort was in three sections. The first joined on 7 September and went through to Archangel arriving on 21 September and consisted of the destroyers ACHATES and MALCOLM, the AA ships ALYNBANK and ULSTER QUEEN, corvettes BERGAMOT, BLUEBELL, BRYONY and CAMELLIA and minesweepers GLEANER and SHARPSHOOTER. This close escort was augmented by the submarines P 614 and P 615 9 to 17 September, and by the trawlers CAPE ARGONA, CAPE MARIATO, DANEMAN and ST KENAN which joined on 9 September and went through to Archangel.

The second element of the escort was the escort carrier AVENGER escorted by the destroyers WHEATLAND and WILTON, while the "fighting escort" consisted of the cruiser SCYLLA(Flag) and destroyers ASHANTI, ESKIMO, FAULKNOR, FURY, IMPULSIVE, INTREPID, MARNE, MARTIN, METEOR, MILNE, OFFA, ONSLAUGHT, ONSLOW, OPPORTUNE, SOMALI and TARTAR. Both the carrier force and the destroyer escort joined on 9 September and remained until 17 September, then detaching to convoy QP 14. FURY and IMPULSIVE remained until 18, while OFFA did not join until 13 September.

The cruiser cover force was formed from LONDON, NORFOLK and SUFFOLK which cruised to the North of the convoy. At Spitzbergen, where a concurrent relief operation was underway, were the cruisers CUMBERLAND and SHEFFIELD and destroyer ECLIPSE; while the establishment of a fuelling base there for the convoy escorts involved the destroyers AMAZON, BULLDOG, COWDRAY, ECHO, OAKLEY, VENOMOUS, WINDSOR and WORCESTER.

Local escort from 17 September was provided by the Russian destroyers GREMYASCHI and KUIBYSHEV, joined on 18 September by SOKRUSHITELNY and URITSKI and the minesweepers BRITOMART, HALCYON, HAZARD and SALAMANDER.

Distant cover for the passage of this convoy and QP 14, and for the Spitzbergen operations, was provided by the Home Fleet made up of battleships ANSON and DUKE OF YORK, cruiser JAMAICA, and destroyers BRAMHAM, KEPPEL, MACKAY and MONTROSE . An additional escort factor was provided by two squadrons of Hampden torpedo bombers specially flown to Russia to operate, if the situation arose, against enemy heavy units attempting to intercept the convoy when within their range.

When the main escort joined, half the destroyers immediately went ahead to Lowe Sound and fuelled, to return and relieve their consorts. The convoy had been located the previous day, 8 September, and twelve U boats were sailed to form three intercept groups. Cruiser movements also took place, but in fact the prior decision had been made not to use surface forces, in view of the success of submarines and aircraft against PQ 17, though of course this fact was unknown to the British. Probably the most potent threat to the convoy however was posed by the Luftwaffe, then disposing of 91 torpedo bombers and 133 high level and dive bombers in Northern Norway.

Between 9 and 13 September fuelling continued for the escorts, either in Lowe Sound or from the oilers in the convoy. The escort had its first success on 12 September when FAULKNOR, with ONSLOW and IMPULSIVE, sank U 88 ahead of the convoy. The enemy drew blood the next day when either U 405 or U 408 sank *STALINGRAD* and *OLIVER ELLSWORTH.*

Air patrols by the AVENGER's aircraft harassed the constant shadowers, and the first air attacks took place on 13 September when Ju 88s bombed without effect. Shortly afterwards 44 torpedo bombers attacked the convoy from the south, pressing home their attack despite an intense AA barrage from all ships. AVENGER had been caught off balance, and was unable to get her Hurricanes airborne in time. Slow reaction by the two starboard columns of the convoy, those ships with numbers in the 90 and 100 series, caused their destruction, six of the eight ships sunk being in those positions, for a loss of only 5 aircraft.

Early on 14 September the oiler *ATHELTEMPLAR* was torpedoed by U 457; severely damaged, she was later sunk by HARRIER after consideration of towing her to Lowe Sound had to be abandoned. Also on that day, ONSLOW, together with a Swordfish from AVENGER and IMPULSIVE and FAULKNOR sank U 589. A further torpedo attack was frustrated with no loss to the convoy and 12 aircraft were brought down. Further attacks developed later in the day by aircraft and, although the *MARY LUCKENBACH* was sunk in a colossal explosion 20 aircraft were claimed destroyed, in fact only 8 were lost.

*PQ 18 under attack on 14 September 1942. The MARY LUCKENBACH in column 8 has just blown up; she had escaped the heavy losses in that column and in column 9 during the attack on the previous day.*

On 15 September air attacks continued, but were driven of with no loss to the convoy and thereafter U boats became the principal threat. On 16 September Russian based Catalina aircraft were able to support the convoy against them, and on that day IMPULSIVE sank U 457.

SCYLLA and her destroyers left PQ 18 on 16 September and transferred their strength to the homeward bound QP 14, the main threat being adjudged past. In fact, there were further air attacks on 18 September in the entrance to the White Sea in which *KENTUCKY* was severely damaged and went ashore; the Russians later attempted to salvage some of her cargo though the ship was a total loss. *EMPIRE MORN* flew off her Hurricane during these attacks; after exhausting his ammunition the RAF pilot succeeded in making a landing at a Russian airfield many miles away from the convoy.

On a final note, an unusual feature of this convoy was the decision of Admiral Burnett in SCYLLA to arrange the transfer of all survivors from ships of the convoy to the cruiser and attendant destroyers before departing to join QP 14. This spared many men the rigours of existing in Russia until the next convoy home, and relieved the British staff in Archangel and Murmansk of considerable problems as, in the event, they had to support only the unfortunate *KENTUCKY's* survivors.

## Convoy QP 14

This convoy brought home survivors from PQ 17, both human and ships, and sailed from Archangel on 13 September as follows:

| | | | | | |
|---|---|---|---|---|---|
| *ALCOA BANNER* | 32 Amer | 5035/19 | *BELLINGHAM* | 61 Amer | 5345/20 |
| *BENJAMIN HARRISON* | 51 Amer | 7191/42 | *BLACK RANGER* | 33 Br | 3417/41 |
| *DEER LODGE* | 42 Amer | 6187/19 | *EMPIRE TIDE* | 11 Br | 6978/41 |
| *GRAY RANGER* | 52 Br | 3313/41 | *HARMATRIS* | 21 Br | 5395/32 |
| *MINOTAUR* | 22 Amer | 4554/18 | *OCEAN FREEDOM* | 41 Br | 7173/42 |
| *OCEAN VOICE* | 31 Br | 7174/41 | *OLIGARCH* | 44 Br | 6894/18 |
| *RATHLIN* | 53 Br | 1600/36 | *SAMUEL CHASE* | 62 Amer | 7191/42 |
| *SILVER SWORD* | 43 Amer | 4937/19 | *TOBRUK* | 13 Pol | 7048/42 |
| *TROUBADOR* | 63 Pan | 6428/20 | *WEST NILUS* | 12 Amer | 5495/20 |
| *WINSTON-SALEM* | Amer | 6223/20 | *ZAMALEK* | 23 Br | 1567/21 |

Commodore was in *OCEAN VOICE,* Vice Commodore in *OCEAN FREEDOM; RATHLIN* and *ZAMALEK* were Rescue Ships. *ALCOA BANNER, EMPIRE TIDE, HARMATRIS, MINOTAUR, OCEAN FREEDOM* and *WEST NILUS* carried a total of 141 passengers.

The oiler *OLIGARCH* joined the convoy during its passage, after operating in Lowe Sound as oiler for the escorts of PQ 18 and QP 14. The position of *WINSTON-SALEM* is not known, Lloyd's records confirm her sailing from Russia on 13 September.

The eastern local escort comprised BRITOMART, HALCYON, HAZARD and SALAMANDER while the ocean escort was BLANKNEY and MIDDLETON from 13 to 25 September, BRAMBLE, LEDA (until her loss) and SEAGULL, trawlers AYRSHIRE, LORD AUSTIN, LORD MIDDLETON and NORTHERN GEM. AA ships ALYNBANK, PALOMARES and POZARICA were present 13 to 26 September as were the corvettes DIANELLA, LA MALOUINE, LOTUS and POPPY. On 17 September SCYLLA , the escort carrier AVENGER, destroyers ASHANTI, ESKIMO, FAULKNOR, FURY, INTREPID, MARNE, METEOR, MILNE, OFFA, ONSLAUGHT, ONSLOW, OPPORTUNE, SOMALI, TARTAR, WHEATLAND and WILTON, the submarines P 614 and P 615 joined from PQ 18. Ships of this last unit detached at varying dates from 20 September (SCYLLA, AVENGER, FURY, WHEATLAND and WILTON), 21st (OPPORTUNE, ESKIMO, SOMALI, ASHANTI and INTREPID, P 614 and P 615). MILNE detached on 22, remaining ships on 25 September. WORCESTER and IMPULSIVE provided local escort to Loch Ewe 25/26 September, the convoy arriving there on the 26th.

Cruiser and distant cover was provided by the ships that had carried out that duty for PQ 18.

The passage of the convoy, in poor weather, was uneventful until 20 September when the minesweeper LEDA was sunk by U 435 while in the stern station of the escort. On the same evening *SILVER SWORD,* a survivor of PQ 17 was sunk by U 255, while U 703 torpedoed the destroyer SOMALI. SOMALI was taken in tow by ASHANTI,

*HMS SOMALI under tow by ASHANTI after being torpedoed on 20 September.*

screened by ESKIMO, INTREPID, OPPORTUNE and LORD MIDDLETON. After a tow of 420 miles, in deteriorating weather, SOMALI broke in two and sank on 24 September.

Air cover was first available on 21 September, the first Catalina being damaged by gunfire from a U boat and having to land near the convoy. On 22 September U 435 penetrated the screen, and sank *OCEAN VOICE* and *BELLINGHAM* and hit *GRAY RANGER* which had later to be sunk. The final event in the passage of the convoy was the sinking of U 253 by a Coastal Command Liberator of 210 Squadron on 23 September. The convoy finally reached Loch Ewe on 26 September.

## Transfer of medical and RAF personnel to and from Russia

Between 13 and 28 October, the cruiser ARGONAUT and destroyers INTREPID and OBDURATE took the previously rejected Medical Unit to Archangel, and brought home the RAF aircrews and ground staff from the two Hampden squadrons, those aircraft having been handed over to the Russians after the completion of the passage of PQ 18.

## Independent passages—Operation FB

Operation "Torch", the North African invasion, required the detachment of so many Home Fleet ships that it became impossible to run convoy PQ 19. As a gesture to the Russians, the decision was taken to attempt a major series of independent passages both east and westbound, the eastbound series being known as Operation FB.

It was planned that twelve merchant ships, then lying in Iceland, should be sailed at twelve hour intervals from 29 October to 2 November, alternating British and American ships. At the last moment, a further Russian ship was also added.

**1942**

While no escorts were provided, the trawlers CAPE PALLISER, NORTHERN PRIDE, NORTHERN SPRAY and ST ELSTAN were disposed along the route from Iceland, while CAPE ARGONA, CAPE MARIATO and ST KENAN were sailed from Murmansk to cover the eastern end of the passage. It was the presence of NORTHERN SPRAY and her attack on a U boat, plus unusual reconnaissance by Catalina aircraft along the route that probably alerted the enemy. In the event, of the 13 ships three returned, five were sunk and only five completed their voyage. However, 22 of the 23 ships sailed westward from Russia arrived safely.

Merchant ships involved were as follows:

**Eastbound, returned to Iceland**

| | | | | | | |
|---|---|---|---|---|---|---|
| *BRIARWOOD* | Br | 4019/30 | | | | |
| *DALDORCH* | Br | 5571/30 | | | | |
| *JOHN H B LATROBE* | Amer | 7191/42 | | | | |
| **Eastbound, sunk** | | | | | | |
| *CHULMLEIGH* | Br | 5445/38 | Stranded and then sunk by U 625 16 November. | | | |
| *DEKABRIST* | Russ | 7363/03 | Sunk by aircraft 4 November. | | | |
| *EMPIRE GILBERT* | Br | 6640/41 | Sunk by U 586 on 2 November. | | | |
| *EMPIRE SKY* | Br | 7455/41 | Sunk by U 625 on 6 November. | | | |
| *WILLIAM CLARK* | Amer | 7176/42 | Sunk by U 354 on 4 November. | | | |
| **Eastbound, arrived** | | | | | | |
| *EMPIRE GALLIARD* | Br | 7170/42 | | *EMPIRE SCOTT* | Br | 6150/41 |
| *HUGH WILLIAMSON* | Amer | 7177/42 | | *JOHN WALKER* | Amer | 7191/42 |
| *RICHARD H ALVEY* | Amer | 7191/42 | | | | |

Between 29 October and 24 January 1943, the following Russian ships were sailed independently. Although not officially titled Operation FB, the term "Op FB West" has been used in our index:

| | | | |
|---|---|---|---|
| *ALDAN* | 2161/12 | *AZERBAIDJAN* | 6114/32 |
| *CHERNYSHEVSK* | 3588/19 | *DONBASS* | 7925/35 |
| *DVINA* | 1773/22 | *ELNA II* | 3221/03 |
| *KARA* | 2325/33 | *KOMSOMOLETS ARCTIKI* | 3450/97 |
| *KRASNOE ZNAMYA* | 2271/01 | *KUZBASS* | 3109/14 |
| *MIRONYCH* | 2274/27 | *MOSSOVET* | 2981/35 |
| *MSTA* | 1984/21 | *OB* | 2198/17 |
| *OKHTA* | 1357/18 | *OSMUSSAAR* | 2229/09 |
| *SAKKO* | 2363/29 | *SHEKSNA* | 2242/18 |
| *SHILKA* | 1388/16 | *SOROKA* | 1718/26 |
| *URITSKI* | 2336/29 | *VANZETTI* | 2363/28 |
| *VETLUGA* | 1717/18 | | |

**Note that *ELNA II*, previously a British ship, went to Murmansk in September 1941 and remained in Russian waters under Russian ownership following transfer. Having returned West as an independent, she proceeded to the American West Coast, and thereafter traded between there and Vladivostok with war material.

All of the ships arrived safely in Iceland except *DONBASS*, sunk by the destroyer Z 27 on 7 November.

## Convoy QP 15

This, the final westbound convoy of 1942 and the last of the PQ/QP series, sailed from Archangel on 17 November with the following ships:

| | | | | | | | |
|---|---|---|---|---|---|---|---|
| *ANDRE MARTI* | 33 | Russ | 2352/18 | *BELOMORCANAL* | 12 | Russ | 2900/36 |
| *CHARLES R McCORMICK* | 62 | Amer | 6027/20 | *COPELAND* | 54 | Br | 1526/23 |
| *DAN-Y-BRYN* | 71 | Br | 5117/40 | *EMPIRE BAFFIN* | 61 | Br | 6978/41 |
| *EMPIRE MORN* | 13 | Br | 7092/41 | *EMPIRE SNOW* | 31 | Br | 6237/41 |
| *EMPIRE TRISTRAM* | 72 | Br | 7167/42 | *ESEK HOPKINS* | 73 | Amer | 7191/42 |
| *EXFORD* | 41 | Amer | 4969/19 | *FRIEDRICH ENGELS* | 23 | Russ | 3972/30 |
| *GOOLISTAN* | 53 | Br | 5851/29 | HMS ULSTER QUEEN | 42 | | |
| *HOLLYWOOD* | 93 | Amer | 5498/20 | *IRONCLAD* | | Amer | 5685/19 |
| *KOMILES* | 21 | Russ | 3962/32 | *KUZNETZ LESOV* | 64 | Russ | 3974/33 |
| *LAFAYETTE* | 43 | Amer | 5887/19 | *MEANTICUT* | | Amer | 6061/21 |
| *NATHANAEL GREENE* | 83 | Amer | 7177/42 | *OCEAN FAITH* | 81 | Br | 7173/42 |
| *PATRICK HENRY* | 82 | Amer | 7191/41 | *PETROVSKI* | 44 | Russ | 3771/21 |
| *SAHALE* | 11 | Amer | 5028/19 | *SCHOHARIE* | 32 | Amer | 4971/19 |
| *ST OLAF* | 22 | Amer | 7191/42 | *TBILISI* | 52 | Russ | 7169/12 |
| *TEMPLE ARCH* | 51 | Br | 5138/40 | *VIRGINIA DARE* | 91 | Amer | 7176/42 |
| *WHITE CLOVER* | 63 | Pan | 5462/20 | *WILLIAM MOULTRIE* | 92 | Amer | 7177/42 |

Commodore was in *TEMPLE ARCH,* Vice Commodore in *DAN-Y-BRYN; COPELAND* was Rescue Ship, and *EMPIRE MORN* CAM ship.

*IRONCLAD* and *MEANTICUT* both grounded after sailing, and although they got off they were too late to overtake the convoy, and returned to Archangel.

The eastern local escort on 17 November comprised the minesweepers BRITOMART, HALCYON, HAZARD and SHARPSHOOTER, and from 18 to 20 November the destroyers BAKU and SOKRUSHITELNY. The ocean escort from sailing to 30 November consisted of corvettes BERGAMOT, BLUEBELL, BRYONY and CAMELLIA and minesweeper SALAMANDER. Destroyers FAULKNOR, INTREPID, ICARUS and IMPULSIVE were present from 20 to 26, ECHO from 20 to 22 and MUSKETEER and ORWELL 23 to 30 November. Destroyers LEDBURY and MIDDLETON joined on 22 and OAKLEY on 23 November, all three staying until 30th.The AA ship ULSTER QUEEN joined 17 and left to fuel 24 November. Cruiser cover west of Bear Island was provided by LONDON and SUFFOLK screened by FORESTER, OBDURATE and ONSLAUGHT while the submarines P 312, P 216, Free French JUNON and Norwegian UREDD patrolled off Altenfjord to intercept any sortie by surface ships.

By the time the convoy reached the vicinity of Bear Island it had been fragmented by a series of violent gales which also had the fortunate effect of preventing any air activity by the enemy. Escorts had their work cut out to maintain even tenuous contact with their charges, and BLUEBELL, CAMELLIA and ULSTER QUEEN were obliged to depart to fuel.

The weather did not thwart all the U boats, and U 625 sank *GOOLISTAN* and U 601 the *KUZNETZ LESOV* on 11 November. The severity of the weather can be judged by the experience of the two Russian destroyers on 20 November: BAKU lost portions of her superstructure and had serious leaks forward and in her boiler room, while SOKRUSHITELNY was pooped while turning, lost all power and sank after two days drifting in appalling weather; 57 men were lost.

*The Russian destroyer SOKRUSHITELNY, which foundered in heavy weather after escorting convoy QP 15.*

The convoy reached Loch Ewe on 30 November, and this completed the series of PQ/QP convoys. With the next sailing a new code was adopted, JW for eastbound convoys, and RA for westbound.

## Convoy JW 51A

This first convoy in the renamed sequence initiated the practice of using Loch Ewe as the UK terminal, dispensing with a call at Iceland as had hitherto been the case. The convoy sailed on 15 December, made up as follows:

| | | | | | | | |
|---|---|---|---|---|---|---|---|
| *BEAUREGARD* | 51 | Amer | 5976/20 | *BRIARWOOD* | 31 | Br | 4019/30 |
| *DYNASTIC* | 13 | Amer | 5773/19 | *EL ALMIRANTE* | 43 | Pan | 5248/17 |
| *EL OCEANO* | 32 | Pan | 6767/25 | *EMPIRE METEOR* | 11 | Br | 7457/40 |
| *GATEWAY CITY* | 21 | Amer | 5432/20 | *GREYLOCK* | 33 | Amer | 7640/21 |
| *J L M CURRY* | 23 | Amer | 7176/42 | *OLIGARCH* | 42 | Br | 6894/18 |
| *OREMAR 52* | | Amer | 6854/19 | *RICHARD BASSETT* | 12 | Amer | 7191/42 |
| *RICHARD BLAND* | 34 | Amer | 7191/42 | *SAN CIPRIANO* | 22 | Br | 7966/37 |
| *WEST GOTOMSKA* | 41 | Amer | 5728/18 | *WIND RUSH* | 53 | Amer | 5586/18 |

Commodore was in *BRIARWOOD,* Vice Commodore in *EMPIRE METEOR, OLIGARCH* was escort oiler.

The western local escorts 15 to 18 December to 66N were the destroyers BLANKNEY, CHIDDINGFOLD and LEDBURY. From 15 to 25 December the escorts were the corvettes HONEYSUCKLE and OXLIP, minesweeper SEAGULL, and trawlers LADY MADELEINE and NORTHERN WAVE. On 18 December the destroyers BOADICEA, ECHO, ECLIPSE, FAULKNOR (SOE), FURY, and INGLEFIELD joined, on 19 December BEAGLE, MATCHLESS and OPPORTUNE arrived together with the cruisers JAMAICA and SHEFFIELD. Between 19 and 22 December the battleship KING GEORGE V, cruiser BERWICK and destroyers MUSKETEER, QUADRANT and RAIDER provided distant cover. The cruiser force, Force R, remained to the westward until the convoy passed Bear Island, then closed the convoy when the three destroyers of Force R fuelled from the escort oiler and joined the escort. The two cruisers then sailed some 60 miles to the south of the convoy, reaching Kola Inlet a day ahead of the main body. The convoy arrived on Christmas Day 1942, not having been discovered by the enemy.

## Convoy JW 51B

This convoy sailed from Loch Ewe on 22 December, 7 days behind the A section, comprising:

| | | | | | |
|---|---|---|---|---|---|
| *BALLOT* | Pan | 6131/22 | *CALOBRE* | Pan | 6891/19 |
| *CHESTER VALLEY* | Amer | 5078/19 | *DALDORCH* | Br | 5571/30 |
| *DOVER HILL* | Br | 5815/18 | *EMPIRE ARCHER* | Br | 7031/42 |
| *EMPIRE EMERALD* | Br | 8032/41 | *EXECUTIVE* | Amer | 4978/20 |
| *JEFFERSON MYERS* | Amer | 7582/20 | *JOHN H B LATROBE* | Amer | 7191/42 |
| *PONTFIELD* | Br | 8319/40 | *PUERTO RICAN* | Amer | 6076/19 |
| *RALPH WALDO EMERSON* | Amer | 7176/42 | *VERMONT* | Amer | 5670/19 |
| *YORKMAR* | Amer | 5612/19 | | | |

Commodore was in *EMPIRE ARCHER,* Vice Commodore was in *CALOBRE* later moving to *DALDORCH. DOVER HILL* was forced to return with weather and boiler damage, *BALLOT* was wrecked in the entrance to Kola Inlet on arrival, *PONTFIELD* went aground also but got off.

The western escort from 22 to 25 December was the destroyers BLANKNEY, CHIDDINGFOLD and LEDBURY. The destroyer BULLDOG was present 22 to 23 December, while the following ships joined 22 December (leaving on the date shown): corvettes HYDERABAD to 2 Jan and RHODODENDRON to 3 Jan, minesweeper BRAMBLE to 29 December and trawlers NORTHERN GEM and VIZALMA to 3 Jan. On Christmas Day the destroyers ACHATES OBEDIENT, OBDURATE, ONSLOW, ORIBI and ORWELL all joined. From 27 to 31 December cruiser cover was provided by SHEFFIELD and JAMAICA from Kola Inlet, screened until 29 December by MATCHLESS and OPPORTUNE. Distant cover was provided by the battleship ANSON, cruiser CUMBERLAND, destroyers BLANKNEY, CHIDDINGFOLD, FORESTER, ICARUS and IMPULSIVE.

The first enemy shadowing report was probably made on 24 December; the convoy was broken up by bad weather the next day, ORIBI, VIZALMA and five merchant ships losing touch. ORIBI arrived in Kola independently on 31 December, one of the merchant ships not turning up there until 5 January. Three other merchantmen rejoined on 29 December, while VIZALMA and the fifth ship, having stayed well to the North, did so on 1 January. In the interval, BRAMBLE was detached to search for the straggling ships astern of the convoy.

The convoy was again reported on 30 December when OBDURATE put down a shadowing U boat, U 354. As a result of her report, the cruiser ADMIRAL HIPPER, armoured ship LUTZOW and destroyers ECKOLDT, BEITZEN, RIEDEL, Z 29, Z 30 and Z 31 were sailed for Operation ''Regenbogen'', to intercept the convoy. On reaching the approximate area of the convoy, the two cruisers divided, with the six destroyers spread out between them to form a line of search and swept on, later separating into two groups of a major ship and three destroyers in each. ECKOLDT made the first sighting at 0800 when the position was that there were five destroyers, two corvettes and a trawler in company with the convoy. VIZALMA was some 45 miles north, BRAMBLE was searching 15 miles astern and the cruiser cover was 30 miles to the north of the convoy.

First contact by the escort was by HYDERABAD twenty minutes after the German sighting, but no report was made as it was thought that the enemy were Russian destroyers. Ten minutes later OBDURATE sighted and reported them; an hour later she was fired on, made an enemy report, and fell back on the main escort. ONSLOW (Captain Sherbrooke) then sighted the HIPPER, and the cruiser cover was advised of the position, altering towards the convoy which also turned to close the cruisers. In doing so it was unwittingly closing the LUTZOW group, a fact observed by HIPPER which was evading a possible torpedo attack. When this did not materialise, a heavy fire was opened on ONSLOW which received several hits and sustained heavy damage and casualties, including the severe wounding of Captain Sherbrooke, the Senior Officer of the Escort. During this interval, BRAMBLE, while closing the convoy, happened upon HIPPER who hit her badly and sent ECKOLDT to finish her off.

The situation then was that ACHATES was covering the rear of the convoy with smoke, while OBEDIENT, OBDURATE and ORWELL covered the convoy to the North from HIPPER, the corvettes the southern flank, and ONSLOW was ahead of the convoy. ACHATES was then ordered to join the crippled ONSLOW, shortly after HIPPER engaged her and inflicted heavy damage killing 40 onboard. The cruiser was then engaged by the three undamaged destroyers and, fearing a torpedo attack, she turned away only to be straddled by fire from the rapidly approaching British cruisers. HIPPER then retired, calling for all ships to join her, ECKOLDT in so doing approaching close to SHEFFIELD out of a snow squall. While the German thought the ship was HIPPER, SHEFFIELD was under no such misapprehension and engaged and sank her at short range.

There was further action between the escort and LUTZOW, damaging OBEDIENT, but the intervention of the cruiser force caused the enemy to retire with damage to HIPPER and the loss of ECKOLDT. By 1240 the enemy was out of touch and the danger past, with only one merchant ship damaged in the action. ACHATES, who had continued screening the convoy with smoke, then suddenly called for assistance from NORTHERN GEM and sank almost at once with heavy casualties, the final loss to the convoy which proceeded without further incident, being met by the minesweepers HARRIER and SEAGULL and arriving at Kola Inlet on 3 and 4 January.

The final result of the action was the loss of ACHATES and BRAMBLE, and damage to OBDURATE, OBEDIENT and ONSLOW. On the German side, ECKOLDT was lost and HIPPER damaged; more importantly the poor results of the large German force led to a far reaching political upheaval culminating in the removal of Admiral Raeder, the Commander-in-Chief and a decision to lay up the German surface fleet. While this last order was not fully implemented, it did cause lasting damage to German operational freedom.

## Convoy RA 51

Sailing from Kola Inlet 30 December 1942, the ships were:

| | | | | | |
|---|---|---|---|---|---|
| *BELORUSSIA* | 13 Russ | 2900/36 | *CAMPFIRE* | 53 Amer | 5671/19 |
| *EMPIRE GALLIARD* | 11 Br | 7200/42 | *EMPIRE SCOTT* | 31 Br | 6150/41 |
| *HOPEMOUNT* | 33 Br | 7434/29 | *HUGH WILLIAMSON* | 43 Amer | 7177/42 |
| *JOHN WALKER* | 32 Amer | 7191/42 | *KOTLIN* | 34 Russ | 2545/21 |
| *MEANTICUT* | 42 Amer | 6061/21 | *OKHTA* | 44 Russ | 1357/18 |
| *OLIGARCH* | 23 Br | 6894/18 | *REVOLUTSIONER* | 22 Russ | 2900/36 |
| *RICHARD H ALVEY* | 52 Amer | 7191/42 | *VOLGA* | 24 Russ | 2847/35 |

Commodore was in *EMPIRE SCOTT,* Vice Commodore in *EMPIRE GALLIARD; OLIGARCH* was escort oiler. *KOTLIN* was forced to return to Kola.

Escort from Kola was (dates of leaving in brackets), minesweeper GLEANER (10 Jan), trawlers CAPE ARGONA, CAPE MARIATO, DANEMAN and ST KENAN (11, 6, 7 and 5 Jan respectively) destroyers ECHO, ECLIPSE, FAULKNOR(SOE), FURY and INGLEFIELD (all to 6 Jan) and BEAGLE (7 Jan). A western local escort from 6 January of the destroyers BLANKNEY and LEDBURY ( 9 and 10 Jan respectively) and MONTROSE (10 Jan) and WORCESTER (7 to 10 Jan) was provided. Cruiser cover comprised JAMAICA and SHEFFIELD from 30 December to 2 January; they arrived at Seidisfjord on 4 January and were relieved by BERWICK and KENT. Distant cover came from battleships KING GEORGE V and HOWE, cruiser BERMUDA and destroyers MONTROSE, MUSKETEER, PIORUN, QUEENBOROUGH, RAIDER and WORCESTER.

Preoccupied with the attack on JW 51B, the enemy did not attempt any attack on RA 51 which arrived at Loch Ewe 11 January. *OKHTA,* having straggled, proceeded to Iceland.

## Transport of wounded

Urgent medical attention being required, OBDURATE and OBEDIENT made an independent passage from Kola to Scapa Flow 11 to 15 January 1943 with the seriously wounded from the Barentz Sea action.

*When the Flower class corvette HMS LOTUS was completed and commissioned, her first duty was to escort convoy PQ 17 to North Russia. This photograph shows HMS LOTUS in January 1943, probably with convoy JW 52. Her acoustic sweep on the A frame right forward is given extra prominence by the covering of ice.*

## Convoy JW 52

This convoy of 15 ships sailed from Loch Ewe 17 January as follows:

| | | | | | |
|---|---|---|---|---|---|
| *ATLANTIC* | 53 Br | 5414/39 | *CORNELIUS HARNETT* | 12 Amer | 7177/42 |
| *DAN-Y-BRYN* | 21 Br | 5117/40 | *DELSUD* | 32 Amer | 4982/19 |
| *EL ORIENTE* | 23 Pan | 6012/10 | *EMPIRE BAFFIN* | 41 Br | 6978/41 |
| *EMPIRE CLARION* | 13 Br | 7031/42 | *EMPIRE PORTIA* | 52 Br | 7058/42 |
| *EMPIRE SNOW* | 51 Br | 6327/41 | *EMPIRE TRISTRAM* | 43 Br | 7167/42 |
| *GULFWING* | 42 Amer | 10217/28 | *NICHOLAS GILMAN* | 33 Amer | 7176/42 |
| *OCEAN FAITH* | 11 Br | 7174/42 | *OLIGARCH* | 22 Br | 6894/18 |
| *TEMPLE ARCH* | 31 Br | 5138/40 | | | |

Commodore was in *EMPIRE CLARION,* Vice Commodore in *DAN-Y-BRYN,* Rear Commodore in *EMPIRE BAFFIN, OLIGARCH* was escort oiler. *ATLANTIC* and *EMPIRE BAFFIN* were obliged to return with defects.

Western local escort 17 to 21 January was destroyers BLANKNEY, LEDBURY and MIDDLETON, ocean escort from 17 to 27 January corvettes LOTUS and STARWORT, minesweeper BRITOMART and trawlers NORTHERN PRIDE and ST ELSTAN. On 21 January the destroyers BEAGLE, BULLDOG, MATCHLESS, MUSKETEER, OFFA, ONSLAUGHT and Polish PIORUN joined. Cruiser cover was provided by BERMUDA, GLASGOW and KENT from 21 January from 10E to Kola, while distant cover on 23/24 January came from battleship ANSON and cruiser SHEFFIELD screened by ECHO, ECLIPSE, FAULKNOR, INGLEFIELD, MONTROSE, QUEENBOROUGH, RAIDER and Polish ORKAN.

The convoy was located and shadowed on 23 January, but U boats making contact were driven under by the escort while the convoy made evasive course alterations. An attack by 4 torpedo bombers on 24 January lost two of their number, and the undamaged convoy arrived in Kola Inlet on 27 January.

## Independent passages by merchant ships

The Russian authorities sailed four ships independently westward to Iceland during January 1943, of which two were lost

| | | | |
|---|---|---|---|
| *UFA* | Russ | 1892/17 | By U 255 on 26 January |
| *KRASNY PARTIZAN* | Russ | 2418/27 | By U 255 on 26 January |

The two ships which succeeded in making a safe passage to Iceland were

| | | | | | |
|---|---|---|---|---|---|
| *BUREYA* | Russ | 2723/08 | *LEONID KRASIN* | Russ | 1840/13 |

Two ships were also sailed independently eastward to the White Sea:

| | | | | | |
|---|---|---|---|---|---|
| *ANDRE MARTI* | Russ | 2352/18 | *MOSSOVET* | Russ | 2981/35 |

Both ships arrived on 20 February but were subsequently damaged in air raids.

## Convoy RA 52

This convoy sailed from Kola Inlet on 29 January 1943 as follows:

| | | | | | |
|---|---|---|---|---|---|
| *BEAUREGARD* | 32 Amer | 5976/20 | *BRIARWOOD* | 21 Br | 4019/30 |
| *DALDORCH* | 31 Br | 5571/30 | *DYNASTIC* | 43 Amer | 5773/19 |
| *EL ALMIRANTE* | 42 Pan | 5248/17 | *EL OCEANO* | 41 Pan | 6767/25 |
| *EMPIRE METEOR* | 11 Br | 7457/40 | *GATEWAY CITY* | 22 Amer | 5432/20 |
| *GREYLOCK* | 12 Amer | 7460/21 | *WIND RUSH* | 33 Amer | 5586/18 |

Commodore was in *DALDORCH,* Vice Commodore in *EMPIRE METEOR.*

Ocean escort from sailing consisted of BEAGLE, BULLDOG, FORESTER, ICARUS, MATCHLESS, MUSKETEER, OFFA, ONSLAUGHT, ONSLOW and PIORUN, all to 5 February except ONSLOW (2 February) and FORESTER (4 February), corvettes HONEYSUCKLE, HYDERABAD, RHODODENDRON and OXLIP and minesweepers HARRIER and SEAGULL. All these ships remained until 8 February except HONEYSUCKLE and SEAGULL who were absent fuelling 6 to 8 Feb. Trawlers LADY MADELEINE, NORTHERN GEM, NORTHERN WAVE and VIZALMA were also present until 8 February. A local escort of destroyers BLANKNEY and MIDDLETON joined from 5 to 8 February, and VIVACIOUS 5 to 7 February. On the destroyers leaving, HARRIER became SOE. ONSLOW was on passage with serious damage after the Barentz Sea action in convoy JW 51B.

From 30 January to 2 February BERMUDA, GLASGOW and KENT provided cruiser cover, and ANSON, SHEFFIELD, INGLEFIELD, ORIBI, OBEDIENT and ORKAN distant cover.

U boat attacks commenced on 1 February, U 255 sinking *GREYLOCK* on the 3rd although her entire crew was rescued. The escorts were somewhat fatigued after a long stint in Arctic weather, some of the ships having been at sea, in action or lying at Kola Inlet for over a month with a consequent lessening of efficiency. The convoy arrived at Loch Ewe between 8 and 9 February.

*Taken from HMS INGLEFIELD, the destroyer HMS LEDBURY oils at Seidisfjord before sailing to meet RA 53.*

*The view looking forward from HMS SHEFFIELD shortly before she sustained the weather damage which prevented her continuing with convoy JW 53.*

## Convoy JW 53

The convoy sailed from Loch Ewe on 15 February with 26 ships, a further 3 ships following the next day as convoy JW 53B to overtake, names of the combined convoy as follows:

| | | | | | |
|---|---|---|---|---|---|
| *ARTIGAS* | Pan | 5613/20 | *ATLANTIC* | Br | 5414/39 |
| *BEACONHILL* | Amer | 6941/19 | *BERING* | Amer | 7631/20 |
| *BRITISH GOVERNOR* | Br | 6840/26 | *CITY OF OMAHA* | Amer | 6124/20 |
| *DOVER HILL* | Br | 5815/18 | *EMPIRE BAFFIN* | Br | 6978/41 |
| *EMPIRE FORTUNE* | Br | 6140/43 | *EMPIRE GALLIARD* | Br | 7200/42 |
| *EMPIRE KINSMAN* | Br | 6744/42 | *EMPIRE SCOTT* | Br | 6150/41 |
| *EXPLORER* | Br | 6235/35 | *FRANCIS SCOTT KEY* | Amer | 7191/42 |
| *ISRAEL PUTNAM* | Amer | 7176/42 | *JAMES BOWIE* | Amer | 7176/42 |
| *JOHN LAURANCE* | Amer | 7176/42 | *JOSEPH E JOHNSTON* | Amer | 7196/42 |
| *KOMILES* | Russ | 3962/32 | *LLANDAFF* | Br | 4825/37 |
| *MARATHON* | Nor | 7208/30 | *MOBILE CITY* | Amer | 6157/20 |
| *OCEAN FREEDOM* | Br | 7173/42 | *PETROVSKI* | Russ | 3771/21 |
| *PIETER DE HOOGH* | Du | 7168/41 | *TBILISI* | Russ | 7169/12 |
| *THOMAS HARTLEY* | Amer | 7176/42 | *TOBRUK* | Pol | 7048/42 |

Unfortunately, documents regarding the composition of the convoy have not survived and it has been necessary to reconstruct the above list from a variety of sources. In every case it is confirmed that the ships named were at Loch Ewe and available for sailing. *EMPIRE BAFFIN, EXPLORER, JAMES BOWIE, JOHN LAURANCE, JOSEPH*

*E JOHNSTON* and *KOMILES* returned with weather damage or engine defects after sailing, such being recorded by Lloyd's; all other ships later returned from Russia with no explicable alternative passage, and in most of the cases an arrival date in Russian waters is available.

Of the ships making the passage, *DOVER HILL* was damaged at Murmansk after arrival, and *OCEAN FREEDOM* sunk in harbour there by air attack.

A western local escort covered the convoy from sailing, consisting of the minesweeper HAZARD for the first day, the corvettes BRYONY, DIANELLA and LORD MIDDLETON to the 17 February, and destroyers MEYNELL, MIDDLETON and PYTCHLEY to 21 and minesweeper HALCYON to the 22 February. The minesweeper JASON, corvettes BERGAMOT and POPPY and the trawler LORD AUSTIN accompanied the convoy throughout the passage.

The corvettes BLUEBELL and CAMELLIA joined from 20 to 27 February, while the destroyer escort of BOADICEA, FAULKNOR, INGLEFIELD, MILNE, OBDURATE, OBEDIENT, OPPORTUNE, ORWELL, was present from 19 to 27 February. Reinforcement commanded by CS 10 in the cruiser SCYLLA accompanied by destroyers ECLIPSE, FURY, IMPULSIVE, INTREPID and the Polish ORKAN joined from 21 to 27 February also.

The cruiser SHEFFIELD and the escort carrier DASHER were also to have joined, but both were obliged to return with severe weather damage—the carrier's flight deck was damaged and SHEFFIELD had one third of the roof of A turret torn away.

Additional heavy cover was provided by the cruisers BELFAST, CUMBERLAND and NORFOLK which cruised to the north of the convoy from 21 to 26 February, while from the 24 to 26 February distant cover was provided by ships of the Home Fleet, battleships KING GEORGE V, HOWE, and the cruiser BERWICK screened by the destroyers ICARUS, METEOR, MUSKETEER, OFFA, ONSLAUGHT and the Polish PIORUN.

A local eastern escort joined the convoy on 26 to 27 February comprising the Russian destroyers GROMKI, GROZNI, KUIBYSHEV, URITSKI and URAGAN, and the minesweeper BRITOMART.

The Kola Run was notorious for its weather conditions, and this convoy was deemed to have experienced almost the worst, if not the worst, of all. Weather, however, also affected the enemy whose aircraft did not locate the convoy until 23 February, maintaining contact each day thereafter and on the 26 February making an ineffective high level attack. U boats made contact on the 24 February, but vigorous follow-up of HF/DF reports by the escorts prevented any attacks developing.

*The escorts of convoy JW 53 lying off Vaenga awaiting the sailing of convoy RA 53. From the left, HM Ships CUMBERLAND, OBDURATE, an unidentified O class destroyer, and BELFAST, with FAULKNOR alongside.*

## Convoy RA 53

The convoy sailed from Kola Inlet on 1 March, composed as follows:

| | | | | | |
|---|---|---|---|---|---|
| *CALOBRE* | Pan | 6891/19 | *CHESTER VALLEY* | Amer | 5078/19 |
| *CORNELIUS HARNETT* | Amer | 7177/42 | *DAN-Y-BRYN* | Br | 5117/40 |
| *DELSUD* | Amer | 4982/19 | *EL ORIENTE* | Pan | 6012/10 |
| *EMPIRE ARCHER* | Br | 7031/41 | *EMPIRE CLARION* | Br | 7031/42 |
| *EMPIRE EMERALD* | Br | 8032/41 | *EMPIRE SNOW* | Br | 6327/41 |
| *EMPIRE TRISTRAM* | Br | 7167/42 | *EXECUTIVE* | Amer | 4978/20 |
| *GULFWING* | Amer | 10217/28 | *J L M CURRY* | Amer | 7167/42 |
| *JEFFERSON MYERS* | Amer | 7582/20 | *JOHN H B LATROBE* | Amer | 7191/42 |
| *MOSSOVET* | Russ | 2981/35 | *NICHOLAS GILMAN* | Amer | 7176/42 |
| *OCEAN FAITH* | Br | 7174/42 | *OLIGARCH* | Br | 6894/18 |
| *OREMAR* | Amer | 6854/19 | *PUERTO RICAN* | Amer | 6076/19 |
| *RALPH WALDO EMERSON* | Amer | 7176/42 | *RICHARD BASSETT* | Amer | 7191/42 |
| *RICHARD BLAND* | Amer | 7191/42 | *SAN CIPRIANO* | Br | 7966/37 |
| *TEMPLE ARCH* | Br | 5138/40 | *VERMONT* | Amer | 5670/19 |
| *WEST GOTOMSKA* | Amer | 5728/18 | *YORKMAR* | Amer | 5612/19 |

*HMS INGLEFIELD at Kola; in the background two freighters await the sailing of convoy RA 53. In fact, the nearer "freighter" is the tanker OLIGARCH disguised with a dummy funnel, deck gear etc, and with her own funnel cut down and fitted with a spark arrestor. A very successful disguise which was adopted by several tankers. The further "freighter" is the tanker EMPIRE EMERALD.*

Commodore was in *TEMPLE ARCH,* Vice Commodore in *DAN-Y-BRYN, OLIGARCH* was escort oiler. Passengers were carried in *DAN-Y- BRYN (4), EMPIRE ARCHER (11), EMPIRE CLARION (20), EMPIRE TRISTRAM (30), OCEAN FAITH (4) and WEST GOTOMSKA (10).*

From 1 March escorts were (dates of leaving are bracketed), SCYLLA (10 March), INTREPID, OBEDIENT and OBDURATE (all 7 March), BOADICEA, ECLIPSE, FAULKNOR, IMPULSIVE and INGLEFIELD (all 12 March). BOADICEA absent fuelling 7 to 11 and INGLEFIELD 10 to 12 March, FURY and OPPORTUNE (11 March), MILNE, ORWELL and ORKAN (10 March). Also present were corvettes BERGAMOT (14 March), POPPY (11 March), LOTUS and STARWORT (12 March) and trawlers NORTHERN PRIDE (10 March) and ST ELSTAN (11 March). On 9 March a local western escort of VIVACIOUS (to 14 March), LEDBURY (to 10 March), MEYNELL and PYTCHLEY (both to 13 March) joined.

From 2 to 9 March BELFAST, CUMBERLAND and NORFOLK provided cruiser cover, while the Home Fleet, the battleships KING GEORGE V, HOWE, and cruiser GLASGOW, screened by the destroyers FORESTER, ICARUS, MUSKETEER, OFFA, ONSLAUGHT and Polish PIORUN were the distant cover.

The convoy was scattered by storms, a factor usually favouring the U boats, which indeed sank three ships. On 5 March U 255 hit *EXECUTIVE* and *RICHARD BLAND.* The former sank at once, the latter stayed afloat and the derelict was sunk by U 255 five days later. On 9 March U 586 sank *PUERTO RICAN* while the *J L M CURRY* foundered on 7 March with hull defects caused by the weather. *JOHN H B LATROBE* broke down and was towed in to Seidisfjord by OPPORTUNE.

On 8 March it became known that SCHARNHORST had cleared Gdynia for Norway and as a precaution ships of the Home Fleet came to short notice, ANSON proceeding to Hvalfjord and INDOMITABLE and FURIOUS standing by on the Clyde. Break out patrols in the Denmark Strait and the Faroes-Iceland passage were restarted and cruisers were sailed from Seidisfjord to meet the convoy and cover it to Loch Ewe, where 26 ships arrived on 14 March.

*An enlargement of EMPIRE EMERALD taken from the preceding illustration.*

## Suspension of Russian convoys

By mid March 1943 TIRPITZ, SCHARNHORST and LUTZOW were all operational and based in northern Norway. As a counter, the USN Task Force 22 assembled at Portland, Maine prepared to reinforce the Home Fleet so that Atlantic convoys had an insurance against an attempted break out. However, the Arctic could not be covered simultaneously, and the long summer days were approaching. Co-operation with the Russians was becoming a problem at this time also, and the losses in the North Atlantic demanded that the Home Fleet destroyer screen be stripped to send Support Groups to Western Approaches. The Russian convoy cycle had therefore to be suspended until the next winter, and the return of resources from the Atlantic.

## Operation FQ

This operation was the relief of the Norwegian garrison at Spitzbergen and was carried out by the US cruiser TUSCALOOSA, and destroyer FITCH and the British destroyers ONSLAUGHT, ORIBI and ORWELL. Arriving at Spitzbergen on 19 October, the relief was carried out during which ONSLAUGHT surprised a U boat and damaged it by ramming. On completion of the relief the force returned to Scapa. Distant cover was provided by the battleship ANSON, aircraft carrier USS RANGER, cruiser NORFOLK and destroyers HARDY, IMPULSIVE, JANUS and VIGILANT, Canadian HURON and IROQUOIS and American CORRY.

## Operations HOLDER and FR

Operation HOLDER was the passage, between 1 and 11 October 1943, of the destroyers ONSLAUGHT and Canadian HURON and IROQUOIS to North Russia , covered by the cruiser LONDON and destroyer IMPULSIVE, with supplies for the escorts which had remained there during the summer months.

Between 20 and 28 October, Operation FR took place, this being the passage of escorts to North Russia to bring back merchant ships which had remained there after the suspension of convoys in the spring. The destroyers MAHRATTA, MATCHLESS, MILNE, MUSKETEER, SAUMAREZ, SAVAGE, SCOURGE, SCORPION and WESTCOTT, corvette EGLANTINE and minesweepers HARRIER and SEAGULL were despatched, covered by the cruisers LONDON and USS AUGUSTA with the destroyer MIDDLETON. Five small minesweepers T 111 to T 115 and six motor launches BO 201, 204 and 208 to 211 received by Russia under Lease/Lend and manned by Russians, accompanied the escorts on their delivery passage to the Northern Fleet.

## Convoy RA 54A

This, the first convoy of the 1943 winter season, sailed from Kola Inlet on 1 November with ships which had summered in Archangel or been employed in trade or supporting Russian activities in the Northern seas. Sailing from Kola Inlet on 1 November, the convoy consisted of:

| | | | | | |
|---|---|---|---|---|---|
| *BEACONHILL* | 21 Amer | 6941/19 | *BRITISH GOVERNOR* | 32 Br | 6840/26 |
| *CITY OF OMAHA* | 51 Amer | 6124/20 | *EMPIRE FORTUNE* | 11 Br | 6140/43 |
| *EMPIRE GALLIARD* | 31 Br | 7200/42 | *EMPIRE KINSMAN* | 41 Br | 6744/42 |
| *EMPIRE PORTIA* | 43 Br | 7058/42 | *FRANCIS SCOTT KEY* | 12 Amer | 7191/42 |
| *ISRAEL PUTNAM* | 23 Amer | 7176/42 | *MOBILE CITY* | 13 Amer | 6157/20 |
| *PONTFIELD* | 42 Br | 8319/40 | *THOMAS HARTLEY* | 22 Amer | 7176/42 |
| *TOBRUK* | 52 Pol | 7048/42 | | | |

Commodore was in *EMPIRE GALLIARD,* Vice Commodore in *EMPIRE KINSMAN,* and *BRITISH GOVERNOR* was escort oiler.

The eastern local escorts 1 to 3 November were the minesweepers HARRIER and SEAGULL from Operation FR, and the Russian destroyers GROMKI and KUIBYSHEV. The ocean escorts were the minesweepers JASON and BRITOMART (who had been based in Russia during the summer) the corvette EGLANTINE and destroyers

MAHRATTA, MATCHLESS, MILNE, MUSKETEER, SAVAGE, SAUMAREZ, SCORPION, SCOURGE and WESTCOTT. WESTCOTT was present 1 to 13 November, the other ships joined 3 until 10 November except MUSKETEER and MATCHLESS who left 8 November, and SAVAGE to 9 November

The minesweeper HALCYON and destroyers BRISSENDEN and MIDDLETON joined as local escorts 10 to 13 November, cruiser cover was provided by BELFAST, KENT and NORFOLK 2 to 8 November and distant cover for the same period by the Home Fleet, battleship ANSON, aircraft carrier FORMIDABLE, cruiser JAMAICA, and destroyers ONSLOW, VENUS, the American CAPPS and HOBSON, Canadian HAIDA, and Norwegian STORD.

Thick fog delayed the convoy, but also hid it from the enemy, and it arrived in Loch Ewe on 14 November without being attacked.

## Convoy JW 54A

The nineteen ships of this convoy, which sailed from Loch Ewe on 15 November were:

| | | | | | |
|---|---|---|---|---|---|
| *COPELAND* | 33 Br | 1526/23 | *DANIEL DRAKE* | 12 Amer | 7176/43 |
| *EDMUND FANNING* | 21 Amer | 7176/43 | *EMPIRE CARPENTER* | 62 Br | 7025/43 |
| *EMPIRE CELIA* | 61 Br | 7025/43 | *EMPIRE NIGEL* | 71 Br | 7067/43 |
| *FORT YUKON* | 41 Br | 7153/43 | *GILBERT STUART* | 23 Amer | 7176/43 |
| *HENRY VILLARD* | 72 Amer | 7176/42 | *JAMES GORDON BENNETT* | 32 Amer | 7176/42 |
| *JAMES SMITH* | 51 Amer | 7181/42 | *JUNECREST* | 11 Br | 6945/42 |
| *MIJDRECHT* | 52 Du | 7493/31 | *NORLYS* | 42 Pan | 9892/36 |
| *OCEAN VANITY* | 22 Br | 7174/42 | *OCEAN VERITY* | 53 Br | 7174/42 |
| *PARK HOLLAND* | 63 Amer | 7176/43 | *THOMAS SIM LEE* | 31 Amer | 7191/42 |
| *WILLIAM WINDOM* | 13 Amer | 7191/43 | | | |

Commodore was in *FORT YUKON,* Vice Commodore in *EMPIRE CARPENTER,* Rear Commodore in *OCEAN VANITY. COPELAND* was Rescue Ship and *NORLYS* escort oiler.

Three Lend/Lease PC craft and two Lend/Lease minesweepers (of the US ''ADMIRABLE'' class) and named as T 116 and T 117 also accompanied the convoy and motor launches BO 206, 207 and 212.

Local escort 15 to 18 November was the destroyers BRISSENDEN, TERMAGANT and Polish BURZA, the ocean escorts destroyers INCONSTANT, WHITEHALL, corvette HEATHER and minesweeper HUSSAR 15 to 24 November, destroyers IMPULSIVE, ONSLAUGHT, ONSLOW, ORWELL and Canadian HAIDA, HURON and IROQUOIS 18 to 25 November and OBEDIENT 18 to 19 November. The minesweeper SEAGULL was present 24 to 26 November, probably escorting the Dvina River section of the convoy.

Cruiser cover was provided by BERMUDA, JAMAICA and KENT 19 to 24 November while the Home Fleet, the battleship ANSON, cruiser USS TUSCALOOSA, and American destroyers CORRY, FITCH, FORREST and HOBSON were the distant cover for the same period.

OBEDIENT returned early with defects; the convoy arrived unmolested at Kola Inlet 24 November the enemy having failed to detect its passage.

## Convoy JW 54B

This convoy, sailing from Loch Ewe on 22 November, consisted of:

| | | | | | |
|---|---|---|---|---|---|
| *ARTHUR L PERRY* | 62 Amer | 7176/43 | *DALDORCH* | 41 Br | 5571/30 |
| *EMPIRE LIONEL* | 22 Br | 7030/42 | *EMPIRE STALWART* | 11 Br | 7050/43 |
| *EUGENE FIELD* | 12 Amer | 7176/43 | *FORT COLUMBIA* | 31 Br | 7181/42 |
| *FORT McMURRAY* | 52 Br | 7133/42 | *FORT POPLAR* | 61 Br | 7134/42 |
| *HORACE GRAY* | 21 Amer | 7200/43 | *JOHN FITCH* | 32 Amer | 7181/42 |
| *OCEAN STRENGTH* | Br | 7173/42 | *RATHLIN* | 33 Br | 1600/36 |
| *SAN ADOLFO* | 42 Br | 7365/35 | *THOMAS KEARNS* | 23 Amer | 7184/43 |
| *WILLIAM L MARCY* | 51 Amer | 7176/42 | | | |

Commodore was in *DALDORCH,* Vice Commodore in *FORT McMURRAY,* Rear Commodore in *EMPIRE LIONEL. RATHLIN* was Rescue ship, *SAN ADOLFO* escort oiler. The position of *OCEAN STRENGTH* in the convoy is unknown.

Local escort 22 to 25 November comprised destroyers MIDDLETON, SALADIN and SKATE and minesweeper SPEEDWELL. The ocean escort, which also sailed on 22 November, consisted of destroyer BEAGLE, corvettes DIANELLA (joined on 23 November), POPPY and RHODODENDRON and the minesweeper HALCYON. These ships were joined on 23 November by the destroyers HARDY, SAUMAREZ, SAVAGE, SCORPION, SCOURGE, VENUS and VIGILANT and the Norwegian STORD.

HALCYON left the convoy 2 December and proceeded to Archangel, BEAGLE and the corvettes remained until the convoy arrived at Archangel on 3 December. The remaining destroyers, having seen the convoy through to the approaches to Archangel, then returned to Scapa Flow as an independent passage.

From 27 November to Archangel, BERMUDA, JAMAICA and KENT provided cruiser cover, and from 28 November to 2 December the battleship ANSON, cruiser BELFAST, screened by the destroyers ASHANTI, MATCHLESS, MUSKETEER and OBDURATE (MATCHLESS 28/29 November only) provided distant cover.

The convoy was neither located nor attacked during its passage.

## Convoy RA 54B

Ten ships formed this convoy, which sailed from Archangel on 26 November:

| | | | | | |
|---|---|---|---|---|---|
| *ARTIGAS* | Pan | 5613/20 | *ATLANTIC* | Br | 5414/39 |
| *BERING* | Amer | 7631/20 | *COPELAND* | Br | 1526/23 |
| *DOVER HILL* | Br | 5815/18 | *EMPIRE SCOTT* | Br | 6150/41 |
| *LLANDAFF* | Br | 4825/37 | *MARATHON* | Nor | 7208/30 |
| *NORLYS* | Pan | 9892/36 | *PIETER DE HOOGH* | Du | 7168/41 |

Commodore was in *EMPIRE SCOTT, COPELAND* was Rescue Ship and *NORLYS* escort oiler.

Minesweepers HUSSAR and SEAGULL formed the local escort 26 to 28 November, trawler LORD AUSTIN also joined 26 November to 9 December. Other escorts for the passage were destroyers INCONSTANT and WHITEHALL, minesweeper HARRIER and corvette HEATHER, all from 27 November to 9 December. On 28 November the destroyers IMPULSIVE, ONSLAUGHT, ONSLOW, ORWELL and Canadian HAIDA, HURON and IROQUOIS joined until 5 December (IROQUOIS left earlier on 4 December). Local escort in the west comprised destroyers BRISSENDEN, MIDDLETON, SALADIN and SKATE 5 to 9 December.

Cruiser cover was provided between 27 November and 3 December by BERMUDA, JAMAICA and KENT, while the Home Fleet distant cover comprised the battleship *ANSON*, and the cruiser BELFAST screened by the destroyers ASHANTI, MATCHLESS, MUSKETEER and ORIBI. MATCHLESS detached on 29 November with weather damage, and the other destroyers were absent from 29 November to 1 December, also due to the weather.

KENT, of the cruiser force, had embarked 54 tons of gold and silver bullion prior to sailing, earmarked for payment for war supplies to Russia.

The convoy arrived at Loch Ewe on 9 December undetected by the enemy, after a passage in very poor weather.

## Convoy JW 55A

The following ships sailed from Loch Ewe on 12 December:

| | | | | | |
|---|---|---|---|---|---|
| *COLLIS P HUNTINGTON* | 31 Amer | 7177/42 | *DANIEL WILLARD* | 71 Amer | 7200/42 |
| *EMPIRE ARCHER* | 22 Br | 7031/42 | *EMPIRE PICKWICK* | 62 Br | 7068/43 |
| *FORT ASTORIA* | 21 Br | 7189/43 | *FORT HALL* | 41 Br | 7157/43 |
| *FORT MISSANABIE* | 53 Br | 7147/43 | *FORT THOMPSON* | 11 Br | 7134/42 |
| *GEORGE WEEMS* | 12 Amer | 7191/42 | *JAMES A FARRELL* | 13 Amer | 7176/43 |
| *JAMES WOODROW* | 23 Amer | 7200/42 | *LAPLAND* | 52 Br | 2897/42 |
| *LEWIS EMERY Jr* | 63 Amer | 7176/43 | *LUCERNA* | 32 Br | 6556/30 |
| *PHILIP LIVINGSTON* | 72 Amer | 7176/42 | *SAN AMBROSIO* | 42 Br | 7410/35 |
| *STAGE DOOR CANTEEN* | 61 Amer | 7176/43 | *THISTLEDALE* | 51 Br | 7241/42 |
| *THOMAS SCOTT* | 33 Amer | 7176/42 | | | |

Commodore was in *FORT HALL,* Vice Commodore in *EMPIRE ARCHER,* Rear Commodore in *EMPIRE PICKWICK, SAN AMBROSIO* was escort oiler. Two Russian minesweepers sailed in company on their delivery passage from America.

Minesweepers COCKATRICE and HARRIER formed the local escort from 12 to 15 December, while the ocean escort from 12 December was destroyer WESTCOTT, minesweeper SPEEDWELL and Norwegian corvette ACANTHUS. On 15 December the destroyers ASHANTI, MATCHLESS, METEOR, MILNE, MUSKETEER, OPPORTUNE, VIRAGO and Canadian ATHABASKAN joined the escort until 21 December. From 20 to 22 December the eastern local escort comprised HUSSAR and three Russian destroyers. Cruiser cover was provided by BELFAST, NORFOLK and SHEFFIELD while the Home Fleet with the battleship DUKE OF YORK and cruiser JAMAICA, screened by the destroyers SAVAGE, SAUMAREZ, SCORPION and Norwegian STORD provided the distant cover.

As the convoy had been sighted and shadowed by aircraft, the Commander-in-Chief considered that a surface attack might develop, he therefore took the Fleet through to Kola Inlet and made use of the opportunity to confer with the Russian Commander of the Northern Fleet, Admiral Golovko. The convoy, unmolested, arrived at Kola Inlet on 22 December.

## Convoy JW 55B, and the sinking of SCHARNHORST

Nineteen ships sailed from Loch Ewe on 20 December forming this convoy:

| | | | | | |
|---|---|---|---|---|---|
| *BERNARD N BAKER* | 21 Amer | 7191/43 | *BRITISH STATESMAN* | 42 Br | 6991/23 |
| *BROCKHOLST LIVINGSTON* | 33 Amer | 7176/42 | *CARDINAL GIBBONS* | 23 Amer | 7191/42 |
| *FORT KULLYSPELL* | 31 Br | 7190/43 | *FORT NAKASLEY* | 11 Br | 7100/43 |
| *FORT VERCHERES* | 22 Br | 7122/42 | *HAROLD L WINSLOW* | 51 Amer | 7176/43 |
| *JOHN J ABEL* | 13 Amer | 7191/43 | *JOHN VINING* | 34 Amer | 7191/42 |
| *JOHN WANAMAKER* | 24 Amer | 7176/43 | *NORLYS* | 32 Pan | 9892/36 |
| *OCEAN GYPSY* | 53 Br | 7178/42 | *OCEAN MESSENGER* | 43 Br | 7178/42 |
| *OCEAN PRIDE* | 52 Br | 7173/42 | *OCEAN VALOUR* | 12 Br | 7174/41 |
| *OCEAN VICEROY* | 61 Br | 7174/42 | *THOMAS U WALTER* | 41 Amer | 7176/43 |
| *WILL ROGERS* | 62 Amer | 7200/42 | | | |

Commodore was in *FORT KULLYSPELL,* Vice Commodore in *FORT NAKASLEY,* Rear Commodore in *OCEAN PRIDE, NORLYS* was escort oiler.

## 1943

Western local escort on sailing to 22 December comprised corvettes BORAGE and WALLFLOWER, and minesweepers HOUND and HYDRA. Ocean escorts which joined the same day were destroyers WHITEHALL and WRESTLER, minesweeper GLEANER and corvettes HONEYSUCKLE and OXLIP. On 22 December the destroyers IMPULSIVE, ONSLOW, ONSLAUGHT, ORWELL, SCOURGE and Canadian HAIDA, HURON and IROQUOIS joined, remaining until 29 December. On 25 December the destroyers MATCHLESS, MUSKETEER, OPPORTUNE and VIRAGO re-inforced the escort after detaching from convoy RA 55A, on the orders of the Commander-in-Chief; they remained until 26 December after the impending action. Eastern local escort from 28 to 30 December was the minesweepers HALCYON and HUSSAR and three Russian destroyers.

Between 23 and 27 December the cruisers BELFAST, NORFOLK and SHEFFIELD provided cover, with the Home Fleet comprising the battleship DUKE OF YORK, cruiser JAMAICA, and destroyers SAVAGE, SAUMAREZ, SCORPION and Norwegian STORD as distant cover.

Enemy aircraft which sighted the convoy on 22 December for some reason described it as a "troop convoy", so that a raid on the Norwegian coast was suspected. Later, realising that it was, in fact, an eastbound Russian convoy, U boats were despatched to the Bear Island area, and shadowing commenced. Expecting a surface attack, the Commander-in-Chief kept a careful eye on the convoy, including breaking wireless silence to make the situation clear and avoid misunderstandings.

The only effective enemy surface vessel was SCHARNHORST, TIRPITZ having been disabled by midget submarines earlier in the year, and a close watch was being kept on the situation including the reading of the current German cypher traffic. By this means, it was apparent by Christmas Day that the westbound convoy RA 55A had not been detected, so that four of its destroyer escort were detached to reinforce JW 55B, while steps were taken to enable the Home Fleet to close on that convoy.

On Christmas Day, the SCHARNHORST, screened by destroyers Z 29, Z 30, Z 33, Z 34 and Z 38, sailed to intercept the convoy, which was reported by U 601 at 0900. The orders were to attack the convoy, but to disengage if heavy units were present; for some reason reports of the presence of DUKE OF YORK in the area were not passed to SCHARNHORST, or were incorrectly evaluated.

By early on 26 December the Commander-in-Chief, knowing that SCHARNHORST was at sea, ordered the cruiser cover, and his own force, to close JW 55B in readiness for the imminent action. At much the same time SCHARNHORST became detached from her destroyers, which took no further part in events.

At 0921 SHEFFIELD sighted the enemy and reported her, the cruisers opening fire eight minutes later. SCHARNHORST turned away without response after being hit by NORFOLK's 8in gunfire, and the cruisers remained between her and the convoy. The Commander-in-Chief then ordered MATCHLESS, MUSKETEER, OPPORTUNE and VIRAGO to leave the convoy and join the cruisers, the force remaining ahead of the convoy which by now was steering north east. At noon SCHARNHORST was again located, and a brisk action ensued twenty minutes later. In that action NORFOLK was hit hard and SHEFFIELD damaged, but SCHARNHORST again withdrew, this time towards the approaching DUKE OF YORK. Meanwhile, the German destroyers narrowly missed the convoy, and were then ordered to return to base.

At 1617 DUKE OF YORK gained radar contact, and at 1650 opened fire on SCHARNHORST. In the following action the Fleet was to the south of the target with the cruiser force closing from the north. Action continued in the form of a spirited chase in very poor weather and visibility, culminating in a torpedo attack by the DUKE OF YORK's screen which slowed and then stopped the battlecruiser. The end of SCHARNHORST was not visible in the Arctic gloom, but she probably sank at 1945. In spite of a search only 35 rating survivors could be found.

The convoy continued its passage without further attack and arrived in Kola Inlet on 30 December, three days after the victorious ships of the Home Fleet.

## Convoy RA 55A

This convoy sailed from Kola Inlet 22 December as follows:

| | | | | | |
|---|---|---|---|---|---|
| *ARTHUR L PERRY* | Amer | 7176/43 | *DANIEL DRAKE* | Amer | 7176/43 |
| *EDMUND FANNING* | Amer | 7176/43 | *EMPIRE CARPENTER* | Br | 7025/43 |
| *EMPIRE CELIA* | Br | 7025/43 | *EMPIRE NIGEL* | Br | 7067/43 |
| *FORT McMURRAY* | Br | 7133/42 | *FORT YUKON* | Br | 7153/43 |
| *GILBERT STUART* | Amer | 7176/43 | *HENRY VILLARD* | Amer | 7176/42 |
| *JAMES SMITH* | Amer | 7181/42 | *JUNECREST* | Br | 6945/42 |
| *MIJDRECHT* | Du | 7493/31 | *OCEAN STRENGTH* | Br | 7173/42 |
| *OCEAN VANITY* | Br | 7174/42 | *OCEAN VERITY* | Br | 7174/42 |
| *PARK HOLLAND* | Amer | 7176/43 | *RATHLIN* | Br | 1600/36 |
| *SAN ADOLFO* | Br | 7365/35 | *THOMAS KEARNS* | Amer | 7184/43 |
| *THOMAS SIM LEE* | Amer | 7191/42 | *WILLIAM L MARCY* | Amer | 7176/42 |
| *WILLIAM WINDOM* | Amer | 7191/43 | | | |

Commodore was in *FORT YUKON*, Vice Commodore in *EMPIRE CARPENTER*, *RATHLIN* was Rescue Ship and *SAN ADOLFO* escort oiler. *THOMAS KEARNS* returned, unable to continue the passage.

Ocean escorts were minesweeper SEAGULL (22 to 31 December), destroyers BEAGLE (23 TO 28) and WESTCOTT (23 to 30 December), corvettes DIANELLA, POPPY and Norwegian ACANTHUS (all 23 December to 1 January) and destroyers METEOR and MILNE (23 to 31 December), MATCHLESS, MUSKETEER, OPPORTUNE and VIRAGO (23 to 25 December), ASHANTI (23 to 30 December) and Canadian ATHABASKAN (23 to 28 December). Local escorts 30 December to 1 January were the minesweepers HOUND and HYDRA, and corvettes BORAGE and WALLFLOWER.

Cruiser cover was provided by BELFAST, NORFOLK and SHEFFIELD with DUKE OF YORK, JAMAICA, SAVAGE, SAUMAREZ, SCORPION and Norwegian STORD as distant cover.

The destroyers MATCHLESS, MUSKETEER, OPPORTUNE and VIRAGO were detached on Christmas Day to reinforce convoy JW 55B prior to the North Cape action in which SCHARNHORST was sunk. Convoy RA 55A was not molested, and arrived at Loch Ewe on 1 January 1944 without loss.

## Convoy RA 55B

This convoy was somewhat smaller than usual, and only eight ships sailed from Kola Inlet on New Year's Eve 1943:

| | | | | | |
|---|---|---|---|---|---|
| *DALDORCH* | 41 Br | 5571/30 | *EMPIRE STALWART* | 11 Br | 7050/43 |
| *FORT COLUMBIA* | 12 Br | 7181/42 | *FORT POPLAR* | 21 Br | 7134/42 |
| *JAMES GORDON BENNETT* | 42 Amer | 7176/42 | *LUCERNA* | 22 Br | 6556/30 |
| *SAN AMBROSIO* | 32 Br | 7410/35 | *THOMAS KEARNS* | 31 Amer | 7184/43 |

Commodore was in *THOMAS KEARNS,* Vice Commodore in *FORT POPLAR,* Rear Commodore in *DALDORCH. SAN AMBROSIO* was escort oiler.

The minesweepers HALCYON, HUSSAR and SPEEDWELL gave local protection to 1 January 1944; the ocean escort was the destroyers WHITEHALL and WRESTLER, corvettes HONEYSUCKLE, OXLIP and RHODODENDRON until 8 January, and the destroyers IMPULSIVE, ONSLAUGHT, ONSLOW, ORWELL and Canadian HAIDA, HURON and IROQUOIS until 7 January. Minesweepers ORESTES and READY met the convoy on 7 January and escorted it into Loch Ewe the following day.

There were only ineffectual U boat attacks, and neither losses nor damage to the convoy.

## Convoy JW 56A

The convoy sailed from Loch Ewe on 12 January with a local escort of the minesweepers ORESTES and READY (to 22 January), corvettes BORAGE and WALLFLOWER (to 18 January) and POPPY and DIANELLA and destroyer INCONSTANT (all three to 27 January). The sloop CYGNET was present from 12 to 15 January and the destroyers SAVAGE and Norwegian STORD 16 to 27 January.

On 15 January the convoy experienced exceptionally heavy weather off the Faroes, and ran for shelter to Akureyri, Iceland, arriving on 18 January. The convoy remained there until 21 January and, on sailing, five ships had fallen out. The initial composition was as follows:

| | | | | | |
|---|---|---|---|---|---|
| *AERT VAN DER NEER* | Du | 7170/42 | *ANDREW G CURTIN* | Amer | 7200/43 |
| *CHARLES BULFINCH* | Amer | 7176/43 | *CHARLES SCRIBNER* | Amer | 7176/43 |
| *EDWIN L DRAKE* | Amer | 7176/43 | *EMPIRE PLOUGHMAN* | Br | 7049/43 |
| *FORT BELLINGHAM* | Br | 7153/42 | *FORT SLAVE* | Br | 7134/42 |
| *JEFFERSON DAVIS* | Amer | 7176/42 | *JOHN A QUITMAN* | Amer | 7176/43 |
| *JOSEPH N NICOLLET* | Amer | 7176/43 | *NATHANIEL ALEXANDER* | Amer | 7177/42 |
| *NOREG* | Nor | 7605/31 | *PENELOPE BARKER* | Amer | 7177/42 |
| *RICHARD H ALVEY* | Amer | 7191/42 | *SAN ADOLFO* | Br | 7365/35 |
| *SAN CIRILO* | Br | 8012/37 | *THORSTEIN VEBLEN* | Amer | 7176/43 |
| *WILLIAM TYLER PAGE* | Amer | 7176/43 | *WOODBRIDGE N FERRIS* | Amer | 7200/43 |

Commodore was in *PENELOPE BARKER* (later *FORT BELLINGHAM*), Vice Commodore in *EMPIRE PLOUGHMAN,* Rear Commodore in *NATHANIEL ALEXANDER. SAN ADOLFO* was escort oiler.

Of the above *CHARLES BULFINCH, JEFFERSON DAVIS, JOHN A QUITMAN, JOSEPH N NICOLLET* and *NATHANIEL ALEXANDER* did not proceed beyond Iceland, or returned to Loch Ewe.

The escorts from Akureyri to Kola Inlet were the destroyers HARDY(SOE), INCONSTANT, OBDURATE, OFFA, SAVAGE, VENUS, VIGILANT, VIRAGO and Norwegian STORD, all present until arrival except OBDURATE, who parted company on 25 January when torpedoed. The corvettes POPPY and DIANELLA were also present until 27 January while the minesweepers ORESTES and READY provided local escort from Akureyri until 22 January.

Cruiser cover was provided by BERMUDA and KENT (BERWICK, which had also sailed, returned with defects), while the Russian destroyers GREMYASCHI, GROZNY and RAZUMNY provided local eastern escort on 27 and 28 January.

While the Luftwaffe failed to locate the convoy, a patrol line of ten U boats could not be evaded, and on 25 January U 278 sank *PENELOPE BARKER,* who was relieved as Commodore by *FORT BELLINGHAM* which was in turn sunk by U 360 and U 957 on 26 January. U 716 sank *ANDREW G CURTIN* on 26 January, and the destroyer OBDURATE was damaged by U 360 on 25 January and left the convoy. The remaining ships arrived at Kola Inlet on 28 January.

## Convoy JW 56B

This convoy sailed from Loch Ewe on 22 January, composed as follows:

| | | | | | |
|---|---|---|---|---|---|
| *ABNER NASH* | 12 Amer | 7177/42 | *ALBERT C RITCHIE* | 42 Amer | 7176/43 |
| *CHARLES A McALLISTER* | 22 Amer | 7176/43 | *EDWARD L GRANT* | 33 Amer | 7176/43 |
| *EMPIRE TOURIST* | 21 Br | 7062/43 | *FORT CREVECOEUR* | 41 Br | 7191/43 |
| *FORT NORFOLK* | 52 Br | 7131/43 | *HENRY BACON* | 51 Amer | 7177/42 |
| *HENRY LOMB* | 32 Amer | 7176/43 | *HENRY WYNKOOP* | 11 Amer | 7176/42 |
| *JOHN H B LATROBE* | 31 Amer | 7191/42 | *JOHN LA FARGE* | 53 Amer | 7176/43 |
| *PAUL HAMILTON HAYNE* | 61 Amer | 7177/42 | *ROBERT LOWRY* | 43 Amer | 7176/43 |
| *SAMUEL McINTYRE* | 13 Amer | 7176/43 | *WILLARD HALL* | 62 Amer | 7200/43 |
| *WINFRED L SMITH* | 23 Amer | 7191/43 | | | |

Commodore was in *FORT CREVECOEUR,* Vice Commodore in *EMPIRE TOURIST,* Rear Commodore in *PAUL HAMILTON HAYNE.*

The local escort from 22 January was as follows: destroyer WRESTLER, corvette HONEYSUCKLE, minesweepers HYDRA and ONYX until 26 January; corvette RHODODENDRON until 25 January, destroyers WHITEHALL and WESTCOTT, sloop CYGNET, corvette OXLIP and minesweeper SEAGULL until 1 February. On 26 January the following destroyers joined: MAHRATTA, MILNE, MUSKETEER, OPPORTUNE, SCOURGE and Canadian HURON. METEOR arrived on 28 January. The destroyer force which had accompanied JW 56A also sailed from Kola Inlet, HARDY, INCONSTANT, OFFA, SAVAGE, VENUS, VIGILANT, VIRAGO and Norwegian STORD and joined the convoy on 29 January, remaining until 1 February. Cruiser cover was provided by BERMUDA, BERWICK and KENT.

*HENRY LOMB* had to return but the remainder of the convoy proceeded and, following sighting by aircraft, fifteen U boats were directed to its track. The enemy subsequently remarked upon the tenacity of the escort. In the series of attacks on this and the preceding convoy 7 destroyers and 4 merchant ships were claimed sunk and 4 destroyers and 6 merchant ships damaged. In fact 1 destroyer had been damaged in the previous convoy and 3 merchant ships sunk; in this convoy the destroyer HARDY was lost when torpedoed by U 278 (her wreck was sunk by VENUS) and no other damage was inflicted. The enemy claims were undoubtedly exaggerated by the use of the Gnat acoustic torpedo which tended to explode when passing through a ship's wake; many of these premature explosions were thought to be hits when relying upon timed runs for interpreting results.

The attackers did not go unscathed, U 314 being sunk by WHITEHALL and METEOR on 30 January. The convoy arrived in Kola Inlet on 1 February, the Archangel ships a day later.

## Convoy RA 56

The ships of the two preceding JW convoys were united into one westbound convoy which sailed on 3 February with the combined escorts of the eastbound convoys plus three extra destroyers. The thirty nine ships which sailed were:

| | | | | | |
|---|---|---|---|---|---|
| *BRITISH STATESMAN* | 72 Br | 6991/23 | *BROCKHOLST LIVINGSTON* | 44 Amer | 7176/42 |
| *CARDINAL GIBBONS* | 84 Amer | 7191/42 | *COLLIS P HUNTINGTON* | 21 Amer | 7177/42 |
| *DANIEL WILLARD* | 33 Amer | 7200/42 | *EMPIRE ARCHER* | 54 Br | 7032/42 |
| *EMPIRE LIONEL* | 43 Br | 7030/42 | *EMPIRE PICKWICK* | Br | 7068/43 |
| *EUGENE FIELD* | 11 Amer | 7176/43 | *FORT ASTORIA* | 13 Br | 7189/43 |
| *FORT HALL* | 32 Br | 7157/43 | *FORT KULLYSPELL* | 73 Br | 7190/43 |
| *FORT MISSANABIE* | 42 Br | 7147/43 | *FORT NAKASLEY* | 82 Br | 7200/43 |
| *FORT THOMPSON* | 74 Br | 7134/42 | *FORT VERCHERES* | 24 Br | 7122/42 |
| *GEORGE WEEMS* | 34 Amer | 7191/42 | *HAROLD L WINSLOW* | 93 Amer | 7176/43 |
| *HORACE GRAY* | 41 Amer | 7200/43 | *JAMES A FARRELL* | 83 Amer | 7161/43 |
| *JAMES WOODROW* | 92 Amer | 7200/42 | *JOHN FITCH* | 23 Amer | 7181/42 |
| *JOHN J ABEL* | 91 Amer | 7191/43 | *JOHN VINING* | 71 Amer | 7191/42 |
| *JOHN WANAMAKER* | 103 Amer | 7176/43 | *LEWIS EMERY Jr* | 22 Amer | 7176/43 |
| *NOREG* | 52 Nor | 7605/31 | *NORLYS* | 62 Pan | 9892/36 |
| *OCEAN GYPSY* | 13 Br | 7178/42 | *OCEAN MESSENGER* | 102 Br | 7178/42 |
| *OCEAN PRIDE* | 94 Br | 7173/42 | *OCEAN VALOUR* | 53 Br | 7174/41 |
| *OCEAN VICEROY* | 101 Br | 7174/42 | *PHILIP LIVINGSTON* | Amer | 7176/41 |
| *STAGE DOOR CANTEEN* | 81 Amer | 7176/43 | *THISTLEDALE* | 51 Br | 7241/42 |
| *THOMAS SCOTT* | 12 Amer | 7176/42 | *THOMAS U WALTER* | 104 Amer | 7176/43 |
| *WILL ROGERS* | 61 Amer | 7200/42 | | | |

Commodore was in *WILL ROGERS,* Vice Commodore in *FORT HALL,* Rear Commodore in *FORT NAKASLEY. NOREG* and *NORLYS* were escort oilers.

*EMPIRE PICKWICK* and *PHILIP LIVINGSTON,* the two unnumbered ships in the listing, returned to Murmansk.

Minesweepers GLEANER and SEAGULL provided local escort from 3 to 5 February; close escort from 3 to 11 February comprised destroyers WESTCOTT and WHITEHALL, sloop CYGNET, corvettes DIANELLA, OXLIP, POPPY and RHODODENDRON, minesweepers HALCYON, HUSSAR and SPEEDWELL (these last three ships until 10 February).

*An example of the surface fog caused by temperature differences of the air and sea, frequently met in Arctic waters. The ships are outward bound to Russia in early 1943.*

Destroyers were present as follows: until 7 February OFFA, OPPORTUNE, SAVAGE, VENUS and VIGILANT, until 9 February INCONSTANT, MAHRATTA, METEOR, MILNE, MUSKETEER and SCOURGE, Canadian HURON and Norwegian STORD, 6 to 9 February OBEDIENT, SWIFT and VERULAM.

Western local escort was destroyer WRESTLER, corvettes BORAGE, HONEYSUCKLE and WALLFLOWER, minesweepers COCKATRICE, LOYALTY, RATTLESNAKE and READY. From 5 to 7 February BERMUDA, BERWICK and KENT provided cruiser cover.

Enemy W/T intercepts alerted U boats to the sailing of the convoy, and a sighting report was made by the Luftwaffe on 6 February, however as the westbound convoy was reported as eastbound no intercepts took place! The convoy arrived in Loch Ewe on 11 February.

## Convoy JW 57

The problems of detecting submerged submarines in Arctic waters had now reached a climax in view of the increasing number of U boats deployed in Norway against the convoy traffic. JW 57 therefore introduced a new concept in escort routine for this route, the provision of a light cruiser equipped as a Flagship specifically for controlling aircraft carrier operations, plus an escort carrier with dedicated A/S squadrons embarked, these ships operating within the convoy itself. Also, hereafter, Western Approaches ships with great A/S experience were involved much more in the escort.

The merchant ships of the convoy, and the included cruiser and escort carrier, were as follows:

| | | | | | | | |
|---|---|---|---|---|---|---|---|
| *ALEXANDER WHITE* | 72 | Amer | 7191/42 | *BRITISH VALOUR* | 33 | Br | 6952/27 |
| *BYRON DARNTON* | 61 | Amer | 7176/43 | *CAESAR RODNEY* | 113 | Amer | 7191/42 |
| *CHARLES BULFINCH* | 42 | Amer | 7176/43 | *CHARLES M SCHWAB* | 92 | Amer | 7191/43 |
| *COPELAND* | 85 | Br | 1526/23 | *DAPHNELLA* | 43 | Br | 8078/38 |
| *EDWARD SPARROW* | 44 | Amer | 7176/43 | *EMPIRE CARPENTER* | 103 | Br | 7025/43 |
| *EMPIRE CELIA* | 51 | Br | 7025/43 | *EMPIRE NIGEL* | 13 | Br | 7067/43 |
| *FORT BRULE* | 31 | Br | 7133/42 | *FORT McMURRAY* | 115 | Br | 7133/42 |
| *FORT ROMAINE* | 71 | Br | 7131/43 | *HENRY B BROWN* | 111 | Amer | 7200/43 |
| *HENRY LOMB* | 23 | Amer | 7176/43 | HMS BLACK PRINCE | 62 | | |
| HMS CHASER | 63 | | | *JEFFERSON DAVIS* | 105 | Amer | 7176/42 |
| *JOHN A DONALD* | 53 | Amer | 7176/43 | *JOHN A QUITMAN* | 82 | Amer | 7176/43 |
| *JOHN LANGDON* | 11 | Amer | 7176/42 | *JOHN RUTLEDGE* | 32 | Amer | 7181/42 |
| *JOHN SHARP WILLIAMS* | 21 | Amer | 7176/43 | *JOHN STEVENSON* | 101 | Amer | 7176/43 |
| *JOHN W POWELL* | 41 | Amer | 7176/43 | *JOHN WOOLMAN* | 75 | Amer | 7191/43 |
| *JOSHUA W ALEXANDER* | 74 | Amer | 7176/43 | *LORD DELAWARE* | 102 | Amer | 7200/43 |
| *LOUIS D BRANDEIS* | 12 | Amer | 7200/43 | *LUCERNA* | 83 | Br | 6556/30 |
| *MARIE M MELONEY* | 81 | Amer | 7176/43 | *MIJDRECHT* | 73 | Du | 7493/31 |
| *NATHAN TOWSON* | 104 | Amer | 7176/43 | *NATHANIEL ALEXANDER* | 52 | Amer | 7177/42 |
| *OCEAN STRENGTH* | 91 | Br | 7173/42 | *PHILIP F THOMAS* | 114 | Amer | 7176/43 |
| *RICHARD M JOHNSON* | 15 | Amer | 7176/43 | *ROBERT EDEN* | 22 | Amer | 7176/43 |
| *ROBERT J COLLIER* | 14 | Amer | 7176/43 | *SAN AMBROSIO* | 93 | Br | 7410/35 |
| *STEVENSON TAYLOR* | 84 | Amer | 7176/43 | *THOMAS HARTLEY* | 54 | Amer | 7176/42 |
| *WILLIAM H WEBB* | 112 | Amer | 7176/43 | | | | |

Commodore was in *FORT ROMAINE,* Vice Commodore in *FORT BRULE,* Rear Commodore in *CHARLES M SCHWAB. COPELAND* was Rescue Ship, *BRITISH VALOUR* and *SAN AMBROSIO* escort oilers. Three Russian manned minesweepers and three small patrol craft accompanied the convoy which sailed on 20 February.

Local escort on sailing until 22 February were minesweepers HYDRA, LOYALTY, ORESTES and RATTLESNAKE and corvettes BURDOCK and DIANELLA. Close escort 20 to 28 February was destroyers BEAGLE, BOADICEA, KEPPEL and WALKER and corvettes BLUEBELL, CAMELLIA, LOTUS and RHODODENDRON. On 22 February the cruiser BLACK PRINCE (Flag) joined with the destroyers IMPULSIVE, MAHRATTA, MATCHLESS, METEOR, MILNE, OBEDIENT, OFFA, ONSLAUGHT, ORIBI, SAVAGE, SERAPIS, SWIFT, VERULAM and VIGILANT. All these ships remained until 28 February except MAHRATTA, lost on 25 February.

Also on 22 February the destroyers WANDERER and WATCHMAN, and frigates BYRON and STRULE escorted the escort carrier CHASER to join the convoy, these ships remained until 26 February. Cruiser cover was provided on 26 and 27 February by BERWICK and JAMAICA.

Two patrol lines of 14 U boats in all were deployed against the convoy, plus air shadowing which was dealt with by CHASER's Wildcat fighters on 23 February. On 24 February the U boats gained contact, and were repelled by the escort, U 713 being sunk by KEPPEL. On 25 February, a Catalina of 210 Squadron, operating at extreme range from Shetland, sank U 601.

On 25 February the U boats gained their first (and only) success, when U 990 sank MAHRATTA. The destroyer sank rapidly when hit, and only 17 survivors were picked up by IMPULSIVE.

No merchant ships were lost and the convoy, complete with *JOHN SHARP WILLIAMS* which had defects, arrived in Kola Inlet on 28 February.

## Convoy RA 57

This convoy sailed from Kola Inlet on 2 March, its 33 ships being joined by BLACK PRINCE and CHASER who had headed the escort for the previous eastbound convoy. The merchant ships were:

| | | | | | | | |
|---|---|---|---|---|---|---|---|
| *ABNER NASH* | 102 | Amer | 7177/42 | *AERT VAN DER NEER* | 33 | Du | 7170/42 |
| *ALBERT C RITCHIE* | 92 | Amer | 7176/43 | *BERNARD N BAKER* | 104 | Amer | 7191/43 |
| *CHARLES A McALLISTER* | 11 | Amer | 7176/43 | *CHARLES SCRIBNER* | 44 | Amer | 7176/43 |
| *COPELAND* | 84 | Br | 1536/23 | *EDWARD L GRANT* | 13 | Amer | 7176/43 |
| *EDWIN L DRAKE* | 103 | Amer | 7176/43 | *EMPIRE BARD* | | Br | 3114/42 |
| *EMPIRE PICKWICK* | 22 | Br | 7068/43 | *EMPIRE PLOUGHMAN* | 61 | Br | 7049/43 |
| *EMPIRE TOURIST* | 31 | Br | 7062/43 | *FORT CREVECOEUR* | 51 | Br | 7191/43 |
| *FORT NORFOLK* | 91 | Br | 7131/43 | *FORT SLAVE* | 12 | Br | 7134/42 |
| *HENRY BACON* | 83 | Amer | 7177/42 | *HENRY WYNKOOP* | 23 | Amer | 7176/42 |
| *JOHN H B LATROBE* | 24 | Amer | 7191/42 | *JOHN LA FARGE* | 93 | Amer | 7176/43 |
| *PAUL HAMILTON HAYNE* | 71 | Amer | 7177/42 | *PHILIP LIVINGSTON* | 43 | Amer | 7176/41 |
| *RICHARD H ALVEY* | 34 | Amer | 7191/42 | *ROBERT LOWRY* | 94 | Amer | 7176/43 |
| *SAMUEL McINTYRE* | 41 | Amer | 7176/43 | *SAN ADOLFO* | 52 | Br | 7365/35 |
| *SAN AMBROSIO* | 72 | Br | 7410/35 | *SAN CIRILO* | 42 | Br | 8012/37 |
| *THORSTEIN VEBLEN* | 21 | Amer | 7176/43 | *WILLARD HALL* | 81 | Amer | 7200/43 |
| *WILLIAM TYLER PAGE* | 82 | Amer | 7176/43 | *WINFRED L SMITH* | 101 | Amer | 7191/43 |
| *WOODBRIDGE N FERRIS* | 14 | Amer | 7200/43 | | | | |

Commodore was in *FORT CREVECOEUR,* Vice Commodore in *EMPIRE TOURIST,* Rear Commodore in *PAUL HAMILTON HAYNE. SAN ADOLFO, SAN AMBROSIO* and *SAN CIRILO* were escort oilers, *COPELAND* was Rescue Ship.

The cruiser BLACK PRINCE and escort carrier CHASER occupied positions 62 and 63 during the passage.

The position regarding *COPELAND* is unclear; she was certainly allocated to this convoy, but is also confirmed as being in position 33 in the next convoy (RA 58) with no known intervening eastbound passage. Either she returned from RA 57 (which is not noted in extant documents), there is an unknown eastbound passage, or the attribution to RA 57 is in error. As the position cannot yet be clarified *COPELAND* appears in both lists.

Close A/S escort from 2 March was the destroyers BEAGLE, BOADICEA, KEPPEL and WALKER, corvettes BLUEBELL, CAMELLIA, LOTUS and RHODODENDRON, and minesweepers GLEANER and SEAGULL, all remaining until 10 March except BEAGLE and SEAGULL who detached on 9 March.

The destroyer escort also sailed on 2 March, comprising BLACK PRINCE* (Flag), CHASER, IMPULSIVE*, MATCHLESS, METEOR*, MILNE, OBEDIENT*, OFFA, ONSLAUGHT, ORIBI, SAVAGE, SERAPIS, SWIFT*, VERULAM* and VIGILANT, these ships leaving the convoy on 7 (indicated as *) and 8 March. Local escort 8 to 10 March were the minesweepers HYDRA, LOYALTY, ONYX, ORESTES and READY.

The U boats which had assembled to attack the previous incoming convoy were avoided thanks to the efforts of Russian aircraft and a wide diversion to the east on leaving Kola Inlet, wise measures as CHASER was prevented by storms from operating her aircraft for the first two days. On 4 March U boats made contact and U 703 sank *EMPIRE TOURIST;* in compensation a Swordfish from CHASER damaged U 472 which ONSLAUGHT then sank. The following day another Swordfish sank U 366, and on the 6th U 973; two other U boats were also damaged. All the attacking aircraft came from 816 Squadron operating from CHASER. The convoy, less *EMPIRE BARD* which returned to Murmansk, and *EMPIRE TOURIST,* sunk, arrived at Loch Ewe on 10 March.

## Convoy JW 58

This convoy sailed from Loch Ewe on 27 March, and was joined at sea by three ships from Iceland. The convoy also included the American cruiser MILWAUKEE (in position 83) on passage to be handed over to the Russian Northern Fleet; within the convoy also steamed the cruiser DIADEM (62) and the escort carriers ACTIVITY (63) and TRACKER (64). The merchant ships of the convoy were:

| | | | | | | | |
|---|---|---|---|---|---|---|---|
| *ANDREW CARNEGIE* | 125 | Amer | 7176/42 | *ARUNAH S ABELL* | 82 | Amer | 7176/43 |
| *BARBARA FRIETCHIE* | 102 | Amer | 7176/43 | *BENJAMIN H LATROBE* | 111 | Amer | 7176/42 |
| *BENJAMIN SCHLESINGER* | 114 | Amer | 7176/44 | *CHARLES GORDON CURTIS* | 112 | Amer | 7176/42 |
| *CHARLES HENDERSON* | 45 | Amer | 7176/43 | *DOLABELLA* | 43 | Br | 8142/39 |
| *EDWARD P ALEXANDER* | 22 | Amer | 7201/43 | *ELOY ALFARO* | | Amer | 7176/44 |
| *EMPIRE PROWESS* | 33 | Br | 7058/43 | *FORT COLUMBIA* | 92 | Br | 7155/43 |
| *FORT HALL* | 34 | Br | 7157/43 | *FORT KULLYSPELL* | 61 | Br | 7190/43 |
| *FORT VERCHERES* | 32 | Br | 7128/43 | *FORT YUKON* | 71 | Br | 7153/43 |
| *FRANCIS SCOTT KEY* | 81 | Amer | 7191/42 | *FRANCIS VIGO* | 35 | Amer | 7176/43 |
| *GEORGE GALE* | 122 | Amer | 7176/42 | *GEORGE M COHAN* | 21 | Amer | 7176/43 |
| *GEORGE T ANGELL* | 84 | Amer | 7176/44 | *GILBERT STUART* | 104 | Amer | 7176/43 |
| *GRACE ABBOTT* | 91 | Amer | 7191/42 | *HAWKINS FUDSKE* | 93 | Amer | 7176/43 |
| *HENRY VILLARD* | 103 | Amer | 7176/42 | *JAMES SMITH* | 14 | Amer | 7181/42 |
| *JOHN B LENNON* | 44 | Amer | 7198/43 | *JOHN CARVER* | 85 | Amer | 7176/42 |
| *JOHN DAVENPORT* | 31 | Amer | 7176/42 | *JOHN McDONOGH* | 51 | Amer | 7176/43 |
| *JOHN T HOLT* | 12 | Amer | 7176/43 | *JOSEPH N NICOLLET* | 41 | Amer | 7176/43 |
| *JOSHUA THOMAS* | 42 | Amer | 7176/43 | *JOYCE KILMER* | 94 | Amer | 7176/43 |
| *JULIEN POYDRAS* | 23 | Amer | 7176/43 | *LACKLAN* | 72 | Br | 8670/29 |
| *MORRIS HILLQUIT* | 113 | Amer | 7210/44 | *NICHOLAS BIDDLE* | 123 | Amer | 7191/42 |
| *NOREG* | 52 | Nor | 7605/31 | *PIERRE S DUPONT* | 115 | Amer | 7176/42 |
| *RATHLIN* | 86 | Br | 1600/36 | *THOMAS SIM LEE* | 121 | Amer | 7191/42 |
| *TOWNSEND HARRIS* | 24 | Amer | 7176/43 | *W R GRACE* | 95 | Amer | 7176/43 |
| *WILLIAM D BYRON* | 124 | Amer | 7210/44 | *WILLIAM MATSON* | 101 | Amer | 7176/43 |
| *WILLIAM McKINLEY* | 13 | Amer | 7200/43 | *WILLIAM MOULTRIE* | 25 | Amer | 7177/42 |
| *WILLIAM PEPPER* | 105 | Amer | 7176/43 | *WILLIAM S THAYER* | 11 | Amer | 7176/43 |

Of the above, *ELOY ALFARO, JOHN T HOLT* and *WILLIAM S THAYER* came from Iceland, escorted by the frigate FITZROY and the minesweepers CHAMOIS and CHANCE which were on delivery passage to the UK from America. *ELOY ALFARO* returned to Iceland prior to joining the main body, hence the omission of her position number in the listing.

Local escort for the main body comprised minesweepers RATTLESNAKE(SOE), ONYX and ORESTES and corvettes RHODODENDRON and STARWORT from 27 to 29 March. Close A/S escorts were destroyers WESTCOTT(SOE), WHITEHALL and WRESTLER and corvettes BLUEBELL, HONEYSUCKLE and LOTUS, these being present from 27 March to 4 April. On 29 March the main body of the escort joined until 4 April, being the cruiser DIADEM, escort carriers ACTIVITY and TRACKER and destroyers IMPULSIVE, INCONSTANT (joined 27 March), OBEDIENT, OFFA, ONSLOW, OPPORTUNE, ORIBI, ORWELL, SAUMAREZ, SERAPIS, SCORPION, VENUS and Norwegian STORD.

Also present from 29 March to 4 April was the Western Approaches 2nd Escort Group commanded by the redoubtable Captain F J Walker, consisting of the sloops STARLING (SO), MAGPIE, WILD GOOSE, WREN and WHIMBREL plus destroyers BEAGLE, BOADICEA, KEPPEL and WALKER. Distant cover was afforded by ships of the Home Fleet, at this time engaged in Operation "Tungsten", the Fleet Air Arm attack on TIRPITZ.

Local eastern escort 3 to 4 April was provided by the Russian destroyers GREMYASCHI, KUIBYSHEV, RAZUMNY and RAZYARENNI and eight smaller vessels.

There was considerable air activity during the passage, and fighters disposed of six long range shadowers. South of Bear Island a patrol line of 16 U boats had been set up, and these received the attention of the A/S aircraft and surface escort. On 29 March U 961 was sunk by STARLING, and on 31 March BEAGLE and TRACKER's aircraft sank U 355. KEPPEL sank U 360 with a Hedgehog attack on 2 April and on 3 April a Swordfish sighted U 288 and, calling up a Wildcat fighter and Avenger A/S aircraft, the three sank her in a combined effort.

The convoy, less *GILBERT STUART* which straggled and returned, and the previously mentioned *ELOY ALFARO*, arrived unscathed at Kola Inlet on 4 April.

## Convoy RA 58

The convoy sailed from Kola Inlet on 7 April, with the cruiser DIADEM and escort carriers ACTIVITY and TRACKER sailing in column 6. Merchant ships of the convoy were as below:

| | | | | | | | |
|---|---|---|---|---|---|---|---|
| *ALEXANDER WHITE* | 14 | Amer | 7191/42 | *BRITISH VALOUR* | 52 | Br | 6952/27 |
| *BYRON DARNTON* | 43 | Amer | 7176/43 | *CAESAR RODNEY* | 81 | Amer | 7191/42 |
| *CHARLES BULFINCH* | 113 | Amer | 7176/43 | *CHARLES M SCHWAB* | 31 | Amer | 7191/43 |
| *COPELAND* | 33 | Br | 1526/23 | *DAPHNELLA* | 92 | Br | 8078/38 |
| *EDWARD SPARROW* | 11 | Amer | 7176/43 | *EMPIRE CELIA* | 32 | Br | 7025/43 |
| *FORT McMURRAY* | 104 | Br | 7133/42 | *FORT ROMAINE* | 71 | Br | 7131/43 |
| *HENRY B BROWN* | 22 | Amer | 7200/43 | *HENRY LOMB* | 44 | Amer | 7176/43 |
| *JEFFERSON DAVIS* | 111 | Amer | 7176/42 | *JOHN A DONALD* | 84 | Amer | 7176/43 |

**1944**

| | | | | | | | |
|---|---|---|---|---|---|---|---|
| *JOHN A QUITMAN* | 91 | Amer | 7176/43 | *JOHN RUTLEDGE* | 23 | Amer | 7181/42 |
| *JOHN SHARP WILLIAMS* | 24 | Amer | 7176/43 | *JOHN STEVENSON* | 94 | Amer | 7176/43 |
| *JOHN W POWELL* | 112 | Amer | 7176/43 | *JOHN WOOLMAN* | 13 | Amer | 7191/43 |
| *JOSHUA W ALEXANDER* | 12 | Amer | 7176/43 | *LORD DELAWARE* | 41 | Amer | 7200/43 |
| *LOUIS D BRANDEIS* | 114 | Amer | 7200/43 | *LUCERNA* | 42 | Br | 6556/30 |
| *MARIE M MELONEY* | 72 | Amer | 7176/43 | *MIJDRECHT* | 82 | Du | 7493/31 |
| *NATHAN TOWSON* | 103 | Amer | 7176/43 | *NATHANIEL ALEXANDER* | 93 | Amer | 7177/42 |
| *OCEAN STRENGTH* | 101 | Br | 7173/42 | *PHILIP F THOMAS* | 51 | Amer | 7176/43 |
| *RATHLIN* | 85 | Br | 1600/36 | *RICHARD M JOHNSON* | 21 | Amer | 7176/43 |
| *ROBERT J COLLIER* | 34 | Amer | 7176/43 | *STEVENSON TAYLOR* | 102 | Amer | 7176/43 |
| *THOMAS HARTLEY* | 61 | Amer | 7176/42 | *WILLIAM H WEBB* | 83 | Amer | 7176/43 |

Commodore was in *FORT ROMAINE,* Vice Commodore in *CHARLES M SCHWAB,* Rear Commodores in *JOHN A DONALD* and *NATHAN TOWSON. BRITISH VALOUR* was escort oiler and *RATHLIN* Rescue Ship.

*COPELAND* is noted in documents as 33 in this convoy, a fact confirmed by several MN personnel who took passage in her. The attribution of the ship to RA57 however, referred to on page 62, is still dubious, but the conflict still cannot be resolved and she remains in the listing for that convoy pending further information.

Ocean escorts were, from 7 to 12 April, destroyers BEAGLE, BOADICEA, INCONSTANT, KEPPEL, VENUS, WALKER, WESTCOTT, WHITEHALL, WRESTLER and escort carrier ACTIVITY; from 7 to 13 April the cruiser DIADEM and destroyers OFFA, ONSLOW, OPPORTUNE, ORWELL, SAUMAREZ, SERAPIS and Norwegian STORD; 7 to 14 April escort carrier TRACKER, and destroyers IMPULSIVE, OBEDIENT, ORIBI, SCORPION, corvettes BLUEBELL and HONEYSUCKLE, sloops STARLING, MAGPIE, WHIMBREL, WILD GOOSE and WREN.

Operation "Tungsten" having, for the moment, eliminated the threat from TIRPITZ, no distant cover was required on this occasion. U boats endeavoured to intercept the convoy but failed to make contact, and it arrived at Loch Ewe on 14 April.

## Passage of escorts to Kola Inlet

There were still a number of empty merchant ships lying in Russian ports; the crew of the USS MILWAUKEE (1,336 in total), now handed over to the Russians, required repatriation, and 1,430 Russian crew for British warships in British ports awaiting transfer to the Red Fleet also required transport. Preparations for Operation "Neptune", the invasion of Normandy, precluded the running of a further JW convoy at this time, so it was decided to pass a strong escort through to Kola Inlet in the shortest possible time to retrieve those ships still there, and transport personnel.

Accordingly the cruiser DIADEM, escort carriers ACTIVITY and FENCER and destroyers BEAGLE, BOADICEA, INCONSTANT, KEPPEL, MARNE, MATCHLESS, METEOR, MILNE, MUSKETEER, ULYSSES, VERULAM, VIRAGO, WALKER, WESTCOTT, WHITEHALL and WRESTLER, Canadian frigates CAPE BRETON, GROU, OUTREMONT and WASKESIU and the personnel ship *NEA HELLAS* were sailed. Unfortunately, the *NEA HELLAS* was forced to return with defects, so that the escort arrived in Kola Inlet on 23 April without transport for the large Russian contingent.

## Convoy RA 59

In order to lift the required number of personnel, a great deal of swift re-organisation had to be undertaken by the British staff in North Russia, with the result that when this convoy sailed on 28 April many of the empty cargo vessels carried considerable numbers of Officers and ratings as passengers. The ships sailing are listed below:

| | | | | | | | |
|---|---|---|---|---|---|---|---|
| *ANDREW CARNEGIE* | 92 | Amer | 7176/42 | *ARUNAH S ABELL* | 104 | Amer | 7176/43 |
| *CHARLES HENDERSON* | 24 | Amer | 7176/43 | *DOLABELLA* | 45 | Br | 8142/39 |
| *EDWARD P ALEXANDER* | 43 | Amer | 7201/43 | *FORT BRULE* | 31 | Br | 7133/42 |
| *FORT COLUMBIA* | 91 | Br | 7181/42 | *FORT HALL* | 101 | Br | 7157/43 |
| *FORT KULLYSPELL* | 51 | Br | 7190/43 | *FORT YUKON* | 71 | Br | 7153/43 |
| *FRANCIS SCOTT KEY* | 61 | Amer | 7191/41 | *FRANCIS VIGO* | 112 | Amer | 7176/43 |
| *GEORGE GALE* | 23 | Amer | 7176/42 | *GEORGE M COHAN* | 124 | Amer | 7176/43 |
| *GEORGE T ANGELL* | 111 | Amer | 7176/44 | *GILBERT STUART* | 105 | Amer | 7176/43 |
| *GRACE ABBOTT* | 121 | Amer | 7191/42 | *HAWKINS FUDSKE* | 12 | Amer | 7176/43 |
| *HENRY VILLARD* | 11 | Amer | 7176/42 | *JAMES SMITH* | 102 | Amer | 7181/42 |
| *JOHN B LENNON* | 42 | Amer | 7198/43 | *JOHN CARVER* | 94 | Amer | 7176/42 |
| *JOHN DAVENPORT* | 122 | Amer | 7176/42 | *JOHN MACDONOGH* | 21 | Amer | 7176/43 |
| *JOHN T HOLT* | 14 | Amer | 7176/43 | *JOSEPH N NICOLLET* | 81 | Amer | 7176/43 |
| *JOSHUA THOMAS* | 114 | Amer | 7176/43 | *JOYCE KILMER* | 84 | Amer | 7176/43 |
| *JULIEN POYDRAS* | 32 | Amer | 7176/43 | *LAPLAND* | 72 | Br | 2897/42 |
| *MORRIS HILLQUIT* | 83 | Amer | 7210/44 | *NICHOLAS BIDDLE* | 103 | Amer | 7191/42 |
| *NOREG* | 52 | Nor | 7605/31 | *PIERRE S DUPONT* | 34 | Amer | 7176/42 |
| *ROBERT EDEN* | 35 | Amer | 7176/43 | *THOMAS SIM LEE* | 123 | Amer | 7191/42 |
| *TOWNSEND HARRIS* | 41 | Amer | 7176/43 | *WILLIAM D BYRON* | 82 | Amer | 7210/44 |

| | | | | | |
|---|---|---|---|---|---|
| *WILLIAM MATSON* | 85 Amer | 7176/43 | *WILLIAM McKINLEY* | 13 Amer | 7200/43 |
| *WILLIAM MOULTRIE* | 44 Amer | 7177/42 | *WILLIAM PEPPER* | 93 Amer | 7176/43 |
| *WILLIAM S THAYER* | 33 Amer | 7176/43 | | | |

Commodore was in *FORT YUKON,* Vice Commodore in *FORT BRULE. NOREG* was escort oiler.

Escorts 28 April to 3 May were the cruiser DIADEM, escort carrier FENCER, and destroyers BOADICEA, ULYSSES, VERULAM, VIRAGO, WALKER and WHITEHALL; 28 April to 4 May carrier ACTIVITY and destroyers MARNE, MATCHLESS, METEOR, MILNE and MUSKETEER; 28 April to 6 May the destroyers BEAGLE, INCONSTANT, KEPPEL, WESTCOTT and WRESTLER, corvette LOTUS, and Canadian frigates CAPE BRETON, GROU, OUTREMONT and WASKESIU. Russian destroyers RAZYARENNI and KUIBYSHEV, three minesweepers and six submarine chasers joined the escort 28 to 29 April.

Passenger levels are worth recording, distributed both in the escort and the convoy. In the main, those in the escorts were USN personnel, and the Russians were in the merchant ships except for the Admiral and his staff who were accommodated in FENCER, where they took a great deal of interest in their first sight of carrier operations. Disposal of personnel was as follows;

In the escorts:
ACTIVITY 19, FENCER 17, MARNE 17, METEOR 17, MUSKETEER 16, MATCHLESS 16, VERULAM 17, VIRAGO 17, BOADICEA 14, BEAGLE 14, WALKER 13, WESTCOTT 12, WRESTLER 14, WHITEHALL 14, WASKESIU 10, CAPE BRETON 13, OUTREMONT 13, GROU 12, ULYSSES 17.

In the convoy:
*ANDREW CARNEGIE 160, ARUNAH S ABELL 120, BENJAMIN H LATROBE 137, BENJAMIN SCHLESINGER 124, CHARLES HENDERSON 112, EDWARD P ALEXANDER 150, FORT YUKON 7, FRANCIS VIGO 114, GEORGE GALE 11, GEORGE T ANGELL 9, GILBERT STUART 10, GRACE ABBOTT 10, HAWKINS FUDSKE 10, HENRY VILLARD 10, JAMES SMITH 114, JOHN B LENNON 156, JOHN CARVER 100, JOHN DAVENPORT 11, JOSHUA THOMAS 108, JOYCE KILMER 91, JULIEN POYDRAS 152, MORRIS HILLQUIT 196, NICHOLAS BIDDLE 110, PIERRE S DUPONT 105, WILLIAM D BYRON 139, WILLIAM MATSON* unknown, *WILLIAM McKINLEY 10, WILLIAM MOULTRIE 112, WILLIAM PEPPER 112, WILLIAM S THAYER 166.*

Atrocious weather made carrier air operations extremely hazardous, up to six inches of snow being recorded on flight decks at one point, but the newly embarked aircrew in ACTIVITY worked hard to approach the efficiency of the seasoned veterans in FENCER. Twelve U boats had been stationed in a patrol line near Bear Island, and one of these, U 711, sank the *WILLIAM S THAYER* on 30 April. 43 of her crew and passengers were lost, 192 being rescued, principally by WHITEHALL.

In the next two days, FENCER's Swordfish sank U 277, U674 and U 959 and prevented any further attack on the convoy, which dispersed to Loch Ewe and the Clyde arriving 6 and 7 May.

## Operation DC

No further convoy being due until after the completion of Operation "Neptune", which absorbed the entire resources of the Royal Navy in Home waters, the destroyers MATCHLESS, METEOR and MUSKETEER sailed on 29 June with supplies, mail etc for personnel and ships still in Russian waters. The passage was without incident, the ships arriving on 3 July, sailing again the next day and arriving back at Scapa Flow 8 July.

## Convoy JW 59

This convoy sailed from Loch Ewe on 15 August consisting of the following ships, the Russian warships for passage joining on 17 August:

| | | | | | |
|---|---|---|---|---|---|
| *BRITISH PROMISE* | 23 Br | 8443/42 | *CHARLES A McALLISTER* | 22 Amer | 7176/43 |
| *CHARLES DAURAY* | 95 Amer | 7176/44 | *CLARK HOWELL* | 21 Amer | 7198/44 |
| *DAVID B JOHNSON* | 71 Amer | 7198/44 | *EDWARD H CROCKETT* | 94 Amer | 7176/44 |
| *EDWARD L GRANT* | 104 Amer | 7176/43 | *ELIJAH KELLOGG* | 33 Amer | 7176/44 |
| *EMPIRE BUTTRESS* | 25 Br | 2905/43 | *F T FRELINGHUYSEN* | 14 Amer | 7176/43 |
| *FORT GLENORA* | 51 Br | 7126/43 | *FRANK GILBRETH* | 24 Amer | 7176/44 |
| *HERBRAND* | 42 Nor | 9108/35 | *JOHN LA FARGE* | 41 Amer | 7176/43 |
| *JOSE MARTI* | 34 Amer | 7176/43 | *JOSEPHINE SHAW LOWELL* | 102 Amer | 7176/44 |
| *LEO J DUSTER* | 84 Amer | 7176/43 | *LUCULUS* | 72 Br | 6546/29 |
| *NACELLA* | 93 Br | 8196/43 | *OAKLEY WOOD* | 83 Amer | 7210/44 |
| *RATHLIN* | 85 Br | 1600/36 | *SAMANNAN* | 11 Br | 7219/44 |
| *SAMCALIA* | 31 Br | 7219/43 | *SAMCONSTANT* | 32 Br | 7219/44 |
| *SAMGARA* | 91 Br | 7219/43 | *SAMIDWAY* | 13 Br | 7219/43 |
| *SAMLOYAL* | 81 Br | 7210/44 | *SAMLYTH* | 101 Br | 7210/44 |
| *SAMSUVA* | 103 Br | 7219/44 | *SAMTREDY* | 61 Br | 7219/43 |
| *SILAS WEIR MITCHELL* | 12 Amer | 7176/43 | *THOMAS DONALDSON* | 82 Amer | 7210/44 |
| *THOMAS H SUMNER* | 92 Amer | 7176/44 | *WARREN DELANO* | 35 Amer | 7210/44 |

**1944**

Commodore was in *SAMTREDY,* Vice Commodore in *SAMGARA,* Rear Commodore in *SAMCALIA. RATHLIN* was Rescue Ship, *HERBRAND* and *LUCULUS* escort oilers.

The battleship ARCHANGELSK (formerly HMS ROYAL SOVEREIGN) took position 52 on joining, 12 Russian manned PT boats were also in company for the voyage. JAMAICA, STRIKER and VINDEX occupied column 6 during the passage.

Close escort from sailing to 25 August was sloop CYGNET, frigate LOCH DUNVEGAN, corvettes BLUEBELL, CAMELLIA, CHARLOCK, HONEYSUCKLE and OXLIP. Also present were the sloops KITE, MERMAID and PEACOCK, and destroyers KEPPEL and WHITEHALL. It is believed WHITEHALL joined the screen, the other ships operating ahead of the convoy.

From 17 to 25 August the following were present: the cruiser JAMAICA, escort carriers STRIKER and VINDEX, and destroyers CAPRICE, MARNE, METEOR, MILNE, and MUSKETEER.

The disposition of the escort was with the cruiser and carriers in the centre of the convoy with freedom of movement, six A/S ships ahead of the convoy with KEPPEL and her three sloop consorts a further 10 miles ahead to port and starboard of the line of advance.

On 20 and 21 August there were several U boat contacts, and at 0644 on 21 August KITE was hit by two torpedoes from U 344 and sank in one minute, only nine survivors being rescued. On 22 August a shadowing flying boat was shot down, and one of VINDEX's Swordfish located and sank U 344. Further sightings were made, but by 23 August the U boats were falling astern. The next day another VINDEX Swordfish found U 354 and, in conjunction with KEPPEL, LOCH DUNVEGAN, MERMAID and PEACOCK it was sunk.

Russian fighter cover was available from the morning of the 24 August, and the convoy arrived in Kola Inlet later that day.

## Convoy RA 59A

During the brief lay over of four days between arrival and departure, the ships' companies of the escorts enjoyed a regatta and a first class Russian concert party. The convoy sailed from Kola Inlet on 28 August comprising the following ships:

| | | | | | |
|---|---|---|---|---|---|
| *BARBARA FRIETCHIE* | Amer | 7176/43 | *EMPIRE BARD* | Br | 3114/42 |
| *EMPIRE ELGAR* | Br | 2847/42 | *EMPIRE PROWESS* | Br | 7058/43 |
| *FORT VERCHERES* | Br | 7128/43 | *HERBRAND* | Nor | 9108/35 |
| *LACKLAN* | Br | 8670/29 | *LUCULUS* | Br | 6546/29 |
| *W R GRACE* | Amer | 7176/43 | | | |

Between 28 August and 4 September sloops MERMAID and PEACOCK, destroyers KEPPEL and WHITEHALL and frigate LOCH DUNVEGAN escorted. Other escorts also joined on departure and remained until the date shown, the cruiser JAMAICA, escort carriers STRIKER, VINDEX, destroyers CAPRICE, MARNE, METEOR, MILNE and MUSKETEER until 5 September, sloop CYGNET, and corvettes BLUEBELL, CAMELLIA, CHARLOCK, HONEYSUCKLE and OXLIP to 6 September.

During the convoy's passage there were many U boat sightings and much carrier aircraft activity. On 1 September an aircraft ran down an HF bearing and remained in contact until KEPPEL, MERMAID, PEACOCK and WHITEHALL arrived and sank U 394 in a massed "creeping" attack. The unscathed convoy arrived at Loch Ewe on 5 September.

## Convoy JW 60

The convoy sailed from Loch Ewe on 15 September as follows:

| | | | | | |
|---|---|---|---|---|---|
| *ADOLPH S OCHS* | Br | 7219/43 | *ARUNAH S ABELL* | Amer | 7176/43 |
| *BRITISH PATIENCE* | Br | 8097/43 | *CARDINAL GIBBONS* | Amer | 7191/42 |
| *DANIEL WILLARD* | Amer | 7200/42 | *DAVID STONE* | Amer | 7177/42 |
| *DEXTER W FELLOWS* | Amer | 7210/44 | *EDWARD A SAVOY* | Amer | 7210/44 |
| *EDWARD E SPAFFORD* | Amer | 7176/44 | *EMPIRE CELIA* | Br | 7025/43 |
| *FRANCIS SCOTT KEY* | Amer | 7191/41 | *FREDERIC A KUMMER* | Amer | 7210/44 |
| *FREDERICK W TAYLOR* | Amer | 7176/44 | *GEORGE T ANGELL* | Amer | 7176/44 |
| *HAWKINS FUDSKE* | Amer | 7176/43 | *HENRY LOMB* | Amer | 7176/43 |
| *JOHN J ABEL* | Amer | 7191/43 | *JOHN VINING* | Amer | 7191/42 |
| *JOHN WOOLMAN* | Amer | 7191/43 | *JOSHUA THOMAS* | Amer | 7176/43 |
| *JULIUS OLSEN* | Amer | 7247/44 | *LEWIS EMERY Jr* | Amer | 7176/43 |
| *LUCERNA* | Br | 6556/30 | *NATHANIEL ALEXANDER* | Amer | 7177/42 |
| *NERITINA* | Br | 8228/43 | *NOREG* | Nor | 7605/31 |
| *RAYMOND B STEVENS* | Amer | 7176/44 | *RICHARD M JOHNSON* | Amer | 7176/43 |
| *SAMARITAN* | Br | 7219/43 | *THOMAS U WALTER* | Amer | 7176/43 |
| *ZAMALEK* | Br | 1567/21 | | | |

Commodore was in *EMPIRE CELIA, ZAMALEK* was Rescue Ship, *LUCERNA* and *NOREG* were escort oilers.

As TIRPITZ still survived, although unknown to the Admiralty no longer in a seagoing condition, the Commander-in-Chief took RODNEY through to Kola Inlet as cover for the convoy and also to meet his Russian colleague, Admiral Golovko.

Close escorts were sloop CYGNET, destroyers BULLDOG, KEPPEL and WHITEHALL, corvettes ALLINGTON CASTLE and BAMBOROUGH CASTLE. The remaining escorts joined on 17 September, the battleship RODNEY, cruiser DIADEM, escort carriers CAMPANIA and STRIKER and destroyers MARNE, METEOR, MILNE, MUSKETEER, SAUMAREZ, SCORPION, VENUS, VERULAM, VIRAGO, VOLAGE and Canadian ALGONQUIN and SIOUX. All ships remained until arrival at Kola Inlet on 23 September.

## Convoy RA 60

The convoy sailed from Kola Inlet on 28 September with the escorts of the previous incoming convoy, merchant ships being as follows:

| | | | | | |
|---|---|---|---|---|---|
| *BRITISH PROMISE* | Br | 8443/42 | *CHARLES A McALLISTER* | Amer | 7176/43 |
| *CHARLES DAURAY* | Amer | 7176/44 | *CLARK HOWELL* | Amer | 7198/44 |
| *DAVID B JOHNSON* | Amer | 7198/44 | *EDWARD H CROCKETT* | Amer | 7176/44 |
| *EDWARD L GRANT* | Amer | 7176/43 | *ELIJAH KELLOGG* | Amer | 7176/44 |
| *FORT GLENORA* | Br | 7126/43 | *FRANK GILBRETH* | Amer | 7176/44 |
| *JOHN LA FARGE* | Amer | 7176/43 | *JOSE MARTI* | Amer | 7176/43 |
| *JOSEPHINE SHAW LOWELL* | Amer | 7176/44 | *LEO J DUSTER* | Amer | 7176/43 |
| *NACELLA* | Br | 8196/43 | *NOREG* | Nor | 7605/31 |
| *OAKLEY WOOD* | Amer | 7210/44 | *RATHLIN* | Br | 1600/36 |
| *SAMANNAN* | Br | 7219/44 | *SAMCALIA* | Br | 7219/43 |
| *SAMCONSTANT* | Br | 7219/44 | *SAMGARA* | Br | 7219/43 |
| *SAMIDWAY* | Br | 7219/43 | *SAMLOYAL* | Br | 7210/44 |
| *SAMLYTH* | Br | 7210/44 | *SAMSUVA* | Br | 7219/44 |
| *SAMTREDY* | Br | 7219/43 | *SILAS WEIR MITCHELL* | Amer | 7176/43 |
| *THOMAS DONALDSON* | Amer | 7210/44 | *THOMAS H SUMNER* | Amer | 7176/44 |
| *WARREN DELANO* | Amer | 7210/44 | *ZAMALEK* | Br | 1567/21 |

Commodore was in *SAMTREDY,* Vice Commodore in *SAMGARA,* Rear Commodore in *SAMCALIA. ZAMALEK* was Rescue Ship, *NACELLA* and *NOREG* escort oilers.

Close escort sailed with the convoy on 28 September; sloop CYGNET, destroyers BULLDOG, KEPPEL and WHITEHALL and corvettes ALLINGTON CASTLE and BAMBOROUGH CASTLE, all remaining with the convoy until 4 October. RODNEY and the remaining ships of JW 60's escort joined at the same time and left for Scapa Flow on 3 October.

The passage of the convoy was quiet after 29 September, on which day U 310 succeeded in penetrating the escort and sinking both *EDWARD H CROCKETT* and *SAMSUVA.* The remainder of the convoy arrived in Loch Ewe on 5 October. Aircraft from HMS CAMPANIA sank U 921 on 30.9.44.

## Convoy JW 61

The convoy sailed from Loch Ewe on 20 October, as follows:

| | | | | | | | |
|---|---|---|---|---|---|---|---|
| *ABNER NASH* | 31 | Amer | 7177/42 | *ANDREW W PRESTON* | 34 | Amer | 7247/44 |
| *BENJAMIN SCHLESINGER* | 81 | Amer | 7176/44 | *COLLIS P HUNTINGTON* | 104 | Amer | 7177/42 |
| *DOLABELLA* | 22 | Br | 8142/39 | *DONALD W BAIN* | 83 | Amer | 7200/44 |
| *ELEAZAR LORD* | 13 | Amer | 7247/44 | *ELOY ALFARO* | 103 | Amer | 7176/44 |
| *FORT CREVECOEUR* | 61 | Br | 7191/43 | *FORT ROMAINE* | 11 | Br | 7131/43 |
| *FORT YUKON* | 92 | Br | 7153/43 | *HAROLD L WINSLOW* | 101 | Amer | 7176/43 |
| *HENRY ADAMS* | 33 | Amer | 7212/44 | *JAMES M GILLIS* | 82 | Amer | 7176/43 |
| *JOHN SHARP WILLIAMS* | 12 | Amer | 7176/43 | *JOYCE KILMER* | 32 | Amer | 7176/43 |
| *KEITH PALMER* | 102 | Amer | 7244/44 | *LAPLAND* | 94 | Br | 2897/42 |
| *LAURELWOOD* | 72 | Br | 7347/29 | *LAWRENCE J BRENGLE* | 14 | Amer | 7209/44 |
| *MARATHON* | 93 | Nor | 7208/30 | *NICHOLAS BIDDLE* | 51 | Amer | 7191/42 |
| *NOREG* | 42 | Nor | 7605/31 | *PARK BENJAMIN* | 24 | Amer | 7176/44 |
| *SAN VENANCIO* | 23 | Br | 8152/42 | *STAGE DOOR CANTEEN* | 21 | Amer | 7176/43 |
| *SYRIAN PRINCE* | 84 | Br | 1990/36 | *WILLIAM PEPPER* | 71 | Amer | 7176/43 |
| *WILLIAM WHEELWRIGHT* | 91 | Amer | 7176/44 | *WINFRED L SMITH* | 41 | Amer | 7191/43 |

Commodore was in *FORT CREVECOEUR,* Vice Commodore in *FORT YUKON* and Rear Commodore in *DOLABELLA. SYRIAN PRINCE* was Rescue Ship, *LAURELWOOD* and *NOREG* escort oilers. Six Russian SC boats also sailed with the convoy.

Action against TIRPITZ by the Fleet Air Arm and the Royal Air Force , by the latter as recently as 15 September, had removed that ship as a menace to convoys, while the Luftwaffe had long ceased to have a viable striking force in north Norway. The main threat to this, and subsequent, convoys was therefore the U boat, especially as experience had demonstrated that the thermal layers in the Arctic seas deprived the escorts of much of their Asdic potential. Escort carriers and their squadrons were increasingly seen as the key factors, and a flagship and three carriers sailed with this convoy, the strongest support to date. These ships occupied the after part of the 4th, 5th and 6th columns of the convoy as their operating area.

**1944**

Close escort, provided by Western Approaches, was 8 Escort Group formed of the destroyer WALKER, sloops LAPWING and LARK, and corvettes CAMELLIA, OXLIP and RHODODENDRON who were present from 20 to 28 October. The main escort joined 22 October and comprised the cruiser DIDO and destroyers OBEDIENT, OFFA, ONSLOW, OPPORTUNE, ORIBI and ORWELL, these ships remaining also until 28 October. Joining on the same day was the third component of three escort carriers NAIRANA, TRACKER and VINDEX and two more Western Approaches Groups, frigates BYRON, CONN, DEANE, FITZROY, INGLIS, LAWSON, LORING, LOUIS, MOUNSEY, NARBOROUGH, REDMILL and RUPERT.

Vigorous action by the ships and aircraft of this powerful escort ensured the safe and undamaged arrival of the convoy in Kola Inlet on 28 October.

## Convoy JW 61A

This convoy was the most unusual of the entire series as it consisted of just two large personnel ships which made a fast passage from Liverpool to Murmansk sailing on 31 October and arriving 6 November. The personnel ships were:

| | | | | | |
|---|---|---|---|---|---|
| *EMPRESS OF AUSTRALIA* | Br | 21833/14 | *SCYTHIA* | Br | 19761/20 |

*The liner EMPRESS OF AUSTRALIA, photographed from HMS BERWICK, as she enters Kola Inlet at the end of convoy JW 61A.*

Escort was strong, the sloop CYGNET, destroyers BEAGLE and WESTCOTT, Canadian manned frigate NENE from sailing as local escort, relieved by the cruiser BERWICK, escort carrier CAMPANIA, and destroyers CAMBRIAN, CAPRICE, CASSANDRA, SAUMAREZ, SCOURGE and SERAPIS, all of which joined on 2 November as ocean escort.

The purpose of the passage was to return to Russia some 11,000 nationals who had been captured in Normandy while serving in the Wehrmacht as part of the armies opposing the Anglo-American landing; doubtless these men were part of the forces raised by the Germans from their prisoners of war ostensibly to fight Communism. As such, their reception in Russia can be imagined. British personnel were prevented from landing on this occasion, neither were the SBNO's staff allowed into the area.

BERWICK also carried a contingent of Norwegian troops who were put ashore at Murmansk to join the Russian forces then about to enter northern Norway, an endeavour on the part of the exiled government to ensure the sovereignty of Norwegian territory.

Additionally, an advance party of Norwegian troops which should have been flown in but whose passage was prevented by weather conditions, was embarked in the destroyers SAVAGE and SCORPION which made an independent passage to Kola under the title Operation FREEMAN. Sailing on 3 November, these ships arrived at Kola at the same time as the convoy, and returned with RA 61A.

## Convoy RA 61

The convoy cleared Kola Inlet on 2 November, some ships having commenced their passage in the White Sea on 30 October. The following were present:

| | | | |
|---|---|---|---|
| *ADOLPH S OCHS* | 91 | Br | 7219/43 |
| *BRITISH PATIENCE* | 83 | Br | 8097/43 |
| *DANIEL WILLARD* | 71 | Amer | 7200/42 |
| *DEXTER W FELLOWS* | 11 | Amer | 7210/44 |
| *EDWARD E SPAFFORD* | 13 | Amer | 7176/44 |
| *F T FRELINGHUYSEN* | 105 | Amer | 7176/43 |
| *FREDERIC A KUMMER* | 14 | Amer | 7210/44 |
| *GEORGE T ANGELL* | 41 | Amer | 7176/44 |
| *HENRY LOMB* | 31 | Amer | 7176/43 |
| *JOHN VINING* | 103 | Amer | 7191/42 |
| *JOSHUA THOMAS* | 102 | Amer | 7176/43 |
| *LAURELWOOD* | 72 | Br | 7347/29 |
| *LUCERNA* | 23 | Br | 6556/30 |
| *NERITINA* | 93 | Br | 8228/43 |
| *RAYMOND B STEVENS* | 84 | Amer | 7176/44 |
| *SAMARITAN* | 51 | Br | 7219/43 |
| *THOMAS U WALTER* | 101 | Amer | 7176/43 |
| *ARUNAH S ABELL* | 81 | Amer | 7176/43 |
| *CARDINAL GIBBONS* | 104 | Amer | 7191/42 |
| *DAVID STONE* | 92 | Amer | 7177/42 |
| *EDWARD A SAVOY* | 61 | Amer | 7210/44 |
| *EMPIRE CELIA* | 82 | Br | 7025/43 |
| *FRANCIS SCOTT KEY* | 21 | Amer | 7191/41 |
| *FREDERICK W TAYLOR* | 24 | Amer | 7176/44 |
| *HAWKINS FUDSKE* | 33 | Amer | 7176/43 |
| *JOHN J ABEL* | 32 | Amer | 7191/43 |
| *JOHN WOOLMAN* | 94 | Amer | 7191/43 |
| *JULIUS OLSEN* | 12 | Amer | 7247/44 |
| *LEWIS EMERY Jr* | 22 | Amer | 7176/43 |
| *NATHANIEL ALEXANDER* | 95 | Amer | 7177/42 |
| *NOREG* | 42 | Nor | 7605/31 |
| *RICHARD M JOHNSON* | 15 | Amer | 7176/43 |
| *SYRIAN PRINCE* | 34 | Br | 1990/36 |

Commodore was in *EDWARD A SAVOY,* Vice Commodore in *EMPIRE CELIA,* Rear Commodore in *JOHN J ABEL. SYRIAN PRINCE* was Rescue Ship, *LAURELWOOD* and *NOREG* escort oilers.

Escort was that provided for JW 61, sloops LAPWING and LARK, destroyer WALKER, and corvettes CAMELLIA, OXLIP and RHODODENDRON from 2 to 9 November, destroyers OBEDIENT, OFFA, ONSLOW, OPPORTUNE, ORIBI and ORWELL and frigates BYRON, CONN, DEANE, FITZROY, REDMILL and RUPERT from 2 to 7 November; INGLIS, LAWSON, LORING, LOUIS and NARBOROUGH from 2 to 6 November. Cruiser DIDO and escort carriers NAIRANA, TRACKER and VINDEX were stationed within the convoy in their own operating area, from 2 to 7 November.

18 U boats were disposed off Kola Inlet in an attempt to attack the convoy from the outset, the frigate force therefore sailed early to ''put down'' these attackers during the merchant ships' exit. Asdic conditions were poor, and there were no successes despite the talent arrayed against the enemy, indeed MOUNSEY was torpedoed by U 295 during these operations and obliged to return to Kola for assistance.

No merchant ships were lost, either in the initial stages or the later passage, the convoy arriving in Loch Ewe on 9 November.

## Convoy RA 61A

The two ships of JW 61A,

| | | |
|---|---|---|
| *EMPRESS OF AUSTRALIA* | Br | 21833/14 |
| *SCYTHIA* | Br | 19761/20 |

left Kola Inlet on 11 November to return to the Clyde where they arrived on 17 November. It is assumed that they sailed empty other than for the returning guards from the outward passage, probably in battalion strength if the normal ratio of 10% guards to PoWs had been observed.

Escort was provided, as on the outward voyage, by the cruiser BERWICK (11 to 16 November), escort carrier CAMPANIA (11 to 17 November) and destroyers CAMBRIAN, CAPRICE, CASSANDRA, SAVAGE, SAUMAREZ, SCORPION, SCOURGE and SERAPIS. There are some reports that an Escort Group of frigates from Western Approaches Command was also attached during the later part of the voyage, but this cannot be confirmed at the time of writing.

## Convoy JW 62

Thirty one ships sailed with this convoy from Loch Ewe on 29 November, as follows:

| | | | |
|---|---|---|---|
| *AMASA DELANO* | 92 | Amer | 7176/44 |
| *AUGUST BELMONT* | 62 | Amer | 7240/44 |
| *BRITISH RESPECT* | 32 | Br | 8479/43 |
| *EDWARD N HURLEY* | 21 | Amer | 7191/43 |
| *EMPIRE STALWART* | 11 | Br | 7050/43 |
| *FORT HIGHFIELD* | 31 | Br | 7129/43 |
| *FORT MASSAC* | 12 | Br | 7157/43 |
| *LAURELWOOD* | 82 | Br | 7347/29 |
| *LONGWOOD* | 33 | Br | 9463/30 |
| *NELSON W ALDRICH* | 91 | Amer | 7176/44 |
| *RATHLIN* | 94 | Br | 1600/36 |
| *ROBERT LOWRY* | 61 | Amer | 7176/43 |
| *ANDREW TURNBULL* | 42 | Amer | 7240/44 |
| *BARBARA FRIETCHIE* | 14 | Amer | 7176/43 |
| *CECIL N BEAN* | 43 | Amer | 7176/44 |
| *EMPIRE GARRICK* | 22 | Br | 8128/42 |
| *FORT BOISE* | 71 | Br | 7151/43 |
| *FORT ISLAND* | 13 | Br | 7167/44 |
| *JOHN GIBBON* | 51 | Amer | 7247/44 |
| *LINN BOYD* | 15 | Amer | 7176/44 |
| *LUCULUS* | 52 | Br | 6546/29 |
| *OWEN WISTER* | 104 | Amer | 7240/43 |
| *RENALD FERNALD* | 81 | Amer | 7176/44 |
| *STANTON H KING* | 102 | Amer | 7176/44 |

**1944**

| | | | | | | |
|---|---|---|---|---|---|---|
| *STEPHEN LEACOCK* | 101 Amer | 7198/44 | *STEVENSON TAYLOR* | 103 Amer | 7176/43 |
| *U.S.O.* | 34 Amer | 7176/43 | *W R GRACE* | 23 Amer | 7176/43 |
| *WILLIAM H WILMER* | 24 Amer | 7191/43 | *WILLIAM TYLER PAGE* | 41 Amer | 7176/43 |
| *WOODBRIDGE N FERRIS* | 44 Amer | 7200/43 | | | |

Commodore was in *FORT BOISE,* Vice Commodore in *EMPIRE STALWART. RATHLIN* was Rescue Ship, and *LAURELWOOD* and *LUCULUS* were escort oilers.

The cruiser BELLONA and escort carriers CAMPANIA and NAIRANA, present from 1 to 7 December, occupied positions in columns 6,7 and 8 during the passage.

The following escorts were present from 29 November to 7 December: sloops CYGNET, LAPWING and LARK, frigates BAHAMAS, LOCH ALVIE, SOMALILAND, TAVY and TORTOLA and Canadian MONNOW, NENE, PORT COLBORNE, ST JOHN and STORMONT, corvettes ALLINGTON CASTLE, BAMBOROUGH CASTLE, and Norwegian TUNSBERG CASTLE and EGLANTINE.

On 1 December the cruiser BELLONA, escort carriers CAMPANIA, NAIRANA and destroyers BEAGLE, BULLDOG, CAESAR, CAMBRIAN, CAPRICE, CASSANDRA, KEPPEL, OBEDIENT, OFFA, ONSLAUGHT, ONSLOW, ORIBI, ORWELL and WESTCOTT joined.

Although TIRPITZ had been eliminated by the Royal Air Force on 12 November, removing the necessity of maintaining the Home Fleet at strength (and using it to support the Russian convoy route), the enemy had replaced one threat with another by moving back to north Norway a substantial force of Ju 88 torpedo bombers in their first attempt to restore the weapon lost in the carnage of the attacks on PQ 18. The U boat threat, of course, also remained great in this theatre. In spite of this formidable strength however, the enemy was not able to make any impression on JW 62 which arrived unscathed in Kola Inlet on 7 December.

## Convoy RA 62

The 29 ships of this convoy sailed from Kola Inlet on 10 December, having within its columns a cruiser and two escort carriers of the escort, and the damaged frigate MOUNSEY returning for permanent repairs. The merchant ships were:

| | | | | | |
|---|---|---|---|---|---|
| *ABNER NASH* | 31 Amer | 7177/42 | *ANDREW W PRESTON* | 42 Amer | 7247/44 |
| *BENJAMIN SCHLESINGER* | 81 Amer | 7176/44 | *COLLIS P HUNTINGTON* | 104 Amer | 7177/42 |
| *DOLABELLA* | 22 Br | 8142/39 | *DONALD W BAIN* | 83 Amer | 7200/44 |
| *ELEAZAR LORD* | 12 Amer | 7247/44 | *ELOY ALFARO* | 103 Amer | 7176/44 |
| *FORT CREVECOEUR* | 61 Br | 7191/43 | *FORT ROMAINE* | 11 Br | 7131/43 |
| *FORT YUKON* | 92 Br | 7153/43 | *HAROLD L WINSLOW* | 101 Amer | 7176/43 |
| *HENRY ADAMS* | 33 Amer | 7212/44 | *JAMES M GILLIS* | 82 Amer | 7176/43 |
| *JOHN SHARP WILLIAMS* | 13 Amer | 7176/43 | *JOYCE KILMER* | 32 Amer | 7176/43 |
| *KEITH PALMER* | 102 Amer | 7244/44 | *LAURELWOOD* | 72 Br | 7347/29 |
| *LAWRENCE J BRENGLE* | 14 Amer | 7209/44 | *LUCULUS* | 52 Br | 6546/29 |
| *MARATHON* | 93 Nor | 7208/30 | *NICHOLAS BIDDLE* | 51 Amer | 7191/42 |
| *PARK BENJAMIN* | 24 Amer | 7176/44 | *RATHLIN* | 84 Br | 1600/36 |
| *SAN VENANCIO* | 23 Br | 8152/42 | *STAGE DOOR CANTEEN* | 21 Amer | 7176/43 |
| *WILLIAM PEPPER* | 71 Amer | 7176/43 | *WILLIAM WHEELWRIGHT* | 91 Amer | 7176/44 |
| *WINFRED L SMITH* | 41 Amer | 7191/43 | | | |

Commodore was in *FORT CREVECOEUR,* Vice Commodore in *FORT YUKON. RATHLIN* was Rescue Ship, *LAURELWOOD* and *LUCULUS* escort oilers.

The escort was that provided for the inward JW 62, sailing from Kola Inlet shortly before the convoy to attack the assembled U boats during which period U 387 was sunk by BAMBOROUGH CASTLE. The Canadian frigates MONNOW, NENE, PORT COLBORNE, ST JOHN and STORMONT and the British LOCH ALVIE left the convoy on 17 December, the remaining escorts on 18 and 19 December.

During the passage of the convoy on 11 December U 365 torpedoed the destroyer CASSANDRA, who lost her bows and was obliged to return to Murmansk for emergency repairs. On 12 December the Norwegian corvette TUNSBERG CASTLE was mined and sunk.

The Luftwaffe re-entered the fray on 12 December with an attack by nine torpedo bombers, to no avail and with the loss of two aircraft. Finally, on 13 December, 813 Squadron from CAMPANIA drew blood by sinking U 365.

The convoy, less *FORT ROMAINE* which proceeded as an independent, arrived at Loch Ewe 19 December.

## Convoy JW 63

This convoy sailed from Loch Ewe on 30 December 1944, composed as follows:

| | | | | | |
|---|---|---|---|---|---|
| *ADOLPH S OCHS* | 106 Br | 7219/43 | *ALANSON B HOUGHTON* | 51 Amer | 7176/44 |
| *BENJAMIN H HILL* | 35 Amer | 7198/44 | *BERNARD N BAKER* | 32 Amer | 7191/43 |
| *BLUE RANGER* | 42 Br | 3417/41 | *BRITISH PROMISE* | 93 Br | 8443/42 |
| *CAESAR RODNEY* | 25 Amer | 7191/42 | *CHARLES M SCHWAB* | 91 Amer | 7191/43 |
| *CHARLES SCRIBNER* | 24 Amer | 7176/43 | *CROSBY S NOYES* | 13 Amer | 7176/43 |
| *EDMUND FANNING* | 14 Amer | 7176/43 | *EMPIRE ARCHER* | 92 Br | 7031/42 |
| *EMPIRE CELIA* | 52 Br | 7025/43 | *FRANCIS C HARRINGTON* | 21 Amer | 7176/43 |
| *GEORGE H PENDLETON* | 71 Amer | 7176/43 | *HENRY BACON* | 12 Amer | 7177/42 |
| *HENRY VILLARD* | 104 Amer | 7176/42 | *HENRY WYNKOOP* | 15 Amer | 7176/42 |
| *HORACE GRAY* | 33 Amer | 7200/43 | *IDEFJORD* | 84 Nor | 4287/21 |
| *J D YEAGER* | 82 Amer | 7247/44 | *JAMES KERNEY* | 85 Amer | 7210/44 |
| *JOHN A QUITMAN* | 103 Amer | 7176/43 | *JOHN IRELAND* | 95 Amer | 7247/44 |
| *JOHN LA FARGE* | 81 Amer | 7176/43 | *JOSE MARTI* | 102 Amer | 7176/43 |
| *JOSHUA W ALEXANDER* | 41 Amer | 7176/43 | *LACKLAN* | 72 Br | 8670/29 |
| *LEBARON RUSSELL BRIGGS* | 105 Amer | 7176/44 | *NACELLA* | 22 Br | 8196/43 |
| *NORFJELL* | 23 Nor | 8129/42 | *PAUL H HARWOOD* | 94 Amer | 6610/18 |
| *PHILIP F THOMAS* | 11 Amer | 7176/43 | *R NEY McNEELY* | 34 Amer | 7198/44 |
| *SAMARITAN* | 61 Br | 7219/43 | *SILAS WEIR MITCHELL* | 31 Amer | 7176/43 |
| *THOMAS SCOTT* | 83 Amer | 7176/42 | *WARREN DELANO* | 101 Amer | 7210/44 |

Commodore was in *SAMARITAN,* Vice Commodore in *EMPIRE ARCHER.* The RFA *BLUE RANGER* and tanker *LAURELWOOD* were the escort oilers.

The escorts from 30 December to 8 January were the destroyers KEPPEL, WALKER and WESTCOTT, sloops CYGNET, LAPWING and LARK and corvettes ALLINGTON CASTLE, ALNWICK CASTLE and BAMBOROUGH CASTLE. On New Year's Day 1945 the cruiser DIADEM and escort carrier VINDEX joined the centre columns of the convoy, and the destroyers MYNGS, SAVAGE, SCOURGE, SERAPIS, ZAMBESI, ZEBRA and Canadian ALGONQUIN and SIOUX and Norwegian STORD formed the outer escort.

Neither this convoy, nor the subsequent RA 63 were detected by the enemy, and JW 63 arrived safely at Kola Inlet on 8 January 1945, less *ADOLPH S OCHS* which had returned to Loch Ewe.

*Seamen clear the flight deck of an escort carrier at Kola, illustrating the conditions which hampered flying in Arctic operations. A Russian TOWN class destroyer can be seen astern of the carrier.*

## Convoy RA 63

Thirty one ships sailed from Kola Inlet on 11 January to be joined within their columns by the cruiser DIADEM and escort carrier VINDEX. The ships were:

| | | | | | | |
|---|---|---|---|---|---|---|
| *AMASA DELANO* | 82 Amer | 7176/44 | | *ANDREW TURNBULL* | 24 Amer | 7240/44 |
| *AUGUST BELMONT* | 14 Amer | 7240/44 | | *BARBARA FRIETCHIE* | 94 Amer | 7176/43 |
| *BERNARD N BAKER* | 11 Amer | 7191/43 | | *BLUE RANGER* | 52 Br | 3417/41 |
| *BRITISH RESPECT* | 61 Br | 8479/43 | | *CECIL N BEAN* | 33 Amer | 7176/44 |
| *EDWARD N HURLEY* | 101 Amer | 7191/43 | | *EMPIRE GARRICK* | 93 Br | 8128/42 |
| *EMPIRE STALWART* | 92 Br | 7050/43 | | *FORT BOISE* | 21 Br | 7151/43 |
| *FORT HIGHFIELD* | 22 Br | 7129/43 | | *FORT ISLAND* | 83 Br | 7167/44 |
| *FORT MASSAC* | 104 Br | 7157/43 | | *JOHN GIBBON* | 41 Amer | 7247/44 |
| *LACKLAN* | 72 Br | 8670/29 | | *LINN BOYD* | 91 Amer | 7176/44 |
| *LONGWOOD* | 23 Br | 9463/30 | | *NELSON W ALDRICH* | 81 Amer | 7176/44 |
| *OWEN WISTER* | 12 Amer | 7240/43 | | *RENALD FERNALD* | 71 Amer | 7176/44 |
| *ROBERT LOWRY* | 51 Amer | 7176/43 | | *STANTON H KING* | 102 Amer | 7176/44 |
| *STEPHEN LEACOCK* | 13 Amer | 7198/44 | | *STEVENSON TAYLOR* | 103 Amer | 7176/43 |
| *U.S.O.* | 32 Amer | 7176/43 | | *W R GRACE* | 11 Amer | 7176/43 |
| *WILLIAM H WILMER* | 34 Amer | 7191/43 | | *WILLIAM TYLER PAGE* | 31 Amer | 7176/43 |
| *WOODBRIDGE N FERRIS* | 42 Amer | 7200/43 | | | | |

Escorts for the convoy were those from JW 63 plus the destroyer SCORPION. Commodore was in *BRITISH RESPECT,*, Vice Commodore in *EMPIRE STALWART. LACKLAN, LONGWOOD* and *BLUE RANGER* were escort oilers.

The convoy proceeded undetected and unmolested, except by the weather. North east of the Faroes, an unusually severe gale forced the convoy to take shelter, reassemble and proceed when the weather abated; it reached Loch Ewe on 21 January, less *FORT HIGHFIELD* which had sheltered in the Faroes with collision damage, and later arrived at Kirkwall.

The destroyers KEPPEL, WALKER and WESTCOTT took ships for the Clyde onwards from Loch Ewe, arriving there on 23 January.

*A general view of convoy JW 64 taken from the bridge of the cruiser HMS BELLONA.*

## Convoy JW 64

The Loch Ewe convoy anchorage having been dispensed with, this next convoy sailed direct from the Clyde Anchorage on 3 February, as below:

| | | | | | | | |
|---|---|---|---|---|---|---|---|
| *ADOLPH S OCHS* | 92 | Br | 7219/43 | *ARUNAH S ABELL* | 71 | Br | 7176/43 |
| *BEN F DIXON* | 14 | Amer | 7176/43 | *BLACK RANGER* | 42 | Br | 3417/41 |
| *BRITISH MERIT* | 22 | Br | 8093/42 | *BYRON DARNTON* | 93 | Amer | 7176/43 |
| *DANIEL WILLARD* | 31 | Amer | 7200/42 | *EDWIN L DRAKE* | 13 | Amer | 7176/43 |
| *EMPIRE FLINT* | 32 | Br | 8129/41 | *F T FRELINGHUYSEN* | 11 | Amer | 7176/43 |
| *FORT CREVECOEUR* | 61 | Br | 7191/43 | *FORT VERCHERES* | 81 | Br | 7128/43 |
| *FRANCIS SCOTT KEY* | 91 | Amer | 7191/41 | *GEORGE STEERS* | 83 | Amer | 7247/44 |
| H Nor M S OKSOY | 111 | Nor | | *HAROLD L WINSLOW* | 41 | Amer | 7176/43 |
| *HAWKINS FUDSKE* | 33 | Amer | 7176/43 | *HENRY LOMB* | 12 | Amer | 7176/43 |
| *JOHN J ABEL* | 103 | Amer | 7191/43 | *JOHN WANAMAKER* | 102 | Amer | 7176/43 |
| *JOYCE KILMER* | 82 | Amer | 7176/43 | *LEWIS EMERY Jr* | 23 | Amer | 7176/43 |
| *LUCERNA* | 72 | Br | 6556/30 | *MARIE M MELONEY* | 101 | Amer | 7176/43 |
| *NATHAN TOWSON* | 21 | Amer | 7176/43 | *NERITINA* | 52 | Br | 8228/43 |
| *SKIENSFJORD* | 104 | Nor | 5922/22 | *TOWNSEND HARRIS* | 51 | Amer | 7176/43 |
| *WILLARD HALL* | 94 | Amer | 7200/43 | | | | |

Commodore was in *FORT CREVECOEUR,* Vice Commodore in *ADOLPH S OCHS* and Rear Commodore in *BRITISH MERIT. BLACK RANGER* and *LUCERNA* were escort oilers.

Close escort on sailing on 3 February was sloops CYGNET and LARK, destroyer WHITEHALL and corvettes ALNWICK CASTLE, BAMBOROUGH CASTLE, BLUEBELL and RHODODENDRON. On 6 February the cruiser BELLONA, escort carriers CAMPANIA and NAIRANA, sloop LAPWING, corvette DENBIGH CASTLE and trawler OKSOY all joined plus destroyers ONSLAUGHT, ONSLOW, OPPORTUNE, ORWELL, SERAPIS, ZAMBESI, ZEALOUS, ZEST and Canadian SIOUX. The destroyer ZEBRA, which sailed with her sisters on 3 February to join, had to return to the Faroes with defects.

A sighting report was made by the Luftwaffe on 6 February, thereafter almost constant contact was maintained. Two Wildcat fighters shot down a Ju 88 on 6, and on 7 February a mass attack by 48 torpedo bombers was foiled with the loss of seven aircraft, six to fighters and one to DENBIGH CASTLE. This was despite the lack of modern fighters in the escort carriers, with old machines operating in conditions of low light and visibility.

On 10 February a further torpedo bomber attack was mounted, again repulsed this time with the loss of five aircraft, and without damage to the convoy. It must be said that, at this time, fire discipline amongst both convoy and escort was poor, and not infrequently our own fighter aircraft were fired upon.

Eleven U boats were deployed against the convoy, and were in action on 13 February when U 992 torpedoed DENBIGH CASTLE. She was towed in to Kola Inlet by BLUEBELL and the Russian tug BUREVESTNIK, but grounded and then capsized on arrival, becoming a total loss.

The convoy arrived at Kola Inlet on 15 February, less the OKSOY which straggled on 11 February. *FORT CREVECOEUR* and *ARUNAH S ABELL* collided during the entry to the Inlet.

On the day prior to arrival U 711 sank *HORACE GRAY* and U 968 sank *NORFJELL* in a local convoy in the White Sea; news was also received that the enemy were attacking the island of Soroy in north Norway. Accordingly, the Flag Officer in JW 64 detached the destroyers SIOUX, ZAMBESI, ZEALOUS and ZEST to Soroy where they embarked the population of 500 and brought them to Murmansk to be distributed amongst homeward bound ships in the next convoy.

## Convoy RA 64

The ships of this convoy, as listed below, sailed from Kola Inlet on 17 February:

| | | | | | | | |
|---|---|---|---|---|---|---|---|
| *ALANSON B HOUGHTON* | 61 | Amer | 7176/44 | *BENJAMIN H HILL* | 13 | Amer | 7198/44 |
| *BLACK RANGER* | 52 | Br | 3417/41 | *BRITISH PROMISE* | 24 | Br | 8443/42 |
| *CAESAR RODNEY* | 22 | Amer | 7191/42 | *CHARLES M SCHWAB* | 101 | Amer | 7191/43 |
| *CHARLES SCRIBNER* | 31 | Amer | 7176/43 | *CROSBY S NOYES* | 14 | Amer | 7176/43 |
| *EDMUND FANNING* | 33 | Amer | 7176/43 | *EMPIRE ARCHER* | 102 | Br | 7031/42 |
| *EMPIRE CELIA* | 92 | Br | 7025/43 | *FRANCIS C HARRINGTON* | 42 | Amer | 7176/43 |
| *GEORGE H PENDLETON* | 113 | Amer | 7176/43 | *HENRY BACON* | 43 | Amer | 7177/42 |
| *HENRY VILLARD* | 62 | Amer | 7176/42 | *HENRY WYNKOOP* | 41 | Amer | 7176/42 |
| *IDEFJORD* | 44 | Nor | 4287/21 | *J D YEAGER* | 103 | Amer | 7247/44 |
| *JAMES KERNEY* | 82 | Amer | 7210/44 | *JOHN A QUITMAN* | 12 | Amer | 7176/43 |
| *JOHN IRELAND* | 104 | Amer | 7247/44 | *JOHN LA FARGE* | 111 | Amer | 7176/43 |
| *JOSE MARTI* | 112 | Amer | 7176/43 | *JOSHUA W ALEXANDER* | 51 | Amer | 7176/43 |
| *LEBARON RUSSELL BRIGGS* | 93 | Amer | 7176/44 | *NACELLA* | 32 | Br | 8196/43 |
| *PAUL H HARWOOD* | 114 | Amer | 6610/18 | *PHILIP F THOMAS* | 21 | Amer | 7176/43 |
| *R NEY McNEELY* | 23 | Amer | 7198/44 | *SAMARITAN* | 71 | Br | 7219/43 |
| *SILAS WEIR MITCHELL* | 81 | Amer | 7176/43 | *THOMAS SCOTT* | 34 | Amer | 7176/42 |
| *WARREN DELANO* | 91 | Amer | 7210/44 | | | | |

*The escort carriers of convoy RA 64 meet heavy seas in the Arctic gloom.*

Commodore was in *SAMARITAN,* Vice Commodore in *EMPIRE ARCHER,* Rear Commodore in *NACELLA.* RFA *BLACK RANGER* was escort oiler.

From 17 February to 1 March close escort was sloops CYGNET and LAPWING, corvettes ALNWICK CASTLE, BAMBOROUGH CASTLE and RHODODENDRON. Sloop LARK and corvette BLUEBELL were also part of this group, but both were torpedoed at the outset (see later narrative). WHITEHALL was also part of the close escort, but detached on 21 February. From 17 to 27 February the cruiser BELLONA, carriers CAMPANIA and NAIRANA and destroyers ONSLAUGHT, ONSLOW, OPPORTUNE, ORWELL, SERAPIS, ZAMBESI, ZEALOUS, ZEST and Canadian SIOUX were present. SAVAGE and SCOURGE were with the escort 21 to 26 February, and ZEBRA 26 to 27 February. The destroyers CAVALIER, MYNGS and SCORPION joined as a reinforcement 25 to 27 February.

Close escorts sailed pm 16 February to conduct an A/S hunt outside Kola Inlet, and Russian aircraft cooperation am 17 was also requested. During this night operation, ALNWICK CASTLE and LARK sank U 425. The convoy took some time to clear the entrance to the Inlet, and during this slow operation the sloop LARK was torpedoed by U 968. Although towed in to Kola, LARK was regarded as a total loss, and she was very thoroughly stripped of all equipment (including major items of machinery) before being abandoned to the Russians as a hulk. U 968 had a good day, for after hitting LARK the U boat went on to sink the freighter *THOMAS SCOTT.* Also on 17 February U 711 hit the corvette BLUEBELL which blew up and sank at once, only one man surviving. Some of the patrolling U boats then remained off the Inlet, while others endeavoured to pursue the convoy.

The weather that followed deserves the description of ''the great gale''; other convoys suffered severe weather but none so bad as this; the convoy was greatly scattered, numerous ships suffering serious weather damage. At its height, two merchant ships were reduced to steering with block and tackle on the rudder head, and twelve destroyers were docked with weather damage on return to Britain.

Escorts had assembled all but four ships by 20 February, when more than 25 enemy aircraft attacked. Despite the weather NAIRANA flew off Wildcat fighters and they and the escorts' AA fire accounted for six enemy. No ships were hit, although wild claims were made by the enemy.

Further hurricane force winds then scattered the convoy again, and it was fortunate that after reassembly, a force of torpedo bombers missed the tired ships on 23 February. Unfortunately, they did find the straggler *HENRY BACON,* one of the ships carrying passengers from Soroy Island. When the ship finally sank, some of her crew and gunners gave up places in the boats to ensure the safety of their guests. When destroyers found the boats all 65 persons who had abandoned ship were still alive, including 19 Norwegian civilians, but 26 of the freighter's crew and USN Armed Guard died in the sinking.

The two ships referred to as lost in the narrative for JW 64 had been intended for RA 64, so that the total losses attributable directly or indirectly to this convoy were large given the late period of the war.

*The "great gale" which struck convoy RA 64: a Liberty ship wallows in the trough of huge seas.*

## Convoy JW 65

Twenty six ships sailed from the Clyde on 11 March as follows:

| | | | | | |
|---|---|---|---|---|---|
| *BENJAMIN SCHLESINGER* | 92 Amer | 7176/44 | *BLUE RANGER* | 32 Br | 3417/41 |
| *CHARLES A McALLISTER* | 61 Amer | 7176/43 | *DOLABELLA* | 62 Br | 8142/39 |
| *ELEAZAR LORD* | 84 Amer | 7247/44 | *ELOY ALFARO* | 71 Amer | 7176/44 |
| *EMPIRE STALWART* | 23 Br | 7045/43 | *FORT BOISE* | 51 Br | 7151/43 |
| *FORT MASSAC* | 83 Br | 7157/43 | *FORT YUKON* | 82 Br | 7153/43 |
| *GRACE ABBOTT* | 31 Amer | 7191/42 | *HORACE BUSHNELL* | 11 Amer | 7176/43 |
| *IDEFJORD* | 95 Nor | 4287/21 | *JAMES M GILLIS* | 94 Amer | 7176/43 |
| *JOHN McDONOGH* | 93 Amer | 7176/43 | *LACKLAN* | 72 Br | 8670/29 |
| *LAWRENCE J BRENGLE* | 13 Amer | 7209/44 | *LEO J DUSTER* | 14 Amer | 7176/43 |
| *NICHOLAS BIDDLE* | 41 Amer | 7191/42 | *SAN VENANCIO* | 42 Br | 8152/42 |
| *STAGE DOOR CANTEEN* | 12 Amer | 7176/43 | *THOMAS DONALDSON* | 21 Amer | 7210/44 |
| *W R GRACE* | 91 Amer | 7176/43 | *WILLIAM PEPPER* | 81 Amer | 7176/43 |
| *WILLIAM WHEELWRIGHT* | 24 Amer | 7176/44 | *WINFRED L SMITH* | 22 Amer | 7191/43 |

Commodore was in *FORT BOISE,* Vice Commodore in *FORT YUKON,* Rear Commodore in *EMPIRE STALWART. BLUE RANGER* and *LACKLAN* were escort oilers.

Close escorts from 11 to 21 March were the corvettes ALLINGTON CASTLE, ALNWICK CASTLE, BAMBOROUGH CASTLE, LANCASTER CASTLE, CAMELLIA, HONEYSUCKLE and OXLIP, destroyers MYNGS and Norwegian STORD and sloop LAPWING. On 12 March the cruiser DIADEM, escort carrier CAMPANIA and destroyers ONSLAUGHT, OPPORTUNE, ORWELL, SCORPION, ZAMBESI and Canadian SIOUX and corvette FARNHAM CASTLE joined. Finally, on 15 March, the escort carrier TRUMPETER and destroyers SAVAGE and SCOURGE arrived. The cruiser and escort carriers, as usual, occupied the central ''box'' within the convoy. All ships stayed until arrival at Kola Inlet except LAPWING, sunk on 20 March, and ONSLAUGHT who returned after collision with *BLUE RANGER* whilst oiling.

The enemy became aware of the convoy's passage, and sailed six U boats to patrol west of Bear Island to supplement the efforts of those off Kola Inlet. Air reconnaissance failed to locate the convoy, and the Bear Island patrol line was evaded. However, heavy snow off Kola inhibited air patrols from the carriers and six U boats closed the convoy. U 995 torpedoed the *HORACE BUSHNELL* which, despite being towed in, became a total loss. U 968 sank *THOMAS DONALDSON* and, probably, the sloop LAPWING although some sources, other than the Germans, credit this last success to U 716.

*The corvette HMS HONEYSUCKLE, alongside the carrier HMS TRUMPETER at Kola on 21 March 1945, showing the atrocious conditions which could be met in Arctic waters.*

## Convoy RA 65

The convoy cleared Kola Inlet on 23 March as follows:

| | | | | | |
|---|---|---|---|---|---|
| *ADOLPH S OCHS* | Br | 7219/43 | *ARUNAH S ABELL* | Amer | 7176/43 |
| *BEN F DIXON* | Amer | 7176/43 | *BLUE RANGER* | Br | 3417/41 |
| *BRITISH MERIT* | Br | 8093/42 | *DANIEL WILLARD* | Amer | 7200/42 |
| *EDWIN L DRAKE* | Amer | 7176/43 | *EMPIRE FLINT* | Br | 8129/41 |
| *F T FRELINGHUYSEN* | Amer | 7176/43 | *FORT CREVECOEUR* | Br | 7191/43 |
| *FORT VERCHERES* | Br | 7128/42 | *FRANCIS SCOTT KEY* | Amer | 7191/41 |
| *GEORGE STEERS* | Amer | 7247/44 | *HAROLD L WINSLOW* | Amer | 7176/43 |
| *HAWKINS FUDSKE* | Amer | 7176/43 | *JOHN J ABEL* | Amer | 7191/43 |
| *JOHN WANAMAKER* | Amer | 7176/43 | *JOYCE KILMER* | Amer | 7176/43 |
| *LACKLAN* | Br | 8670/29 | *LEWIS EMERY Jr* | Amer | 7176/43 |
| *LUCERNA* | Br | 6556/30 | *MARIE M MELONEY* | Amer | 7176/43 |
| *NATHAN TOWSON* | Amer | 7176/43 | *NERITINA* | Br | 8228/43 |
| *SKIENSFJORD* | Nor | 5922/22 | *TOWNSEND HARRIS* | Amer | 7176/43 |

Commodore was in *FORT CREVECOEUR; BLUE RANGER* and *LACKLAN* were escort oilers.

Twenty escorts also sailed on 23 March, the corvettes ALLINGTON CASTLE, ALNWICK CASTLE, BAMBOROUGH CASTLE, FARNHAM CASTLE, LANCASTER CASTLE, CAMELLIA, HONEYSUCKLE and OXLIP staying with the convoy until arrival at Scapa Flow on 1 April. The remainder of the escort, cruiser DIADEM, escort carriers CAMPANIA and TRUMPETER, and destroyers MYNGS, OPPORTUNE, ORWELL, SAVAGE, SCORPION, SCOURGE, ZAMBESI, Canadian SIOUX and Norwegian STORD left on 30 March.

At British request, the Russians cleared a channel through the minefields north of Kola Inlet to offer an alternative exit, avoiding the U boats lying in wait off the usual route. The close escort sailed early and harassed the nine U boats off the original route while four destroyers arranged a pyrotechnic display in the same area. As a result, the actual sailing was undetected, air and sea searches failed to locate the convoy on passage, and it arrived at Scapa Flow on 1 April.

## Convoy JW 66

The twenty seven ships of this convoy left the Clyde on 16 April as follows:

| | | | | | | | |
|---|---|---|---|---|---|---|---|
| *ALBERT C RITCHIE* | 34 | Amer | 7176/43 | *AUGUST BELMONT* | 33 | Amer | 7240/44 |
| *BENJAMIN H HILL* | 61 | Amer | 7198/44 | *BLACK RANGER* | 42 | Br | 3417/41 |
| *BLUE RANGER* | | Br | 3417/41 | *BRITISH RESPECT* | 32 | Br | 8479/43 |
| *CECIL N BEAN* | 63 | Amer | 7176/44 | *COPELAND* | 24 | Br | 1526/23 |
| *DAVID B JOHNSON* | 43 | Amer | 7198/44 | *EMPIRE GARRICK* | 23 | Br | 8128/42 |
| *JOHN GIBBON* | 31 | Amer | 7247/44 | *JOSHUA THOMAS* | 52 | Amer | 7176/43 |
| *KEITH PALMER* | 11 | Amer | 7244/44 | *KONG HAAKON VII* | 73 | Nor | 7073/42 |
| *KRONPRINSEN* | 72 | Nor | 7073/42 | *LAURELWOOD* | 53 | Br | 7347/29 |
| *LINN BOYD* | 22 | Amer | 7176/44 | *LORD DELAWARE* | 71 | Amer | 7200/42 |
| *NELSON W ALDRICH* | 62 | Amer | 7176/44 | *OWEN WISTER* | 64 | Amer | 7240/43 |
| *PARK BENJAMIN* | 21 | Amer | 7176/44 | *RENALD FERNALD* | 13 | Amer | 7176/44 |
| *SAMARITAN* | 41 | Br | 7219/43 | *STEVENSON TAYLOR* | 14 | Amer | 7176/43 |
| *WILLIAM D BYRON* | 54 | Amer | 7210/44 | *WILLIAM TYLER PAGE* | 51 | Amer | 7176/43 |
| *WOODBRIDGE N FERRIS* | 12 | Amer | 7200/43 | | | | |

Commodore was in *SAMARITAN,* Vice Commodore in *BENJAMIN HILL,* Rear Commodore in *LINN BOYD. COPELAND* was Rescue Ship, *BLACK RANGER, BLUE RANGER* and *LAURELWOOD* were escort oilers. It is probable that the *BLUE RANGER* detached en route, she is noted as joining the next homeward convoy late in its passage.

The close escort from 16 to 25 April comprised the sloop CYGNET, corvettes ALNWICK CASTLE, BAMBOROUGH CASTLE, FARNHAM CASTLE, HONEYSUCKLE, LOTUS, OXLIP and RHODODENDRON. Also attached were the 19 Escort Group, frigates LOCH INSH, LOCH SHIN, COTTON, GOODALL and ANGUILLA. On 18 April the cruiser BELLONA, escort carriers PREMIER and VINDEX and destroyers OFFA, ZEALOUS, ZEPHYR, ZEST, ZODIAC, Canadian HAIDA, HURON and IROQUOIS and Norwegian STORD joined. All escorts remained until arrival at Kola Inlet on 25 April.

There were no incidents on passage, but it became apparent that U boats were now habitually lying off the restricted access to Kola Inlet. The convoy was, therefore, "blasted into harbour" with the escort proceeding ahead and using all forms of A/S weapons in a blind barrage to discourage a patrol line of, it appears, at least eleven U boats. The limitations of Asdic caused by thermal layers meant that, despite the intensity of attack, only one U boat received even minor damage; the convoy however arrived unscathed.

## Operation TRAMMEL

The Germans knew that the approach route to Kola Inlet, which ran west south westerly for 40 miles, had to be used by the convoys. When, early in 1945, U boats were sent to lie off this focal point, several merchant ships and escorts were lost. Given the poor behaviour of Asdic due to thermal layering in the area, "swamping" techniques by large numbers of experienced escorts and aircraft were resorted to. This enabled a convoy to enter or leave while U boats were kept down and therefore restricted in their opportunity to attack. However it did not, usually, result in a "kill". A further refinement was therefore added, that of the "deep trap minefield". This required the laying of a field in the area of submarine operations, at such a depth that surface ships would not be in danger. Submarines driven deep by escort action however, could expect to be caught in such an area and suffer loss.

The Russians were asked to permit such a lay off Kola Inlet and, after some delay, permission was granted and on 16 April Commander-in-Chief, Home Fleet issued the necessary orders. The minelaying force consisted of the minelayer APOLLO and the destroyers OBEDIENT, OPPORTUNE and ORWELL, all three fitted with mine rails, plus the cruiser DIDO for AA defence. The force sailed from Scapa Flow at 2200 on 17 April and arrived at Kola midday on 21 April to fuel and lay that night. Arrangements for fuelling were, however, chaotic and the ships were not ready to proceed until pm on 22 April.

It was necessary to complete the lay before the arrival of JW 66, and fortunately there was just time for the 19 Escort Group (LOCH INSH, LOCH SHIN, COTTON, GOODALL and ANGUILLA) to arrive and give A/S cover to the minelayers, the Russians providing air cover. The lay, of 276 mines in six lines at sixty feet, was without incident; following it the force returned to harbour and again fuelled. Sailing from Kola on 23 April, the force arrived at Scapa Flow on 26 April, APOLLO proceeding to the Faroes to fuel, thence to Milford Haven.

## Convoy RA 66

Twenty six ships sailed from Kola Inlet on 29 April, being joined on 5 May by a second RFA tanker. The ships were:

| | | | | | | | |
|---|---|---|---|---|---|---|---|
| *BENJAMIN SCHLESINGER* | 72 | Amer | 7176/44 | *BLACK RANGER* | 32 | Br | 3417/41 |
| *BLUE RANGER* | 63 | Br | 3417/41 | *BYRON DARNTON* | 24 | Amer | 7176/43 |
| *CHARLES A McALLISTER* | 61 | Amer | 7176/43 | *COPELAND* | 34 | Br | 1526/23 |
| *DOLABELLA* | 53 | Br | 8142/39 | *ELEAZAR LORD* | 64 | Amer | 7247/44 |
| *ELOY ALFARO* | 71 | Amer | 7176/44 | *EMPIRE STALWART* | 23 | Br | 7045/43 |

**1945**

| | | | | | |
|---|---|---|---|---|---|
| *FORT BOISE* | 42 Br | 7151/43 | *FORT MASSAC* | 54 Br | 7157/43 |
| *FORT YUKON* | 51 Br | 7153/43 | *GRACE ABBOTT* | 31 Amer | 7191/42 |
| *HENRY LOMB* | 14 Amer | 7176/43 | *JAMES M GILLIS* | 52 Amer | 7176/43 |
| *JAMES McDONOGH* | 73 Amer | 7176/43 | *LAWRENCE J BRENGLE* | 21 Amer | 7209/44 |
| *LEO J DUSTER* | 13 Amer | 7176/43 | *NICHOLAS BIDDLE* | 41 Amer | 7191/42 |
| *SAN VENANCIO* | 62 Br | 8152/42 | *STAGE DOOR CANTEEN* | 12 Amer | 7176/43 |
| *W R GRACE* | 43 Amer | 7176/43 | *WILLARD HALL* | 44 Amer | 7200/43 |
| *WILLIAM PEPPER* | 33 Amer | 7176/43 | *WILLIAM WHEELWRIGHT* | 11 Amer | 7176/44 |
| *WINFRED L SMITH* | 22 Amer | 7191/43 | | | |

Commodore was in *FORT YUKON,* Vice Commodore in *SAN VENANCIO,* Rear Commodore in *EMPIRE STALWART. COPELAND* was Rescue Ship, *BLACK RANGER* and *BLUE RANGER* (the latter joining 5 May) were escort oilers.

The escorts all sailed with the convoy, leaving on the dates indicated in brackets—CYGNET, ALNWICK CASTLE, BAMBOROUGH CASTLE, FARNHAM CASTLE, HONEYSUCKLE, LOTUS, OXLIP and RHODODENDRON (all to 7 May), BELLONA, PREMIER, VINDEX (to 6 May), ZEALOUS, ZEST, ZODIAC (to 5 May), ZEPHYR, HAIDA, HURON, IROQUOIS, STORD (to 7 May), OFFA (8 May). ORWELL and OBEDIENT brought out *BLUE RANGER* from Scapa Flow and were present 5 to 8 May. The 19 Escort Group, involved in JW 66 and Operation "Trammel" were also present on the sailing of the convoy.

About 10 U boats were lying off Kola Inlet waiting for the convoy, but the escort groups that preceded the convoy succeeded in swamping the opposition and driving it deep during the passage. Two boats did get close to the convoy, U 968 and U 307. LOCH SHIN succeeded in sinking U 307 on 29 April; shortly afterwards U 968 torpedoed the frigate GOODALL. HONEYSUCKLE went alongside the stricken ship to embark survivors, and was damaged when GOODALL was sinking, she left the wreck with her paintwork alight, and was later commended for her actions. ANGUILLA sank the wreck with shell fire, GOODALL blowing up when the magazine was hit. On 30 April, LOCH SHIN, ANGUILLA and COTTON located and sank U 286. There were no further attacks on the convoy, which arrived in the Clyde on VE Day, 8 May 1945.

## Convoy JW 67

The following ships sailed from the Clyde on 12 May, four days after the end of hostilities in Europe. As the Royal Navy had had no time to account for all submarines, the principle of convoy was maintained for several weeks. Ships sailing were:

| | | | | | |
|---|---|---|---|---|---|
| *ADOLPH S OCHS* | 22 Br | 7219/43 | *ALANSON B HOUGHTON* | 92 Amer | 7176/44 |
| *BARBARA FRIETCHIE* | 41 Amer | 7176/43 | *BERNARD N BAKER* | 101 Amer | 7191/43 |
| *BRITISH PROMISE* | 52 Br | 8443/42 | *CAESAR RODNEY* | 51 Amer | 7191/42 |
| *CARDINAL GIBBONS* | 12 Amer | 7191/42 | *CHARLES BULFINCH* | 23 Amer | 7176/43 |
| *EDWARD N HURLEY* | 21 Amer | 7191/43 | *EGERO* | 71 Nor | 7590/29 |
| *EMPIRE EMERALD* | 32 Br | 8032/41 | *EMPIRE PROWESS* | 61 Br | 7058/43 |
| *FORT HIGHFIELD* | 82 Br | 7129/43 | *GEORGE H PENDLETON* | 94 Amer | 7176/43 |
| *GEORGE WEEMS* | 11 Amer | 7191/42 | *HENRY WYNKOOP* | 31 Amer | 7176/42 |
| *IVARAN* | 103 Nor | 4955/38 | *JOHN IRELAND* | 81 Amer | 7247/44 |
| *JOSHUA W ALEXANDER* | 71 Amer | 7176/43 | *JULIEN POYDRAS* | 102 Amer | 7176/43 |
| *PHILIP F THOMAS* | 91 Amer | 7176/43 | *RATHLIN* | 24 Br | 1600/36 |
| *ROALD AMUNDSEN* | 104 Nor | 7191/43 | *ROBERT J COLLIER* | 13 Amer | 7176/43 |
| *SAMUEL McINTYRE* | 14 Amer | 7176/43 | *THOMAS SIM LEE* | 93 Amer | 7191/42 |

Commodore was in *EMPIRE PROWESS,* Vice Commodore in *FORT HIGHFIELD,* Rear Commodore in *ADOLPH S OCHS. RATHLIN* was Rescue Ship and *EGERO* escort oiler.

The convoy was escorted between 12 and 20 May by the escort carrier QUEEN, destroyers OBDURATE and ONSLOW, and frigates BAZELEY, BENTINCK, BYARD, DRURY and PASLEY of 4th Escort Group. The U boats still at sea obeyed their orders, and there were no incidents, the convoy entering Kola Inlet on 20 May.

## Convoy RA 67

The final sailing of a Russian convoy took place on 23 May 1945, when these ships sailed from Kola inlet:

| | | | | | |
|---|---|---|---|---|---|
| *ALBERT C RITCHIE* | 41 Amer | 7176/43 | *AUGUST BELMONT* | 32 Amer | 7240/44 |
| *BENJAMIN H HILL* | 21 Amer | 7198/44 | *BRITISH RESPECT* | 72 Br | 8479/43 |
| *CECIL N BEAN* | 73 Amer | 7176/44 | *DAVID B JOHNSON* | 92 Amer | 7198/44 |
| *EGERO* | 42 Nor | 7590/29 | *EMPIRE GARRICK* | 22 Br | 8128/42 |
| *JOHN GIBBON* | 62 Amer | 7247/44 | *JOSHUA THOMAS* | 31 Amer | 7176/43 |
| *KEITH PALMER* | 91 Amer | 7244/44 | *KRONPRINSEN* | 12 Nor | 7073/42 |
| *LAURELWOOD* | 23 Br | 7347/29 | *LINN BOYD* | 14 Amer | 7176/44 |
| *LORD DELAWARE* | 93 Amer | 7200/42 | *NELSON W ALDRICH* | 82 Amer | 7176/44 |
| *OWEN WISTER* | 94 Amer | 7240/43 | *PARK BENJAMIN* | 11 Amer | 7176/44 |
| *RATHLIN* | 84 Br | 1600/36 | *RENALD FERNALD* | 83 Amer | 7176/44 |
| *SAMARITAN* | 51 Br | 7219/43 | *STEVENSON TAYLOR* | 13 Amer | 7176/43 |
| *WILLIAM D BYRON* | 81 Amer | 7210/44 | *WILLIAM TYLER PAGE* | 71 Amer | 7176/43 |
| *WOODBRIDGE N FERRIS* | 61 Amer | 7200/43 | | | |

Commodore was in *SAMARITAN,* Vice Commodore in *WILLIAM D BYRON,* Rear Commodore in *EMPIRE GARRICK. RATHLIN* was Rescue Ship, *EGERO* and *LAURELWOOD* escort oilers.

The escorts during the passage, from 23 to 30 May, were those from JW 67, QUEEN, OBDURATE, ONSLOW, BAZELEY, BENTINCK, BYARD, DRURY and PASLEY. There were no incidents and, with navigation lights burning, the ships arrived in the Clyde on 30 May 1945.

# Post war sailings from Russia

It will have been noted, if comparisons have been made between inward and outward bound ships, that there are certain apparent discrepancies. In fact, these can be resolved by noting post war sailings, and ships which were retained, or lost, in Russia.

| Ship's name | Date sailed from Russia |
|---|---|
| *BRITISH PROMISE* | 2 June 1945 |
| *EMPIRE EMERALD* | 2 June 1945 |
| *FORT HIGHFIELD* | 4 June 1945 |
| *BERNARD N BAKER* | 7 June 1945 |
| *BARBARA FRIETCHIE* | 7 June 1945 |
| *GEORGE H PENDLETON* | 8 June 1945 |
| *JOSHUA W ALEXANDER* | 8 June 1945 |
| *PHILIP F THOMAS* | 8 June 1945 |
| *ALANSON B HOUGHTON* | 9 June 1945 |
| *SAMTRUSTY* | 23 June 1945 |
| *DANIEL WILLARD* | 8 July 1945 |
| *EMPIRE BUTTRESS* | 1 August 1945 |
| *LAPLAND* | unknown, but post August 1945 |

**Ships retained in Russia**

| | |
|---|---|
| *CHARLES GORDON CURTIS* | became *SERGEI KIROV* |
| *IRONCLAD* | became *MARINA RASKOVA* |
| *PANAMA CITY* | became *NOVGOROD* |
| *EMPIRE CARPENTER* | became *DICKSON* |
| *EMPIRE NIGEL* | became *ARCHANGELSK* |

# BRITISH & ALLIED WARSHIPS LOST DURING ARCTIC CONVOY OPERATIONS

**Cruisers**

| | |
|---|---|
| EDINBURGH | Finally sunk 2.5.42 by FORESIGHT, after being torpedeod by U 456 on 30.4.42. |
| TRINIDAD | Damaged by her own torpedo 29.3.42, bombed while returning to the UK 14.5.42, abandoned, and sunk by MATCHLESS. |

**Destroyers**

| | |
|---|---|
| ACHATES | Capsized due to damage from HIPPER 31.12.42. |
| HARDY | Torpedoed by U 278, wreck sunk by VENUS 30.1.44. |
| MAHRATTA | Torpedoed by U 990 25.2.44. |
| MATABELE | Torpedoed by U 454 17.1.42. |
| PUNJABI | In collision with KING GEORGE V 1.5.42. |
| SOKRUSHITELNY | Foundered in a gale 22.11.42 |
| SOMALI | Torpedoed by U 703 20.9.42, sank in tow 24.9.42 during a gale. |

**Sloops**

| | |
|---|---|
| KITE | Torpedoed by U 344 21.8.44. |
| LARK | Torpedoed by U 968 17.2.45, towed in to Kola, wreck abandoned. |
| LAPWING | Torpedoed by U 968 20.3.45. |

**Frigate**

| | |
|---|---|
| GOODALL | Torpedoed by U 968 29.4.45. |

**Corvettes**

| | |
|---|---|
| BLUEBELL | Torpdeoed by U 711 17.2.45. |
| DENBIGH CASTLE | Torpedoed by U 992 13.2.45, towed in to Kola, wreck abandoned. |
| TUNSBERG CASTLE | Mined 12.12.44. |

**Minesweepers**

| | |
|---|---|
| BRAMBLE | Sunk by HIPPER and ECKOLDT 31.12.42. |
| GOSSAMER | Bombed in Kola Inlet 24.6.42. |
| LEDA | Torpedoed by U 435 20.9.42. |
| NIGER | Lost in a British minefield 5.7.42. |

*HMS LEDA, an escort of QP 14, sinking. Torpedoed by U435, she had been abandoned, and the wreck was then investigated by the submarine which took this photograph as the LEDA finally sank.*

**Submarine**

| | |
|---|---|
| P 551 (JASTRZAB) | Sunk by ST ALBANS and SEAGULL in error, 2.5.42. |

**Armed whaler**

| | |
|---|---|
| SHERA | Iced up and capsized 9.3.42. |
| SULLA | Probably torpedoed by U 436 1.4.42 |

# GERMAN LOSSES INCURRED DURING ARCTIC OPERATIONS

**Battlecruiser**

| | |
|---|---|
| SCHARNHORST | Sunk in action with the Home Fleet 26.12.43. |

**Destroyers**

| | |
|---|---|
| FRIEDRICH ECKOLDT | Sunk in action with SHEFFIELD 31.12.42. |
| SCHOEMANN | Scuttled after severe damage inflicted by EDINBURGH 2.5.42. |
| Z 26 | Sunk in action with TRINIDAD and ECLIPSE 29.3.42. |

**Auxiliary vessels/escorts**

| | |
|---|---|
| BREMSE | Sunk by AURORA and NIGERIA 7.9.41. |
| ULM | Sunk by MARNE, MARTIN and ONSLAUGHT 25.8.42. |

**Submarines**

| | |
|---|---|
| U 88 | Sunk by ONSLOW and Swordfish of 825 Sqdn in AVENGER, 12.9.42 |
| U 286 | Sunk by ANGUILLA, COTTON and LOCH SHIN 29.4.45. |
| U 277 | Sunk by Swordfish from FENCER 1.5.44. |
| U 288 | Sunk by aircraft from ACTIVITY and TRACKER 3.4.44. |
| U 307 | Sunk by CYGNET, LOCH INSH and LOCH SHIN 29.4.45. |
| U 314 | Sunk by METEOR and WHITEHALL 30.1.44. |
| U 344 | Sunk by Swordfish of 825 Sqdn from VINDEX 22.8.44. |
| U 347 | Sunk by Catalina of 210 Sqdn 17.7.44. |
| U 354 | Sunk by KEPPEL, LOCH DUNVEGAN, MERMAID, PEACOCK and Swordfish of 825 Sqdn from VINDEX 24.8.44. |
| U 355 | Sunk by BEAGLE & Avenger of 846 Sqdn from TRACKER 1.4.44. |
| U 360 | Sunk by KEPPEL 2.4.44. |
| U 361 | Sunk by Catalina of 210 Sqdn 17.7.44. |
| U 365 | Sunk by Swordfish of 813 Sqdn from CAMPANIA 13.12.44. |
| U 366 | Sunk by Swordfish of 816 Sqdn from CHASER 5.3.44. |
| U 387 | Sunk by BAMBOROUGH CASTLE 9.12.44. |
| U 394 | Sunk by KEPPEL, MERMAID, PEACOCK, WHITEHALL and Swordfish of 825 Sqdn from VINDEX 2.9.44. |
| U 425 | Sunk by ALNWICK CASTLE and LARK 17.2.45. |
| U 457 | Sunk by IMPULSIVE 16.9.42. |
| U 472 | Sunk by ONSLAUGHT and Swordfish of 816 Sqdn from CHASER 4.3.44. |
| U 585 | Mined off Murmansk 30.3.42. |
| U 589 | Sunk by ONSLOW and Swordfish of 825 Sqdn from AVENGER 14.9.42. |
| U 601 | Sunk by Catalina of 210 Sqdn 25.2.44. |
| U 644 | Sunk by TUNA 7.4.43. |
| U 655 | Sunk by SHARPSHOOTER 24.3.42. |
| U 674 | Sunk by Swordfish of 842 Sqdn from FENCER 2.5.44. |
| U 713 | Sunk by KEPPEL 24.2.44. |
| U 742 | Sunk by Catalina of 210 Sqdn 18.7.44. |
| U 921 | Sunk by Swordfish of 813 Sqdn from CAMPANIA 30.9.44. |
| U 959 | Sunk by Swordfish of 842 Sqdn from FENCER 2.5.44. |
| U 961 | Sunk by STARLING 29.3.44. |
| U 973 | Sunk by Swordfish of 816 Sqdn from CHASER 6.3.44. |

It will be noted that some of the details of losses given above differ from the those previously published, the information given here is based on the latest research by the Ministry of Defence (Navy) into contemporary signals and records, and can be taken as authoritative wherever it differs from previously published work. Nevertheless, it is still subject to ongoing research, as resources permit, and cannot even now be regarded as final.

# ALPHABETICAL LIST OF MERCHANT SHIP LOSSES

| Ship's Name | GRT | Year | Flag | Date of loss | Cause of loss | Convoy | Comment |
|---|---|---|---|---|---|---|---|
| AFRICANDER | 5,441 | 21 | Pan | 13/09/42 | AIRCRAFT | PQ 18 | |
| ALAMAR | 5,689 | 16 | Amer | 27/05/42 | AIRCRAFT | PQ 16 | |
| ALCOA CADET | 4,823 | 19 | Amer | 21/06/42 | MINED | | At Murmansk after arrival. Air laid mine |
| ALCOA RANGER | 5,116 | 19 | Amer | 07/07/42 | U 255 | PQ 17 | Post dispersal |
| ALDERSDALE | 8,402 | 37 | Br | 07/07/42 | U 457 | PQ 17 | Post dispersal |
| ANDREW G CURTIN | 7,200 | 43 | Amer | 25/01/44 | U 716 | JW 56A | |
| ATHELTEMPLAR | 8,992 | 30 | Br | 14/09/42 | U 457 | PQ 18 | Wreck Sunk by HARRIER |
| BALLOT | 6,131 | 22 | Pan | 02/01/43 | WRECKED | JW 51B | Aground 2.1, Abandoned 13.1.43 off Kola Inlet |
| BATEAU | 4,687 | 26 | Pan | 29/03/42 | Z 26 | PQ 13 | After straggling |
| BELLINGHAM | 5,349 | 20 | Amer | 22/09/42 | U 435 | QP 14 | |
| BOLTON CASTLE | 5,203 | 39 | Br | 05/07/42 | AIRCRAFT | PQ 17 | Post dispersal |
| BOTAVON | 5,848 | 12 | Br | 03/05/42 | AIRCRAFT | PQ 15 | Wreck sunk by BADSWORTH |
| CAPE CORSO | 3,807 | 29 | Br | 02/05/42 | AIRCRAFT | PQ 15 | |
| CARLTON | 5,127 | 20 | Amer | 05/07/42 | U 88 | PQ 17 | Post dispersal |
| CHRISTOPHER NEWPORT | 7,191 | 42 | Amer | 04/07/42 | AIRCRAFT | PQ 17 | Prior to dispersal, wreck sunk by P 614 & U 457 |
| CHULMLEIGH | 5,445 | 38 | Br | 16/11/42 | U 625 | OP FB | Stranded on ice, and air attack, Independent |
| CITY OF JOLIET | 6,617 | 20 | Amer | 27/05/42 | AIRCRAFT | PQ 16 | Wreck sank 28.5.42 |
| DANIEL MORGAN | 7,177 | 42 | Amer | 05/07/42 | U 88 | PQ 17 | Post dispersal |
| DEKABRIST | 7,363 | 03 | Russ | 04/11/42 | AIRCRAFT | OP FB | Independent passage |
| DONBASS | 7,925 | 35 | Russ | 07/11/42 | Z 27 | OPFBWEST | Only ship lost in westbound passage of OP FB |
| EARLSTON | 7,195 | 41 | Br | 05/07/42 | U 334 | PQ 17 | Post dispersal |
| EDWARD H CROCKETT | 7,176 | 44 | Amer | 29/09/44 | U 310 | RA 60 | |
| EFFINGHAM | 6,421 | 19 | Amer | 30/03/42 | U 435 | PQ 13 | Straggler |
| EL CAPITAN | 5,255 | 17 | Pan | 10/07/42 | U 251 | PQ 17 | Post dispersal, previously damaged by Aircraft |
| EL OCCIDENTE | 6,008 | 10 | Pan | 13/04/42 | U 435 | QP 10 | |
| EMPIRE BEAUMONT | 7,044 | 42 | Br | 13/09/42 | AIRCRAFT | PQ 18 | |
| EMPIRE BYRON | 6,645 | 41 | Br | 05/07/42 | U 703 | PQ 17 | Post dispersal |
| EMPIRE COWPER | 7,164 | 41 | Br | 11/04/42 | AIRCRAFT | QP 10 | |
| EMPIRE GILBERT | 6,640 | 41 | Br | 02/11/42 | U 586 | OP FB | Independent passage |
| EMPIRE HOWARD | 6,985 | 41 | Br | 16/04/42 | U 403 | PQ 14 | |
| EMPIRE LAWRENCE | 7,457 | 41 | Br | 27/05/42 | AIRCRAFT | PQ 16 | |
| EMPIRE PURCELL | 7,049 | 42 | Br | 27/05/42 | AIRCRAFT | PQ 16 | |
| EMPIRE RANGER | 7,008 | 42 | Br | 28/03/42 | AIRCRAFT | PQ 13 | Straggler |
| EMPIRE SKY | 7,455 | 41 | Br | 06/11/42 | U 625 | QP FB | Independent passage |
| EMPIRE STARLIGHT | 6,850 | 41 | Br | 03/04/42 | AIRCRAFT | | At Murmansk, CTL 1.6.42 after further damage |
| EMPIRE STEVENSON | 6,209 | 41 | Br | 13/09/42 | AIRCRAFT | PQ 18 | |
| EMPIRE TOURIST | 7,062 | 43 | Br | 04/03/44 | U 703 | RA 57 | |
| EXECUTIVE | 4,978 | 20 | Amer | 05/03/43 | U 255 | RA 53 | |
| EXTERMINATOR | 6,115 | 24 | Pan | 05/07/42 | MINED | QP 13 | In British minefield |
| FAIRFIELD CITY | 5,686 | 21 | Amer | 05/07/42 | AIRCRAFT | PQ 17 | Post dispersal |
| FORT BELLINGHAM | 7,153 | 42 | Br | 26/01/44 | U360, U957 | JW 56A | First damaged on 25.01, Sank 26.01 |
| GOOLISTAN | 5,851 | 29 | Br | 23/11/42 | U 625 | QP 15 | |
| GRAY RANGER | 3,318 | 41 | Br | 22/09/42 | U 435 | QP 14 | |
| GREYLOCK | 7,460 | 21 | Amer | 03/02/43 | U 255 | RA 52 | |
| HARPALION | 5,486 | 32 | Br | 13/04/42 | AIRCRAFT | QP 10 | |
| HARTLEBURY | 5,082 | 34 | Br | 07/07/42 | U 355 | PQ 17 | Post dispersal |
| HEFFRON | 7,611 | 19 | Amer | 05/07/42 | MINED | QP 13 | In British minefield |
| HENRY BACON | 7,177 | 42 | Amer | 23/02/45 | AIRCRAFT | RA 64 | After straggling |
| HONOMU | 6,977 | 19 | Amer | 05/07/42 | U 456 | PQ 17 | Post dispersal |
| HOOSIER | 5,060 | 20 | Amer | 10/07/42 | U 376 | PQ 17 | Post dispersal |
| HORACE BUSHNELL | 7,716 | 43 | Amer | 20/03/45 | U 995 | JW 65 | Towed in and beached, but total loss |

| Ship's Name | GRT | Year | Flag | Date of loss | Cause of loss | Convoy | Comment |
|---|---|---|---|---|---|---|---|
| HORACE GRAY | 7,200 | 43 | Amer | 14/02/45 | U 711 | | En route in White Sea, to join RA 64 |
| HYBERT | 6,120 | 20 | Amer | 05/07/42 | MINED | QP 13 | In British minefield |
| IJORA | 2,815 | 21 | Russ | 07/03/42 | SURFACE | QP 8 | Straggler, sunk by FRIEDRICH IHN |
| INDUNA | 5,086 | 25 | Br | 30/03/42 | U 376 | PQ 13 | Straggler |
| J L M CURRY | 7,176 | 42 | Amer | 07/03/42 | FOUNDERED | RA 53 | |
| JOHN PENN | 7,177 | 42 | Amer | 13/09/42 | AIRCRAFT | PQ 18 | |
| JOHN WITHERSPOON | 7,191 | 42 | Amer | 06/07/42 | U 255 | PQ 17 | Post dispersal |
| JUTLAND | 6,153 | 28 | Br | 02/05/42 | AIRCRAFT | PQ 15 | Wreck sunk 3.5.42 by U 251 |
| KENTUCKY | 5,446 | 21 | Amer | 18/09/42 | AIRCRAFT | PQ 18 | Wreck ashore, part cargo salved by Russians |
| KIEV | 5,823 | 17 | Russ | 13/04/42 | U 435 | QP 10 | |
| KRASNY PARTIZAN | 2,418 | 27 | Russ | 29/01/43 | U 255 | INDEP | |
| KUZNETZ LESOV | 3,974 | 33 | Russ | 23/11/42 | U 601 | QP 15 | |
| LANCASTER CASTLE | 5,172 | 37 | Br | 14/04/42 | AIRCRAFT | | Lost at Murmansk after arrival |
| LOWTHER CASTLE | 5,171 | 37 | Br | 27/05/42 | AIRCRAFT | PQ 16 | |
| MACBETH | 4,941 | 20 | Pan | 13/09/42 | AIRCRAFT | PQ 18 | |
| MARY LUCKENBACH | 5,049 | 19 | Amer | 14/09/42 | AIRCRAFT | PQ 18 | |
| MASSMAR | 5,829 | 20 | Amer | 05/07/42 | MINED | QP 13 | In British minefield |
| MORMACSUL | 5,481 | 20 | Amer | 27/05/42 | AIRCRAFT | PQ 16 | |
| NAVARINO | 4,841 | 37 | Br | 04/07/42 | AIRCRAFT | PQ 17 | Prior to dispersal |
| NEW WESTMINSTER CITY | 4,747 | 29 | Br | 03/04/42 | AIRCRAFT | | After arrival at Murmansk |
| NORFJELL | 8,129 | 42 | Nor | 14/02/45 | U 968 | | En route in White Sea, to join RA 64 |
| OCEAN FREEDOM | 7,123 | 42 | Br | 13/03/43 | AIRCRAFT | | Lost after arrival at Murmansk |
| OCEAN VOICE | 7,174 | 41 | Br | 22/09/42 | U 435 | QP 14 | |
| OLIVER ELLSWORTH | 7,191 | 42 | Amer | 13/09/42 | U405 or 408 | PQ 18 | |
| OLOPANA | 6,069 | 20 | Amer | 08/07/42 | U 255 | PQ 17 | Post dispersal |
| OREGONIAN | 4,862 | 17 | Amer | 13/09/42 | AIRCRAFT | PQ 18 | |
| PAN ATLANTIC | 5,411 | 19 | Amer | 06/07/42 | AIRCRAFT | PQ 17 | Post dispersal |
| PAN KRAFT | 5,644 | 19 | Amer | 05/07/42 | AIRCRAFT | PQ 17 | Post dispersal |
| PAULUS POTTER | 7,168 | 42 | Du | 05/07/42 | AIRCRAFT | PQ 17 | Post dispersal, derelict sunk by U 255 13.7.42 |
| PENELOPE BARKER | 7,177 | 42 | Amer | 25/01/44 | U 278 | JW 56A | |
| PETER KERR | 6,476 | 20 | Amer | 05/07/42 | AIRCRAFT | PQ 17 | Post dispersal |
| PUERTO RICAN | 6,076 | 19 | Amer | 09/03/43 | U 586 | RA 53 | |
| RACELAND | 4,807 | 10 | Pan | 28/03/42 | AIRCRAFT | PQ 13 | Straggler |
| RICHARD BLAND | 7,191 | 42 | Amer | 05/03/43 | U 255 | RA 53 | Derelict sunk 10.3.43 also by U 255 |
| RIVER AFTON | 5,479 | 35 | Br | 05/07/42 | U 703 | PQ 17 | Post dispersal |
| RODINA | 4,441 | 22 | Russ | 05/07/42 | MINED | QP 13 | In British minefield |
| SAMSUVA | 7,219 | 44 | Br | 29/09/44 | U 310 | RA 60 | |
| SILVER SWORD | 4,937 | 19 | Amer | 20/09/42 | U 255 | QP 14 | |
| STALINGRAD | 3,559 | 31 | Russ | 13/09/42 | U 589 | PQ 18 | |
| STEEL WORKER | 5,685 | 20 | Amer | 03/06/42 | MINED | | At Murmansk after arrival, air laid mine |
| SUKHONA | 3,124 | 18 | Russ | 13/09/42 | AIRCRAFT | PQ 18 | |
| SYROS | 6,191 | 20 | Amer | 26/05/42 | U 703 | PQ 16 | |
| THOMAS DONALDSON | 7,210 | 44 | Amer | 20/03/45 | U 968 | JW 65 | |
| THOMAS SCOTT | 7,176 | 42 | Amer | 17/02/45 | U 968 | RA 64 | |
| TSIOLKOVSKY | 2,847 | 35 | Russ | 01/05/42 | Z24 & Z25 | QP 11 | |
| UFA | 1,892 | 17 | Russ | 26/01/43 | U 255 | INDEP | |
| WACOSTA | 5,432 | 20 | Amer | 13/09/42 | AIRCRAFT | PQ 18 | |
| WASHINGTON | 5,564 | 19 | Amer | 05/07/42 | AIRCRAFT | PQ 17 | Post dispersal |
| WAZIRISTAN | 5,135 | 24 | Br | 02/01/42 | U 134 | PQ 7A | Unescorted, detached. 47 dead |
| WILLIAM CLARK | 7,176 | 42 | Amer | 04/11/42 | U 354 | OP FB | Independent passage |
| WILLIAM HOOPER | 7,177 | 42 | Amer | 04/07/42 | AIRCRAFT | PQ 17 | Prior to dispersal, wreck sunk by U 334 |
| WILLIAM S THAYER | 7,176 | 43 | Amer | 30/04/44 | U 711 | RAS 59 | |
| ZAAFARAN | 1,559 | 21 | Br | 05/07/42 | AIRCRAFT | PQ 17 | Post dispersal |

**No. of ships lost between 21/06/41 & 08/05/45 = 104**

# CHRONOLOGICAL LIST OF MERCHANT SHIP LOSSES

| Date of loss | Ship's Name | GRT | Year | Flag | Cause of loss | Convoy | Comments |
|---|---|---|---|---|---|---|---|
| 02/01/42 | WAZIRISTAN | 5,135 | 24 | Br | U 134 | PQ 7A | Unescorted, detached |
| 07/03/42 | IJORA | 2,815 | 21 | Russ | SURFACE | QP 8 | Straggler, sunk by FRIEDRICH IHN |
| 28/03/42 | RACELAND | 4,807 | 10 | Pan | AIRCRAFT | PQ 13 | Straggler |
| 28/03/42 | EMPIRE RANGER | 7,008 | 42 | Br | AIRCRAFT | PQ 13 | Straggler |
| 29/03/42 | BATEAU | 4,687 | 26 | Pan | Z 26 | PQ 13 | After straggling |
| 30/03/42 | INDUNA | 5,086 | 25 | Br | U 376 | PQ 13 | Straggler |
| 30/03/42 | EFFINGHAM | 6,421 | 19 | Amer | U 435 | PQ 13 | Straggler |
| 03/04/42 | NEW WESTMINSTER CITY | 4,747 | 29 | Br | AIRCRAFT | | After arrival at Murmansk |
| 03/04/42 | EMPIRE STARLIGHT | 6,850 | 41 | Br | AIRCRAFT | | At Murmansk, CTL 1.6.42 after further damage |
| 11/04/42 | EMPIRE COWPER | 7,164 | 41 | Br | AIRCRAFT | QP 10 | |
| 13/04/42 | HARPALION | 5,486 | 32 | Br | AIRCRAFT | QP 10 | |
| 13/04/42 | KIEV | 5,823 | 17 | Russ | U 435 | QP 10 | |
| 13/04/42 | EL OCCIDENTE | 6,008 | 10 | Pan | U 435 | QP 10 | |
| 14/04/42 | LANCASTER CASTLE | 5,172 | 37 | Br | AIRCRAFT | | Lost at Murmansk after arrival |
| 16/04/42 | EMPIRE HOWARD | 6,985 | 41 | Br | U 403 | PQ 14 | |
| 01/05/42 | TSIOLKOVSKY | 2,847 | 35 | Russ | Z24 & Z25 | QP 11 | |
| 02/05/42 | JUTLAND | 6,153 | 28 | Br | AIRCRAFT | PQ 15 | Wreck sunk 3.5.42 by U 251 |
| 02/05/42 | CAPE CORSO | 3,807 | 29 | Br | AIRCRAFT | PQ 15 | |
| 03/05/42 | BOTAVON | 5,848 | 12 | Br | AIRCRAFT | PQ 15 | Wreck sunk by BADSWORTH |
| 26/05/42 | SYROS | 6,191 | 20 | Amer | U 703 | PQ 16 | |
| 27/05/42 | ALAMAR | 5,689 | 16 | Amer | AIRCRAFT | PQ 16 | |
| 27/05/42 | CITY OF JOLIET | 6,167 | 20 | Amer | AIRCRAFT | PQ 16 | Wreck sank 28.5.42 |
| 27/05/42 | MORMACSUL | 5,481 | 20 | Amer | AIRCRAFT | PQ 16 | |
| 27/05/42 | EMPIRE LAWRENCE | 7,457 | 41 | Br | AIRCRAFT | PQ 16 | |
| 27/05/42 | LOWTHER CASTLE | 5,171 | 37 | Br | AIRCRAFT | PQ 16 | |
| 27/05/42 | EMPIRE PURCELL | 7,049 | 42 | Br | AIRCRAFT | PQ 16 | |
| 03/06/42 | STEEL WORKER | 5,685 | 20 | Amer | MINED | | At Murmansk after arrival, air laid mine |
| 21/06/42 | ALCOA CADET | 4,823 | 19 | Amer | AIRCRAFT | | At Kola Inlet after arrival |
| 04/07/42 | NAVARINO | 4,841 | 37 | Br | AIRCRAFT | PQ 17 | Prior to dispersal |
| 04/07/42 | WILLIAM HOOPER | 7,177 | 42 | Amer | AIRCRAFT | PQ 17 | Prior to dispersal, wreck sunk by U 334 |
| 04/07/42 | CHRISTOPHER NEWPORT | 7,191 | 42 | Amer | AIRCRAFT | PQ 17 | Prior to dispersal, wreck sunk by P614 & U457 |
| 05/07/42 | EMPIRE BYRON | 6,645 | 41 | Br | U 703 | PQ 17 | Post dispersal |
| 05/07/42 | PAULUS POTTER | 7,168 | 42 | Du | AIRCRAFT | PQ 17 | Post dispersal, derelict sunk by U 255 13.7.42 |
| 05/07/42 | RIVER AFTON | 5,479 | 35 | Br | U 703 | PQ 17 | Post dispersal |
| 05/07/42 | BOLTON CASTLE | 5,203 | 39 | Br | AIRCRAFT | PQ 17 | Post dispersal |
| 05/07/42 | DANIEL MORGAN | 7,177 | 42 | Amer | U 88 | PQ 17 | Post dispersal |
| 05/07/42 | PAN KRAFT | 5,644 | 19 | Amer | AIRCRAFT | PQ 17 | Post dispersal |
| 05/07/42 | PETER KERR | 6,476 | 20 | Amer | AIRCRAFT | PQ 17 | Post dispersal |
| 05/07/42 | FAIRFIELD CITY | 5,686 | 21 | Amer | AIRCRAFT | PQ 17 | Post dispersal |
| 05/07/42 | ZAAFARAN | 1,559 | 21 | Br | AIRCRAFT | PQ 17 | Post dispersal |
| 05/07/42 | WASHINGTON | 5,564 | 19 | Amer | AIRCRAFT | PQ 17 | Post dispersal |
| 05/07/42 | RODINA | 4,441 | 22 | Russ | MINED | QP 13 | In British minefield |
| 05/07/42 | EXTERMINATOR | 6,115 | 24 | Pan | MINED | QP 13 | In British minefield |
| 05/07/42 | MASSMAR | 5,828 | 20 | Amer | MINED | QP 13 | In British minefield |
| 05/07/42 | HEFFRON | 7,611 | 19 | Amer | MINED | QP 13 | In British minefield |
| 05/07/42 | HYBERT | 6,120 | 20 | Amer | MINED | QP 13 | In British minefield |
| 05/07/42 | CARLTON | 5,127 | 20 | Amer | U 88 | PQ 17 | Post dispersal |
| 05/07/42 | HONOMU | 6,977 | 19 | Amer | U 456 | PQ 17 | Post dispersal |
| 05/07/42 | EARLSTON | 7,195 | 41 | Br | U 334 | PQ 17 | Post dispersal |
| 06/07/42 | PAN ATLANTIC | 5,411 | 19 | Amer | AIRCRAFT | PQ 17 | Post dispersal |
| 06/07/42 | JOHN WITHERSPOON | 7,191 | 42 | Amer | U 255 | PQ 17 | Post dispersal |
| 07/07/42 | HARTLEBURY | 5,082 | 34 | Br | U 355 | PQ 17 | Post dispersal |

| Date of loss | Ship's Name | GRT | Year | Flag | Cause of loss | Convoy | Comments |
|---|---|---|---|---|---|---|---|
| 07/07/42 | ALDERSDALE | 8,402 | 37 | Br | U 457 | PQ 17 | Post dispersal |
| 07/07/42 | ALCOA RANGER | 5,116 | 19 | Amer | U 255 | PQ 17 | Post dispersal |
| 08/07/42 | OLOPANA | 6,069 | 20 | Amer | U 255 | PQ 17 | Post dispersal |
| 10/07/42 | EL CAPITAN | 5,255 | 17 | Pan | U 251 | PQ 17 | Post dispersal, previously damaged by aircraft |
| 10/07/42 | HOOSIER | 5,060 | 20 | Amer | U 376 | PQ 17 | Post dispersal |
| 13/09/42 | EMPIRE BEAUMONT | 7,044 | 42 | Br | AIRCRAFT | PQ 18 | |
| 13/09/42 | JOHN PENN | 7,177 | 42 | Amer | AIRCRAFT | PQ 18 | |
| 13/09/42 | SUKHONA | 3,124 | 18 | Russ | AIRCRAFT | PQ 18 | |
| 13/09/42 | AFRICANDER | 5,441 | 21 | Pan | AIRCRAFT | PQ 18 | |
| 13/09/42 | MACBETH | 4,941 | 20 | Pan | AIRCRAFT | PQ 18 | |
| 13/09/42 | EMPIRE STEVENSON | 6,209 | 41 | Br | AIRCRAFT | PQ 18 | |
| 13/09/42 | OREGONIAN | 4,862 | 17 | Amer | AIRCRAFT | PQ 18 | |
| 13/09/42 | WACOSTA | 5,432 | 20 | Amer | AIRCRAFT | PQ 18 | |
| 13/09/42 | STALINGRAD | 3,559 | 31 | Russ | U 589 | PQ 18 | |
| 13/09/42 | OLIVER ELLSWORTH | 7,191 | 42 | Amer | U405 or 408 | PQ 18 | |
| 14/09/42 | ATHELTEMPLAR | 8,992 | 30 | Br | U 457 | PQ 18 | Wreck sunk by HARRIER |
| 14/09/42 | MARY LUCKENBACH | 5,049 | 19 | Amer | AIRCRAFT | PQ 18 | |
| 18/09/42 | KENTUCKY | 5,446 | 21 | Amer | AIRCRAFT | PQ 18 | Wreck ashore, part cargo salved by Russians |
| 20/09/42 | SILVER SWORD | 4,937 | 19 | Amer | U 255 | QP 14 | |
| 22/09/42 | BELLINGHAM | 5,345 | 20 | Amer | U 435 | QP 14 | |
| 22/09/42 | OCEAN VOICE | 7,174 | 41 | Br | U 435 | QP 14 | |
| 22/09/42 | GRAY RANGER | 3,313 | 41 | Br | U 435 | QP 14 | |
| 02/11/42 | EMPIRE GILBERT | 6,640 | 41 | Br | U 586 | OP FB | Independent passage |
| 04/11/42 | WILLIAM CLARK | 7,176 | 42 | Amer | U 354 | OP FB | Independent passage |
| 04/11/42 | DEKABRIST | 7,363 | 03 | Russ | AIRCRAFT | OP FB | Independent passage |
| 06/11/42 | EMPIRE SKY | 7,455 | 41 | Br | U 625 | OP FB | Independent passage |
| 07/11/42 | DONBASS | 7,925 | 35 | Russ | Z 27 | OPFBWEST | Only ship lost in westbound passage of OP FB |
| 16/11/42 | CHULMLEIGH | 5,445 | 38 | Br | U 625 | OP FB | Stranded on ice, and air attack. Independent |
| 23/11/42 | GOOLISTAN | 5,851 | 29 | Br | U 625 | QP 15 | |
| 23/11/42 | KUZNETZ LESOV | 3,974 | 33 | Russ | U 601 | QP 15 | |
| 02/01/43 | BALLOT | 6,131 | 22 | Pan | WRECKED | JW 51B | Aground 2.1, abandoned 13.1.43 off Kola Inlet |
| 26/01/43 | UFA | 1,892 | 17 | Russ | U 255 | INDEP | |
| 29/01/43 | KRASNY PARTIZAN | 2,418 | 27 | Russ | U 225 | INDEP | |
| 03/02/43 | GREYLOCK | 7,460 | 21 | Amer | U 255 | RA 52 | |
| 05/03/43 | EXECUTIVE | 4,978 | 20 | Amer | U 255 | RA 53 | |
| 05/03/43 | RICHARD BLAND | 7,191 | 42 | Amer | U 255 | RA 53 | Derelict sunk 10.3.43 also by U 255 |
| 07/03/43 | J L M CURRY | 7,176 | 42 | Amer | FOUNDERED | RA 53 | |
| 09/03/43 | PUERTO RICAN | 6,076 | 19 | Amer | U 586 | RA 53 | |
| 13/03/43 | OCEAN FREEDOM | 7,173 | 42 | Br | AIRCRAFT | | Lost after arrival at Murmansk |
| 25/01/44 | ANDREW G CURTIN | 7,200 | 43 | Amer | U 716 | JW 56A | |
| 25/01/44 | PENELOPE BARKER | 7,177 | 42 | Amer | U 278 | JW 56A | |
| 26/01/44 | FORT BELLINGHAM | 7,153 | 42 | Br | U 360,U957 | JW 56A | First damaged on 25.1, sank 26.1 |
| 04/03/44 | EMPIRE TOURIST | 7,062 | 43 | Br | U 703 | RA 57 | |
| 30/04/44 | WILLIAM S THAYER | 7,176 | 43 | Amer | U 711 | RA 59 | |
| 29/09/44 | EDWARD H CROCKETT | 7,176 | 44 | Amer | U 310 | RA 60 | |
| 29/09/44 | SAMSUVA | 7,219 | 44 | Br | U 310 | RA 60 | |
| 14/02/45 | HORACE GRAY | 7,200 | 43 | Amer | U 711 | | En route in White Sea, to join RA 64 |
| 14/02/45 | NORFJELL | 8,129 | 42 | Nor | U 968 | | En route in White Sea, to join RA 64 |
| 17/02/45 | THOMAS SCOTT | 7,176 | 42 | Amer | U 968 | RA 64 | |
| 23/02/45 | HENRY BACON | 7,177 | 42 | Amer | AIRCRAFT | RA 64 | After straggling |
| 20/03/45 | HORACE BUSHNELL | 7,176 | 43 | Amer | U 995 | JW 65 | Towed in and beached, but total loss |
| 20/03/45 | THOMAS DONALDSON | 7,210 | 44 | Amer | U 968 | JW 65 | |

**No. of ships lost between 21/06/41 & 08/05/45 = 104**

# INDEX OF WARSHIPS SHOWING THE CONVOYS WHICH THEY ESCORTED OR SUPPORTED

**(including where the ship operated for only part of the passage.)**

|  |  |
|---|---|
| ACHATES | PQ 16, PQ 18, QP 13, JW 51B. |
| ACANTHUS | JW 55A, RA 55A. |
| ACTIVE | QP 1. |
| ACTIVITY | JW 58, RA 58, RA 59. |
| AIREDALE | PQ 11. |
| ALGONQUIN | JW 60, JW 63, RA 60, RA 63. |
| ALLINGTON CASTLE | JW 60, JW 62, JW 63, JW 65, RA 60, RA 62, RA 63, RA 65. |
| ALNWICK CASTLE | JW 63, JW 64, JW 65, JW 66, RA 63, RA 64, RA 65, RA 66. |
| ALYNBANK | PQ 16, PQ 18, QP 13, QP 14. |
| AMAZON | PQ 14, PQ 18, QP 11, QP 14. |
| ANGLE | PQ 12. |
| ANGUILLA | JW 66, RA 66. |
| ANSON | PQ 18, QP 14, JW 51B, JW 52, JW 54A, JW 54B, RA 52, RA 54A, RA 54B. |
| ANTELOPE | PQ 1. |
| ANTHONY | PQ 1, QP 1. |
| ARAB | PQ 18. |
| ASHANTI | PQ 12, PQ 13, PQ 16, PQ 17, PQ 18, QP 9, QP 13, QP 14, JW 54B, JW 55A, RA 54B, RA 55A. |
| ATHABASKAN | JW 55A, RA 55A. |
| AURORA | DERVISH |
| AVENGER | PQ 18, QP 14. |
| AYRSHIRE | PQ 17, QP 14. |
| | |
| BADSWORTH | PQ 15, QP 12. |
| BAHAMAS | JW 62, RA 62. |
| BAKU | QP 15. |
| BAMBOROUGH CASTLE | JW 60, JW 62, JW 63, JW 64, JW 65, JW 66, RA 60, RA 62, RA 63, RA 64, RA 65, RA 66. |
| BAZELEY | JW 67, RA 67. |
| BEAGLE | PQ 14, QP 11, JW 51A, JW 52, JW 54B, JW 57, JW 58, JW 61A, JW 62, RA 51, RA 52, RA 55A, RA 57, RA 58, RA 59, RA 62. |
| BEDOUIN | PQ 3, PQ 12, PQ 13, PQ 14, QP 3, QP 9, QP 10. |
| BELFAST | JW 53, JW 54B, JW 55A, JW 55B, RA 53, RA 54A, RA 54B, RA 55A. |
| BELLONA | JW 62, JW 64, JW 66, RA 62, RA 64, RA 66. |
| BELVOIR | PQ 14, PQ 15, QP 10, QP 11. |
| BENTINCK | JW 67, RA 67. |
| BERGAMOT | PQ 18, QP 15, JW 53, RA 53. |
| BERMUDA | JW 52, JW 54A, JW 54B, JW 56A, JW 56B, RA 51, RA 52, RA 54B, RA 56. |
| BERWICK | PQ 4, PQ 12, JW 51A, JW 53, JW 56A, JW 56B, JW 57, JW 61A, RA 56, RA 61A. |
| BEVERLEY | PQ 14, QP 11. |
| BLACKFLY | PQ 11, PQ 13, QP 10. |
| BLACK PRINCE | JW 57, RA 57. |
| BLANKNEY | PQ 16, PQ 17, QP 12, QP 13, QP 14, JW 51A, JW 51B, JW 52, RA 51, RA 52. |
| BLUEBELL | PQ 18, QP 15, JW 53, JW 57, JW 58, JW 59, JW 64, RA 57, RA 58, RA 59A, RA 64. |
| BLYSKAWICA | PQ 13. |
| BOADICEA | PQ 15, QP 12, JW 51A, JW 53, JW 57, JW 58, RA 53, RA 57, RA 58, RA 59. |
| BORAGE | JW 55B, JW 56A, RA 55A, RA 56. |
| BRAMBLE | PQ 2, PQ 3, PQ 5, PQ 15, PQ 16, QP 2, QP 3, QP 4, QP 6, QP 12, QP 13, QP 14, JW 51B. |
| BRAMHAM | PQ 18, QP 14. |
| BRISSENDEN | JW 54A, RA 54A, RA 54B. |
| BRITOMART | PQ 1, PQ 9, PQ 17, PQ 18, QP 7, QP 9, QP 14, QP 15, JW 52, JW 53, RA 54A. |
| BRYONY | PQ 18, QP 15, JW 53. |

| | |
|---|---|
| BULLDOG | PQ 14, PQ 18, QP 11, QP 14, JW 51B, JW 52, JW 60, JW 62, RA 52, RA 60, RA 62. |
| BURDOCK | JW 57. |
| BURZA | JW 54A. |
| BUTE | PQ 4, QP 4. |
| BYARD | JW 67,RA 67. |
| BYRON | JW 57, JW 61, RA 61. |
| | |
| CAESAR | JW 62, RA 62. |
| CAMBRIAN | JW 61A, JW 62, RA 61A, RA 62. |
| CAMELLIA | PQ 18, QP 15, JW 53, JW 57, JW 59, JW 61, JW 65, RA 57, RA 59A, RA 61, RA 65. |
| CAMPANIA | JW 60, JW 61A, JW 62, JW 64, JW 65, RA 60, RA 61A, RA 62, RA 64, RA 65. |
| CAMPANULA | PQ 14, QP 11. |
| CAMPBELL | PQ 18. |
| CAPE ARGONA | PQ 6, PQ 7B, PQ 11, PQ 18, RA 51. |
| CAPE BRETON | RA 59. |
| CAPE MARIATO | PQ 11, PQ 18, RA 51. |
| CAPE PALLISER | PQ 15, QP 12. |
| CAPPS | RA 54A. |
| CAPRICE | JW 59, JW 61A, JW 62, RA 59A, RA 61A, RA 62. |
| CASSANDRA | JW 61A, JW 62, RA 61A, RA 62. |
| CAVALIER | RA 64. |
| CELIA | DERVISH, QP 2. |
| CHAMOIS | JW 58. |
| CHANCE | JW 58. |
| CHARLOCK | JW 59, RA 59A. |
| CHASER | JW 57, RA 57. |
| CHIDDINGFOLD | JW 51A, JW 51B. |
| CHILTERN | PQ 12, PQ 14, PQ 15. |
| COCKATRICE | JW 55A, RA 56. |
| CONN | JW 61, RA 61. |
| CORRY | JW 54A. |
| COTTON | JW 66, RA 66. |
| COWDRAY | PQ 18, QP 14. |
| CUMBERLAND | PQ 17, PQ 18, QP 5, QP 13, QP 14, JW 51B, JW 53, RA 53. |
| CYGNET | JW 56A, JW 56B, JW 59, JW 60, JW 61A, JW 63, JW 64, JW 66, RA 56, RA 59A, RA 60, RA 62, RA 63, RA 64, RA 66. |
| | |
| DANEMAN | PQ 18, RA 51. |
| DEANE | JW 61, RA 61. |
| DENBIGH CASTLE | JW 64. |
| DIADEM | JW 58, JW 60, JW 63, JW 65, RA 58, RA 59, RA 60, RA 63, RA 65. |
| DIANELLA | PQ 17, QP 14, JW 53, JW 54B, JW 56A, JW 57, RA 55A, RA 56. |
| DIDO | JW 61, RA 61. |
| DOUGLAS | PQ 17, QP 13. |
| DRURY | JW 67, RA 67. |
| DUKE OF YORK | PQ 12, PQ 13, PQ 14, PQ 15, PQ 16, PQ 17, PQ 18, QP 9, QP 10, QP 11, QP 12, QP 13, QP 14, JW 55A, JW 55B, RA 55A. |
| DUNCTON | PQ 14, PQ 18. |
| | |
| ECHO | PQ 6, PQ 12, PQ 13, PQ 18, QP 4, QP 9, QP 14, QP 15, JW 51A, JW 52, RA 51. |
| ECLIPSE | PQ 2, PQ 12, PQ 13, PQ 16, PQ 18, QP 2, QP 10, QP 12, QP 14, JW 51A, JW 52, JW 53, RA 51, RA 53. |
| EDINBURGH | PQ 6, PQ 13, QP 4, QP 9, QP 11. |
| EGLANTINE | JW 62, RA 54A, RA 62. |
| ELECTRA | QP 1. |
| ESCAPADE | PQ 1, PQ 6, PQ 13, PQ 14, PQ 15, PQ 17, QP 4, QP 9, QP 10, QP 11, QP 12. |
| ESKDALE | PQ 18. |
| ESKIMO | PQ 13, PQ 14, PQ 18, QP 9, QP 10, QP 14. |
| | |
| FARNDALE | PQ 18. |
| FARNHAM CASTLE | JW 65, JW 66, RA 65, RA 66. |
| FAULKNOR | PQ 9, PQ 12, PQ 13, PQ 14, PQ 15, PQ 16, PQ 17, PQ 18, QP 7, QP 9, QP 10, QP 11, QP 12, QP 13, QP 14, QP 15, JW 51A, JW 52, JW 53, RA 51, RA 53. |

| | |
|---|---|
| FENCER | RA 59. |
| FITCH | JW 54A. |
| FITZROY | JW 58, JW 61, RA 61. |
| FORESIGHT | PQ 13, PQ 14, QP 9, QP 11. |
| FORESTER | PQ 14, QP 11, QP 15, JW 51B, RA 52, RA 53. |
| FORREST | JW 54A. |
| FORMIDABLE | RA 54A. |
| FURY | PQ 12, PQ 13, PQ 16, PQ 17, PQ 18, QP 10, QP 12, QP 14, JW 51A, JW 53, RA 51, RA 53. |
| GARLAND | PQ 16, QP 13. |
| GLASGOW | JW 52, RA 52, RA 53. |
| GLEANER | PQ 18, JW 55B, RA 51, RA 56, RA 57. |
| GOODALL | JW 66, RA 66. |
| GOSSAMER | PQ 1, PQ 2, PQ 4, PQ 12, PQ 13, PQ 14, PQ 16, QP 3, QP 9, QP 10, QP 11, QP 12. |
| GREMYASCHI | PQ 12, PQ 13, PQ 18, QP 6, QP 8, QP 9, QP 13, JW 56A, JW 58. |
| GROMKI | PQ 11, QP 8, JW 53, RA 54A. |
| GROU | RA 59. |
| GROVE | PQ 12. |
| GROZNI | PQ 11, PQ 16, QP 12, QP 13, JW 53, JW 56A. |
| HAIDA | JW 54A, JW 55B, JW 66, RA 54A, RA 54B, RA 55B, RA 66. |
| HALCYON | PQ 17, PQ 18, QP 1, QP 14, QP 15, JW 53, JW 54B, JW 55B, RA 54A, RA 55B, RA 56. |
| HAMLET | DERVISH, PQ 3, QP 1, QP 3. |
| HARDY | JW 54B, JW 56A, JW 56B. |
| HARRIER | PQ 1, PQ 8, PQ 11, PQ 12, PQ 14, QP 1, QP 6, QP 8, QP 9, QP 10, QP 11, QP 12, JW 51B, JW 55A, RA 52, RA 54A, RA 54B. |
| HAV | PQ 9. |
| HAZARD | PQ 5, PQ 6, PQ 8, PQ 11, PQ 16, PQ 18, QP 7, QP 8, QP 13, QP 14, QP 15, JW 53. |
| HEATHER | JW 54A, RA 54B. |
| HEBE | PQ 5, PQ 14, QP 4, QP 6. |
| HOBSON | JW 54A, RA 54A. |
| HONEYSUCKLE | PQ 16, QP 13, JW 51A, JW 55B, JW 56B, JW 58, JW 59, JW 65, JW 66, RA 52, RA 55B, RA 56, RA 58, RA 59A, RA 65, RA 66. |
| HOUND | JW 55B, RA 55A. |
| HOWE | JW 53, RA 51, RA 53. |
| HUGH WALPOLE | PQ 6, PQ 7A, PQ 18. |
| HURSLEY | PQ 15, QP 11. |
| HURON | JW 54A, JW 55B, JW 56B, JW 66, RA 54B, RA 55B, RA 56, RA 66. |
| HUSSAR | PQ 1, PQ 2, PQ 11, PQ 12, PQ 13, PQ 14, QP 3, QP 9, QP 10, QP 11, QP 13, JW 54A, JW 55A, JW 55B, RA 54B, RA 55B, RA 56. |
| HYDERABAD | PQ 16, QP 13, JW 51B, RA 52. |
| HYDRA | JW 55B, JW 56B, JW 57, RA 55A, RA 57. |
| ICARUS | PQ 2, PQ 7B, PQ 12, PQ 13, PQ 16, QP 2, QP 5, QP 9, QP 12, QP 15, JW 51B, JW 53, RA 52, RA 53. |
| IMPULSIVE | PQ 1, PQ 18, QP 14, QP 15, JW 51B, JW 53, JW 54A, JW 55B, JW 57, JW 58, RA 53, RA 54B, RA 55B, RA 57, RA 58. |
| INCONSTANT | PQ 12, JW 54A, JW 56A, JW 56B, JW 58, RA 54B, RA 56, RA 58, RA 59. |
| INGLEFIELD | PQ 13, PQ 15, QP 9, QP 11, QP 12, QP 13, JW 51A, JW 52, JW 53, RA 51, RA 52, RA 53. |
| INGLIS | JW 61, RA 61. |
| INTREPID | PQ 3, PQ 9, PQ 12, PQ 16, PQ 18, QP 3, QP 7, QP 12, QP 13, QP 14, QP 15, JW 53, RA 53. |
| IROQUOIS | JW 54A, JW 55B, JW 66, RA 54B, RA 55B, RA 66. |
| JAMAICA | PQ 18, QP 14, JW 51A, JW 51B, JW 54A, JW 54B, JW 55A, JW 55B, JW 57, JW 59, RA 51, RA 54A, RA 54B, RA 55A, RA 59A. |
| JAVELIN | PQ 12. |
| JASON | JW 53, RA 54A |
| JUNON | QP 15. |
| KENT | PQ 13, PQ 14, PQ 16, QP 9, QP 10, QP 12, JW 52, JW 54A, JW 54B, JW 56A, JW 56B, RA 52, RA 54A, RA 54B, RA 56. |
| KENYA | PQ 3, PQ 12, PQ 15, QP 3, QP 11. |
| KEPPEL | PQ 17, PQ 18, QP 14, JW 57, JW 58, JW 59, JW 60, JW 62, JW 63, RA 57, RA 58, RA 59, RA 59A, RA 60, RA 62, RA 63. |

| | |
|---|---|
| KING GEORGE V | PQ 12, PQ 13, PQ 14, PQ 15, QP 9, QP 10, QP 11, JW 51A, JW 53, RA 51, RA 53. |
| KING SOL | PQ 18. |
| KITE | JW 59, |
| KUIBYSHEV | PQ 16, PQ 18, QP 11, QP 13, JW 53, JW 58, RA 54A, RA 59. |
| | |
| LA MALOUINE | PQ 17, QP 14. |
| LADY MADELEINE | PQ 16, QP 13, JW 51A, RA 52. |
| LAMERTON | PQ 13, PQ 15, PQ 16, QP 11, QP 12. |
| LANCASTER | PQ 12. |
| LANCASTER CASTLE | JW 65, RA 65. |
| LAPWING | JW 61, JW 62, JW 63, JW 64, JW 65, RA 61, RA 62, RA 63, RA 64. |
| LARK | JW 61, JW 62, JW 63, JW 64, RA 61, RA 62, RA 63, RA 64. |
| LAWSON | JW 61, RA 61. |
| LEAMINGTON | PQ 17. |
| LEDA | PQ 1, PQ 2, PQ 6, PQ 15, PQ 16, QP 2, QP 4, QP 12, QP 13, QP 14. |
| LEDBURY | PQ 12, PQ 13, PQ 14, PQ 15, PQ 16, PQ 17, QP 9, QP 10, QP 15, JW 51A, JW 51B, JW 52, RA 51, RA 53. |
| LIVERPOOL | PQ 16, QP 10, QP 12. |
| LOCH ALVIE | JW 62, RA 62. |
| LOCH DUNVEGAN | JW 59, RA 59A. |
| LOCH INSH | JW 66, RA 66. |
| LOCH SHIN | JW 66, RA 66. |
| LONDON | PQ 15, PQ 16, PQ 17, PQ 18, QP 1, QP 12, QP 14, QP 15. |
| LOOKOUT | PQ 12. |
| LORD AUSTIN | PQ 14, PQ 17, QP 14, JW 53, RA 54B. |
| LORD MIDDLETON | PQ 14, QP 11, QP 14, JW 53. |
| LORING | JW 61, RA 61. |
| LOTUS | PQ 17, QP 14, JW 52, JW 57, JW 58, JW 66, RA 53, RA 57, RA 58, RA 59, RA 66. |
| LOUIS | JW 61, RA 61. |
| LOYALTY | JW 57, RA 56, RA 57. |
| | |
| MACBETH | DERVISH, PQ 3, QP 1, QP 3. |
| MACKAY | PQ 18, QP 14. |
| MADISON | PQ 15. |
| MAGPIE | JW 58, RA 58. |
| MAHRATTA | JW 56B, JW 57, RA 54A, RA 56. |
| MARNE | PQ 13, PQ 15, PQ 16, PQ 17, PQ 18, QP 9, QP 10, QP 11, QP 12, QP 13, QP 14, JW 59, JW 60, RA 59, RA 59A, RA 60. |
| MARTIN | PQ 15, PQ 16, PQ 17, PQ 18, QP 11, QP 13. |
| MATABELE | PQ 8. |
| MATCHLESS | PQ 14, PQ 15, QP 10, JW 51A, JW 51B, JW 52, JW 54B, JW 55A, JW 55B, JW 57, RA 52, RA 54A, RA 54B, RA 55A, RA 57, RA 59. |
| MAYRANT | PQ 16, PQ 17, QP 12, QP 13. |
| MERMAID | JW 59, RA 59A. |
| METEOR | PQ 18, QP 14, JW 53, JW 55A, JW 56B, JW 57, JW 59, JW 60, RA 55A, RA 56, RA 57, RA 59, RA 59A, RA 60. |
| MEYNELL | JW 53, RA 53. |
| MIDDLETON | PQ 11, PQ 13, PQ 14, PQ 15, PQ 16, PQ 17, QP 9, QP 10, QP 11, QP 12, QP 13, QP 14, QP 15, JW 52, JW 53, JW 54B, RA 52, RA 54A, RA 54B. |
| MILNE | PQ 18, QP 14, JW 53, JW 55A, JW 56B, JW 57, JW 59, JW 60, RA 53, RA 54A, RA 55A, RA 56, RA 57, RA 59, RA 59A, RA 60. |
| MINERVE | PQ 15. |
| MONNOW | JW 62, RA 62. |
| MONTROSE | PQ 18, QP 14, JW 52, RA 51. |
| MOUNSEY | JW 61, RA 61, RA 62. |
| MUSKETEER | QP 15, JW 51A, JW 52, JW 53, JW 54B, JW 55A, JW 55B, JW 56B, JW 59, JW 60, RA 51, RA 52, RA 53, RA 54A, RA 54B, RA 55A, RA 56, RA 59, RA 59A, RA 60. |
| MYNGS | JW 63, JW 65, RA 63, RA 64, RA 65. |
| | |
| NAIRANA | JW 61, JW 62, JW 64, RA 61, RA 62, RA 64. |
| NARBOROUGH | JW 61, RA 61. |
| NENE | JW 61A, JW 62, RA 62. |
| NIGER | PQ 11, PQ 14, QP 9, QP 11, QP 13. |
| NIGERIA | PQ 9, PQ 11, PQ 14, PQ 15, PQ 16, PQ 17, QP 7, QP 8, QP 10, QP 12, QP 13. |

| | |
|---|---|
| NORFOLK | PQ 2, PQ 14, PQ 16, PQ 17, PQ 18, QP 2, QP 12, QP 14, JW 53, JW 55A, JW 55B, RA 53, RA 54A, RA 55A. |
| NORTHERN GEM | PQ 17, QP 14, JW 51B, RA 52. |
| NORTHERN PRIDE | PQ 15, QP 12, JW 52, RA 53. |
| NORTHERN SPRAY | PQ 16. |
| NORTHERN WAVE | PQ 14, QP 12, JW 51A, RA 52. |
| NOTTS COUNTY | PQ 12. |
| OAKLEY | PQ 18, QP 14, QP 15. |
| OBDURATE | QP 15, JW 51B, JW 53, JW 54B, JW 56A, JW 67, RA 53, RA 57. |
| OBEDIENT | JW 51B, JW 53, JW 54A, JW 57, JW 58, JW 61, JW 62, RA 52, RA 53, RA 56, RA 57, RA 58, RA 61, RA 62, RA 66. |
| OFFA | PQ 4, PQ 12, PQ 14, PQ 17, PQ 18, QP 9, QP 10, QP 14, JW 52, JW 53, JW 56A, JW 56B, JW 57, JW 58, JW 61, JW 62, JW 66, RA 52, RA 53, RA 56, RA 57, RA 58, RA 61, RA 62, RA 66. |
| ONSLAUGHT | PQ 17, PQ 18, QP 13, QP 14, QP 15, JW 52, JW 53, JW 54A, JW 55B, JW 57, JW 62, JW 64, JW 65, RA 52, RA 53, RA 54B, RA 55B, RA 57, RA 62, RA 64. |
| ONSLOW | PQ 4, PQ 12, PQ 13, PQ 14, PQ 16, PQ 17, PQ 18, QP 9, QP 10, QP 12, QP 13, QP 14, JW 51B, JW 54A, JW 55B, JW 58, JW 61, JW 62, JW 64, JW 67, RA 52, RA 54A, RA 54B, RA 55B, RA 58, RA 61, RA 62, RA 64, RA 67. |
| ONYX | JW 56B, JW 58, RA 57. |
| OPHELIA | DERVISH, PQ 7A, QP 1. |
| OPPORTUNE | PQ 18, QP 14, JW 51A, JW 51B, JW 53, JW 55A, JW 55B, JW 56B, JW 58, JW 61, JW 64, JW 65, RA 53, RA 55A, RA 56, RA 58, RA 61, RA 64, RA 65. |
| ORESTES | JW 56A, JW 57, JW 58, RA 55B, RA 57. |
| ORIBI | PQ 12, PQ 13, PQ 15, PQ 16, QP 10, QP 11, JW 51B, JW 57, JW 58, JW 61, JW 62, RA 52, RA 54B, RA 57, RA 58, RA 61, RA 62. |
| ORKAN | JW 52, JW 53, RA 52, RA 53. |
| ORWELL | QP 15, JW 51B, JW 53, JW 54A, JW 55B, JW 58, JW 61, JW 62, JW 64, JW 65, RA 53, RA 54B, RA 55B, RA 58, RA 61, RA 62, RA 64, RA 65, RA 66. |
| OUTREMONT | RA 59. |
| OXLIP | PQ 11, PQ 14, QP 8, QP 11, JW 51A, JW 55B, JW 56B, JW 59, JW 61, JW 65, JW 66, RA 52, RA 55B, RA 56, RA 59A, RA 61, RA 65, RA 66. |
| P 43 | PQ 15. |
| P 216 | QP 15. |
| P 312 | QP 15. |
| P 551 | PQ 15. |
| P 614 | PQ 17, PQ 18, QP 14. |
| P 615 | PQ 17, PQ 18, QP 14. |
| PALOMARES | PQ 17, QP 14. |
| PASLEY | JW 67, RA 67. |
| PAYNTER | PQ 13, PQ 18, QP 10. |
| PEACOCK | JW 59, RA 59A. |
| PIORUN | JW 52, JW 53, RA 51, RA 52, RA 53. |
| PLUNKETT | PQ 15. |
| POPPY | PQ 17, QP 14, JW 53, JW 54B, JW 56A, RA 53, RA 55A, RA 56. |
| PORT COLBOURNE | JW 62, RA 62. |
| POZARICA | PQ 17, QP 14. |
| PREMIER | JW 66, RA 66. |
| PUNJABI | PQ 12, PQ 13, PQ 15, QP 9, QP 10. |
| PYTCHLEY | JW 53, RA 53. |
| QUADRANT | JW 51A. |
| QUEEN | JW 67, RA 67. |
| QUEENBOROUGH | JW 52, RA 51. |
| RAIDER | JW 51A, JW 52, RA 51. |
| RATTLESNAKE | JW 57, JW 58, RA 56. |
| RAZUMNY | JW 56A, JW 58. |
| RAZYARENNI | JW 58, RA 59. |
| READY | JW 56A, RA 55B, RA 56, RA 57. |
| REDMILL | JW 61, RA 61. |
| RENOWN | PQ 12, PQ 13, QP 9. |
| RETRIEVER | PQ 16. |

| | |
|---|---|
| RHIND | PQ 16, PQ 17, QP 12, QP 13. |
| RHODODENDRON | JW 51B, JW 54B, JW 56B, JW 57, JW 58, JW 61, JW 64, JW 66, RA 52, RA 55B, RA 56, RA 57, RA 61, RA 64, RA 66. |
| RODNEY | JW 60, RA 60. |
| ROSELYS | PQ 16, QP 13. |
| ROWAN | PQ 16, PQ 17, QP 12. |
| RUPERT | JW 61, RA 61. |
| | |
| SABRE | PQ 13. |
| SALADIN | PQ 13, JW 54B, RA 54B. |
| SALAMANDER | PQ 11, PQ 17, PQ 18, QP 1, QP 8, QP 14, QP 15. |
| SAUMAREZ | JW 54B, JW 55A, JW 55B, JW 58, JW 60, JW 61A, RA 54A, RA 55A, RA 58, RA 60, RA 61A. |
| SAVAGE | JW 54B, JW 55A, JW 55B, JW 56A, JW 56B, JW 57, JW 63, JW 65, RA 54A, RA 55A, RA 56, RA 57, RA 61A, RA 63, RA 64, RA 65, Op FREEMAN. |
| SAXIFRAGE | PQ 14, QP 11. |
| SCORPION | JW 54B, JW 55A, JW 55B, JW 58, JW 60, JW 65, RA 54A, RA 55A, RA 58, RA 60, RA 61A, RA 63, RA 64, RA 65, Op FREEMAN. |
| SCOURGE | JW 54B, JW 55B, JW 56B, JW 61A, JW 63, JW 65, RA 54A, RA 56, RA 61A, RA 63, RA 64, RA 65. |
| SCYLLA | PQ 18, QP 14, JW 53, RA 53. |
| SEAGULL | PQ 2, PQ 3, PQ 4, PQ 5, PQ 15, PQ 16, QP 2, QP 4, QP 12, QP 13, QP 14, JW 51A, JW 51B, JW 54A, JW 56B, RA 52, RA 54A, RA 55A, RA 56, RA 57. |
| SEAWOLF | PQ 16. |
| SERAPIS | JW 57, JW 58, JW 61A, JW 63, JW 64, RA 57, RA 58, RA 61A, RA 63, RA 64. |
| SHARPSHOOTER | PQ 5, PQ 8, PQ 12, PQ 18, QP 6, QP 9, QP 15, JW 53. |
| SHEFFIELD | PQ 5, PQ 18, QP 14, JW 51A, JW 51B, JW 52, JW 55A, JW 55B, RA 51, RA 52, RA 55A. |
| SHERA | PQ 12. |
| SHIKA | PQ 9. |
| SHROPSHIRE | QP 1. |
| SHUSA | PQ 12. |
| SILJA | PQ 13. |
| SIOUX | JW 60, JW 63, JW 64, JW 65, RA 60, RA 63, RA 64, RA 65. |
| SKATE | JW 54B, RA 54B. |
| SNOWFLAKE | PQ 14, QP 11. |
| SOKRUSHITELNY | PQ 13, PQ 16, PQ 18, QP 6, QP 11, QP 12, QP 15. |
| SOMALI | PQ 8, PQ 14, PQ 15, PQ 18, QP 6, QP 10, QP 14. |
| SOMALILAND | JW 62, RA 62. |
| SPEEDWELL | PQ 8, PQ 12, PQ 13, QP 6, QP 7, QP 9, QP 10, JW 54B, JW 55A, RA 55B, RA 56. |
| SPEEDY | PQ 2, PQ 3, PQ 4, PQ 14, QP 4. |
| ST ALBANS | PQ 15, QP 12. |
| ST ELSTAN | PQ 16, QP 13, JW 52, RA 53. |
| ST JOHN | JW 62, RA 62. |
| ST KENAN | PQ 18, RA 51. |
| STARLING | JW 58, RA 58. |
| STARWORT | PQ 16, QP 13, JW 52, JW 58, RA 53. |
| STEFA | PQ 12. |
| STELLA CAPELLA | PQ 4, PQ 6, PQ 12, QP 4. |
| STORD | JW 54B, JW 55A, JW 55B, JW 56A, JW 56B, JW 58, JW 63, JW 65, JW 66, RA 54A, RA 55A, RA 56, RA 58, RA 63, RA 65, RA 66. |
| STORMONT | JW 62, RA 62. |
| STRIKER | JW 59, JW 60, RA 59A, RA 60. |
| STRULE | JW 57. |
| STURGEON | PQ 15. |
| SUFFOLK | PQ 1, PQ 18, QP 14, QP 15. |
| SULLA | PQ 12, PQ 13. |
| SUMBA | PQ 13. |
| SVEGA | PQ 12. |
| SWEETBRIAR | PQ 11, QP 8. |
| SWIFT | JW 57, RA 56, RA 57. |
| | |
| TARTAR | PQ 7B, PQ 12, PQ 13, PQ 18, QP 5, QP 9, QP 14. |
| TAVY | JW 62, RA 62. |

| | |
|---|---|
| TERMAGANT | JW 54A. |
| TORTOLA | JW 62, RA 62. |
| TRACKER | JW 58, JW 61, RA 58, RA 61. |
| TRIDENT | PQ 16, QP 13. |
| TRINIDAD | PQ 8, PQ 13, QP 6. |
| TRUANT | PQ 15. |
| TRUMPETER | JW 65, RA 65. |
| TUNSBERG CASTLE | JW 62, RA 62. |
| TUSCALOOSA | PQ 15, PQ 17, JW 54A. |
| | |
| ULSTER QUEEN | PQ 15, PQ 18, QP 12, QP 15. |
| ULYSSES | RA 59. |
| URAGAN | JW 53. |
| UREDD | PQ 15, QP 15. |
| URITSKI | PQ 18, JW 53. |
| | |
| VENOMOUS | PQ 15, PQ 18, QP 12, QP 14. |
| VENUS | JW 54B, JW 56A, JW 56B, JW 58, JW 60, RA 54A, RA 56, RA 58, RA 60. |
| VERDUN | PQ 12. |
| VERULAM | JW 57, JW 60, RA 56, RA 57, RA 59, RA 60. |
| VICTORIOUS | PQ 12, PQ 13, PQ 14, PQ 15, PQ 16, PQ 17, QP 9, QP 10, QP 11, QP 12, QP 13. |
| VIGILANT | JW 54B, JW 56A, JW 56B, JW 57, RA 56, RA 57. |
| VINDEX | JW 59, JW 61, JW 63, JW 66, RA 59A, RA 61, RA 63, RA 66. |
| VIRAGO | JW 55A, JW 55B, JW 56A, JW 56B, JW 60, RA 55A, RA 59, RA 60. |
| VIVACIOUS | RA 52, RA 53. |
| VIZALMA | PQ 15, QP 12, JW 51B, RA 52. |
| VOLAGE | JW 60, RA 60. |
| VOLUNTEER | PQ 16, QP 13. |
| | |
| WAINWRIGHT | PQ 15, PQ 16, PQ 17, QP 12. |
| WALKER | JW 57, JW 58, JW 61, JW 63, RA 57, RA 58, RA 59, RA 61, RA 63. |
| WALLFLOWER | JW 55B, JW 56A, RA 55A, RA 56. |
| WALPOLE | PQ 18. |
| WANDERER | JW 57. |
| WATCHMAN | JW 57. |
| WASHINGTON | PQ 15, PQ 16, PQ 17, QP 12, QP 13. |
| WASKESIU | RA 59. |
| WASTWATER | PQ 7B. |
| WELLS | PQ 12. |
| WESTCOTT | JW 55A, JW 56B, JW 58, JW 61A, JW 62, JW 63, RA 54A, RA 55A, RA 56, RA 58, RA 59, RA 62, RA 63. |
| WHEATLAND | PQ 13, PQ 14, PQ 16, PQ 17, PQ 18, QP 9, QP 10, QP 12, QP 13, QP 14. |
| WHIMBREL | JW 58, RA 58. |
| WHITEHALL | JW 54A, JW 55B, JW 56B, JW 58, JW 59, JW 60, JW 64, RA 54B, RA 55B, RA 56, RA 58, RA 59, RA 59A, RA 60, RA 64. |
| WILD GOOSE | JW 58, RA 58. |
| WICHITA | PQ 15, PQ 16, PQ 17, QP 12. |
| WILSON | PQ 15. |
| WILTON | PQ 14, PQ 17, PQ 18, QP 14. |
| WINDERMERE | QP 2. |
| WINDSOR | PQ 18, QP 14. |
| WOOLSTON | PQ 12. |
| WORCESTER | PQ 18, QP 14, RA 51. |
| WREN | JW 58, RA 58. |
| WRESTLER | JW 55B, JW 56B, JW 58, RA 55B, RA 56, RA 58, RA 59. |
| | |
| ZAMBESI | JW 63, JW 64, JW 65, RA 63, RA 64, RA 65. |
| ZEALOUS | JW 64, JW 66, RA 64, RA 66. |
| ZEBRA | JW 63, JW 64, RA 63, RA 64. |
| ZEPHYR | JW 66, RA 66. |
| ZEST | JW 64, JW 66, RA 66. |
| ZODIAC | JW 66, RA 66. |

# H.M.S. ONSLAUGHT, ARCTIC WINTER 1943

Four photographs by G. Swanson showing the extent of icing on board

# INDEX OF MERCHANT SHIPS SHOWING THE CONVOYS IN WHICH THEY PARTICIPATED

**(including where the ship returned from a convoy.)**

|  |  |
|---|---|
| *ABNER NASH* | JW 56B, JW 61, RA 57, RA 62. |
| *ADOLPH S OCHS* | JW 60, JW 63, JW 64, JW 67, RA 61, RA 65. |
| *AERT VAN DER NEER* | JW 56A, RA 57. |
| *AFRICANDER* | PQ 18. |
| *ALAMAR* | PQ 16. |
| *ALANSON B HOUGHTON* | JW 63, JW 67, RA 64. |
| *ALBERT C RITCHIE* | JW 56B, JW 66, RA 57, RA 67. |
| *ALCHIBA* | DERVISH, QP 01. |
| *ALCOA BANNER* | PQ 16, QP 14. |
| *ALCOA CADET* | PQ 15. |
| *ALCOA RAMBLER* | PQ 15, QP 12. |
| *ALCOA RANGER* | PQ 17. |
| *ALDAN* | Op FB West. |
| *ALDERSDALE* | DERVISH, PQ 14, PQ 17. |
| *ALEXANDER WHITE* | JW 57, RA 58. |
| *ALMA ATA* | PQ 4, QP 1, QP 13. |
| *AMASA DELANO* | JW 62, RA 63. |
| *AMERICAN PRESS* | PQ 16, QP 13. |
| *AMERICAN ROBIN* | PQ 16, QP 13. |
| *ANDRE MARTI* | PQ 14, PQ 18, QP 3, QP 15. |
| *ANDREW CARNEGIE* | JW 58, RA 59. |
| *ANDREW G CURTIN* | JW 56A. |
| *ANDREW TURNBULL* | JW 62, RA 63. |
| *ANDREW W PRESTON* | JW 61, RA 62. |
| *ANEROID* | PQ 7B, QP 6. |
| *ARCHANGEL* | QP 13. |
| *ARCOS* | PQ 14, PQ 16, QP 3, QP 5. |
| *ARTHUR L PERRY* | JW 54B, RA 55A. |
| *ARTIGAS* | PQ 12, QP 10, JW 53, RA 54B. |
| *ARUNAH S ABELL* | JW 58, JW 60, JW 64, RA 59, RA 61, RA 65. |
| *ASHKHABAD* | PQ 11, QP 9. |
| *ATHELTEMPLAR* | PQ 14, PQ 18, QP 11. |
| *ATLANTIC* | PQ 1, PQ 9, PQ 16, QP 2, QP 8, QP 13, JW 52, JW 53, RA 54B. |
| *AUGUST BELMONT* | JW 62, JW 66, RA 63, RA 67. |
| *AZERBAIDJAN* | Op FB West, PQ 17. |
| | |
| *BALLOT* | PQ 12, QP 11, JW 51B. |
| *BARBARA FRIETCHIE* | JW 58, JW 62, JW 67, RA 59A, RA 63. |
| *BARRWHIN* | PQ 11, QP 9. |
| *BATEAU* | PQ 12, PQ 13. |
| *BAYOU CHICO* | PQ 15, QP 12. |
| *BEACONHILL* | JW 53, RA 54A. |
| *BEACONSTREET* | PQ 12, QP 10. |
| *BEAUREGARD* | JW 51A, RA 52. |
| *BELLINGHAM* | PQ 17, QP 14. |
| *BELOMORCANAL* | PQ 12, QP 10, QP 15. |
| *BELORUSSIA* | RA 51. |
| *BEN F DIXON* | JW 64, RA 65. |
| *BENJAMIN H HILL* | JW 63, JW 66, RA 64, RA 67. |
| *BENJAMIN H LATROBE* | JW 58, RA 59. |
| *BENJAMIN HARRISON* | PQ 17, QP 14. |

| | |
|---|---|
| *BENJAMIN SCHLESINGER* | JW 58, JW 61, JW 65, RA 59, RA 62, RA 66 |
| *BERING* | JW 53, RA 54B. |
| *BERNARD N BAKER* | JW 55B, JW 63, JW 67, RA 57, RA 63. |
| *BLACK RANGER* | PQ 1, PQ 16, PQ 18, QP 1, QP 14, JW 64, JW 66, RA 64, RA 66. |
| *BLAIRNEVIS* | PQ 1, QP 2. |
| *BLUE RANGER* | JW 63, JW 65, JW 66, RA 63, RA 65, RA 66. |
| *BOLTON CASTLE* | PQ 17. |
| *BOTAVON* | PQ 7B, PQ 15, QP 7. |
| *BRIARWOOD* | PQ 3, PQ 5, PQ 14, Op FB, QP 4, QP 11, JW 51A, RA 52. |
| *BRITISH CORPORAL* | PQ 14. |
| *BRITISH GOVERNOR* | JW 53, RA 54A. |
| *BRITISH MERIT* | JW 64, RA 65. |
| *BRITISH PATIENCE* | JW 60, RA 61. |
| *BRITISH PRIDE* | PQ 8, QP 8. |
| *BRITISH PROMISE* | JW 59, JW 63, JW 67, RA 60, RA 64. |
| *BRITISH RESPECT* | JW 62, JW 66, RA 63, RA 67. |
| *BRITISH STATESMAN* | JW 55B, RA 56. |
| *BRITISH VALOUR* | JW 57, RA 58. |
| *BRITISH WORKMAN* | PQ 8, QP 8. |
| *BROCKHOLST LIVINGSTON* | JW 55B, RA 56. |
| *BUDENNI* | PQ 4, QP 1, QP 13. |
| *BYRON DARNTON* | JW 57, JW 64, RA 58, RA 66. |
| | |
| *CAESAR RODNEY* | JW 57, JW 63, JW 67, RA 58, RA 64. |
| *CALOBRE* | JW 51B, RA 53. |
| *CAMPFIRE* | PQ 18, RA 51. |
| *CAPE CORSO* | PQ 3, PQ 14, PQ 15, QP 4. |
| *CAPE RACE* | PQ 3, PQ 15, QP 4, QP 12. |
| *CAPIRA* | PQ 1, PQ 15, QP 2, QP 13. |
| *CAPULIN* | PQ 12, QP 10. |
| *CARDINAL GIBBONS* | JW 55B, JW 60, JW 67, RA 56, RA 61. |
| *CARLTON* | PQ 16, PQ 17, |
| *CECIL N BEAN* | JW 62, JW 66, RA 63, RA 67. |
| *CHARLES A McALLISTER* | JW 56B, JW 59, JW 65, RA 57, RA 60, RA 66. |
| *CHARLES BULFINCH* | JW 56A, JW 57, JW 67, RA 58. |
| *CHARLES DAURAY* | JW 59, RA 60. |
| *CHARLES GORDON CURTIS* | JW 58. |
| *CHARLES HENDERSON* | JW 58, RA 59. |
| *CHARLES M SCHWAB* | JW 57, JW 63, RA 58, RA 64. |
| *CHARLES R McCORMICK* | PQ 18, QP 15. |
| *CHARLES SCRIBNER* | JW 56A, JW 63, RA 57, RA 64. |
| *CHERNYSHEVSKI* | PQ 7B, PQ 16, QP 2, QP 6, Op FB West. |
| *CHESTER VALLEY* | JW 51B, RA 53. |
| *CHRISTOPHER NEWPORT* | PQ 17. |
| *CHULMLEIGH* | PQ 5, QP 13, Op FB. |
| *CITY OF FLINT* | PQ 11, QP 9. |
| *CITY OF JOLIET* | PQ 14, PQ 16, QP 10. |
| *CITY OF OMAHA* | PQ 16, QP 13, JW 53, RA 54A. |
| *CLARK HOWELL* | JW 59, RA 60. |
| *COCLE* | PQ 3, QP 4. |
| *COLD HARBOR* | PQ 7A, QP 8. |
| *COLLIS P HUNTINGTON* | JW 55A, JW 61, RA 56, RA 62. |
| *COPELAND* | PQ 18, QP 15, JW 54A, JW 57, JW 66, RA 54B, RA 57, RA 58, RA 66. |
| *CORNELIUS HARNETT* | JW 52, RA 53. |
| *CROSBY S NOYES* | JW 63, RA 64. |
| | |
| *DALDORCH* | PQ 11, QP 9, OP FB, JW 51B, JW 54B, RA 52, RA 55B. |
| *DAN-Y-BRYN* | PQ 4, PQ 14, PQ 18, QP 4, QP 11, QP 15, JW 52, RA 53. |
| *DANIEL MORGAN* | PQ 17. |
| *DANIEL DRAKE* | JW 54A, RA 55A. |
| *DANIEL WILLARD* | JW 55A, JW 60, JW 64, RA 56, RA 61, RA 65. |
| *DAPHNELLA* | JW 57, RA 58. |
| *DARTFORD* | PQ 8, QP 7. |
| *DAVID B JOHNSON* | JW 59, JW 66, RA 60, RA 67. |

| | |
|---|---|
| *DAVID STONE* | JW 60, RA 61. |
| *DEER LODGE* | PQ 15, QP 14. |
| *DEKABRIST* | PQ 6, QP 5, Op FB. |
| *DELSUD* | JW 52, RA 53. |
| *DEXTER W FELLOWS* | JW 60, RA 61. |
| *DNEPROSTROI* | PQ 12, QP 10. |
| *DOLABELLA* | JW 58, JW 61, JW 65, RA 59, RA 62, RA 66 |
| *DONALD W BAIN* | JW 61, RA 62. |
| *DONBASS* | PQ 17, Op FB West. |
| *DOVER HILL* | JW 51B, JW 53, RA 54B. |
| *DUNBOYNE* | PQ 13, QP 11. |
| *DVINA* | Op FB West. |
| *DYNASTIC* | JW 51A, RA 52. |
| | |
| *EARLSTON* | PQ 12, PQ 17, QP 9. |
| *EDMUND FANNING* | JW 54A, JW 63, RA 55A, RA 64. |
| *EDWARD A SAVOY* | JW 60, RA 61. |
| *EDWARD E SPAFFORD* | JW 60, RA 61. |
| *EDWARD H CROCKETT* | JW 59, RA 60. |
| *EDWARD L GRANT* | JW 56B, JW 59, RA 57, RA 60. |
| *EDWARD N HURLEY* | JW 62, JW 67, RA 63. |
| *EDWARD P ALEXANDER* | JW 58, RA 59 |
| *EDWARD SPARROW* | JW 57, RA 58. |
| *EDWIN L DRAKE* | JW 56A, JW 64, RA 57, RA 65. |
| *EFFINGHAM* | PQ 13. |
| *EGERO* | JW 67, RA 67. |
| *EL ALMIRANTE* | PQ 8, QP 7, JW 51A, RA 52. |
| *EL CAPITAN* | PQ 3, PQ 17, QP 4. |
| *EL COSTON* | PQ 12, QP 10. |
| *EL ESTERO* | PQ 13, QP 11. |
| *EL LAGO* | PQ 9, QP 8. |
| *EL MIRLO* | PQ 6, PQ 14, QP 4, QP 10. |
| *EL OCCIDENTE* | PQ 12, QP 10. |
| *EL OCEANO* | PQ 6, JW 51A, RA 52. |
| *EL ORIENTE* | JW 52, RA 53 |
| *ELEAZAR LORD* | JW 61, JW 65, RA 62, RA 66. |
| *ELDENA* | PQ 13, QP 11. |
| *ELNA II* | PQ 1. |
| *ELIJAH KELLOGG* | JW 59, RA 60. |
| *ELONA* | PQ 6, QP 8. |
| *ELOY ALFARO* | JW 58, JW 61, JW 65, RA 62, RA 66. |
| *EMPIRE ACTIVITY* | PQ 7B, QP 6. |
| *EMPIRE ARCHER* | JW 51B, JW 55A, JW 63, RA 53, RA 56, RA 64. |
| *EMPIRE BAFFIN* | PQ 2, PQ 11, PQ 16, PQ 18, QP 3, QP 9, QP 13, QP 15, JW 52, JW 53. |
| *EMPIRE BARD* | PQ 14, PQ 15, RA 57, RA 59A. |
| *EMPIRE BEAUMONT* | PQ 18. |
| *EMPIRE BUTTRESS* | JW 59. |
| *EMPIRE BYRON* | PQ 12, PQ 17, QP 9. |
| *EMPIRE CARPENTER* | JW 54A, JW 57, RA 55A. |
| *EMPIRE CELIA* | JW 54A, JW 57, JW 60, JW 63, RA 55A, RA 58, RA 61, RA 64. |
| *EMPIRE CLARION* | JW 52, RA 53. |
| *EMPIRE COWPER* | PQ 13, QP 10. |
| *EMPIRE ELGAR* | PQ 16, RA 59A. |
| *EMPIRE EMERALD* | JW 51B, JW 67, RA 53. |
| *EMPIRE FLINT* | JW 64, RA 65. |
| *EMPIRE FORTUNE* | JW 53, RA 54A. |
| *EMPIRE GALLIARD* | JW 53, Op FB, RA 51, RA 54A. |
| *EMPIRE GILBERT* | Op FB. |
| *EMPIRE GARRICK* | JW 62, JW 66, RA 63, RA 67. |
| *EMPIRE HALLEY* | PQ 7B, QP 7. |
| *EMPIRE HOWARD* | PQ 7B, PQ 14, QP 6. |
| *EMPIRE KINSMAN* | JW 53, RA 54A. |
| *EMPIRE LAWRENCE* | PQ 16. |
| *EMPIRE LIONEL* | JW 54B, RA 56. |

| | |
|---|---|
| *EMPIRE MAGPIE* | PQ 11, QP 9. |
| *EMPIRE MAVIS* | PQ 6, QP 13. |
| *EMPIRE METEOR* | PQ 4, QP 13, JW 51A, RA 52. |
| *EMPIRE MORN* | PQ 15, PQ 18, QP 12, QP 15. |
| *EMPIRE NIGEL* | JW 54A, JW 57, RA 55A. |
| *EMPIRE PICKWICK* | JW 55A, RA 56, RA 57. |
| *EMPIRE PLOUGHMAN* | JW 56A, RA 57. |
| *EMPIRE PORTIA* | JW 52, RA 54A. |
| *EMPIRE PROWESS* | JW 58, JW 67, RA 59A. |
| *EMPIRE PURCELL* | PQ 16. |
| *EMPIRE RANGER* | PQ 13. |
| *EMPIRE REDSHANK* | PQ 7B, QP 6. |
| *EMPIRE SCOTT* | Op FB, JW 53, RA 51, RA 54B. |
| *EMPIRE SELWYN* | PQ 9, PQ 16, QP 8, QP 13. |
| *EMPIRE SKY* | Op FB. |
| *EMPIRE SNOW* | PQ 18, QP 15, JW 52, RA 53. |
| *EMPIRE STALWART* | JW 54B, JW 62, JW 65, RA 55B, RA 63, RA 66. |
| *EMPIRE STARLIGHT* | PQ 13. |
| *EMPIRE STEVENSON* | PQ 5, PQ 18, QP 13. |
| *EMPIRE TIDE* | PQ 17, QP 14. |
| *EMPIRE TOURIST* | JW 56B, RA 57. |
| *EMPIRE TRISTRAM* | PQ 18, QP 15, JW 52, RA 53. |
| *EMPRESS OF AUSTRALIA* | JW 61A, RA 61A. |
| *ESEK HOPKINS* | PQ 18, QP 15. |
| *EUGENE FIELD* | JW 54B, RA 56. |
| *ESNEH* | DERVISH, QP 1. |
| *EULIMA* | PQ 4, QP 4, QP 5. |
| *EXECUTIVE* | JW 51B, RA 53. |
| *EXFORD* | PQ 18, QP 15. |
| *EXPLORER* | PQ 6, QP 8, JW 53. |
| *EXPOSITOR* | PQ 15, QP 12. |
| *EXTERMINATOR* | PQ 14, PQ 16, QP 13. |
| | |
| *F T FRELINGHUYSEN* | JW 59, JW 64, RA 61, RA 65. |
| *FAIRFIELD CITY* | PQ 17. |
| *FORT ASTORIA* | JW 55A, RA 56. |
| *FORT BELLINGHAM* | JW 56A. |
| *FORT BOISE* | JW 62, JW 65, RA 63, RA 66. |
| *FORT BRULE* | JW 57, RA 59. |
| *FORT COLUMBIA* | JW 54B, JW 58, RA 55B, RA 59. |
| *FORT CREVECOEUR* | JW 56B, JW 61, JW 64, RA 57, RA 62, RA 65. |
| *FORT GLENORA* | JW 59, RA 60. |
| *FORT HALL* | JW 55A, JW 58, RA 56, RA 59. |
| *FORT HIGHFIELD* | JW 62, JW 67, RA 63. |
| *FORT ISLAND* | JW 62, RA 63. |
| *FORT KULLYSPELL* | JW 55B, JW 58, RA 56, RA 59. |
| *FORT MASSAC* | JW 62, JW 65, RA 63, RA 66. |
| *FORT McMURRAY* | JW 54B, JW 57, RA 55A, RA 58. |
| *FORT MISSANABIE* | JW 55A, RA 56. |
| *FORT NAKASLEY* | JW 55B, RA 56. |
| *FORT NORFOLK* | JW 56B, RA 57. |
| *FORT POPLAR* | JW 54B, RA 55B. |
| *FORT ROMAINE* | JW 57, JW 61, RA 58, RA 62. |
| *FORT SLAVE* | JW 56A, RA 57. |
| *FORT THOMPSON* | JW 55A, RA 56. |
| *FORT VERCHERES* | JW 55B, JW 58, JW 64, RA 56, RA 59A, RA 65. |
| *FORT YUKON* | JW 54A, JW 58, JW 61, JW 65, RA 55A, RA 59, RA 62, RA 66. |
| *FRANCIS C HARRINGTON* | JW 63, RA 64. |
| *FRANCIS SCOTT KEY* | PQ 14, PQ 15, QP 10, QP 12, JW 53, JW 58, JW 60, JW 64, RA 54A, RA 59, RA 61, RA 65. |
| *FRANCIS VIGO* | JW 58, RA 59. |
| *FRANK GILBRETH* | JW 59, RA 60. |
| *FREDERIC A KUMMER* | JW 60, RA 61. |
| *FREDERICK W TAYLOR* | JW 60, RA 61. |
| *FRIEDRICH ENGELS* | PQ 9, QP 8, QP 15. |

| | |
|---|---|
| *GALLANT FOX* | PQ 13, QP 11. |
| *GATEWAY CITY* | JW 51A, RA 52. |
| *GEMSTONE* | PQ 1, QP 2. |
| *GEORGE GALE* | JW 58, RA 59. |
| *GEORGE H PENDLETON* | JW 63, JW 67, RA 64. |
| *GEORGE M COHAN* | JW 58, RA 59. |
| *GEORGE STEERS* | JW 64, RA 65. |
| *GEORGE T ANGELL* | JW 58, JW 60, RA 59, RA 61. |
| *GEORGE WEEMS* | JW 55A, JW 67, RA 56. |
| *GILBERT STUART* | JW 54A, JW 58, RA 55A, RA 59. |
| *GOOLISTAN* | PQ 18, QP 15. |
| *GRACE ABBOTT* | JW 58, JW 65, RA 59, RA 66. |
| *GRAY RANGER* | PQ 15, PQ 17, PQ 18, QP 14, |
| *GREYLOCK* | JW 51A, RA 52. |
| *GULFWING* | JW 52, RA 53. |
| | |
| *HARMATRIS* | PQ 8, QP 14. |
| *HARMONIC* | PQ 1, QP 2. |
| *HAROLD L WINSLOW* | JW 55B, JW 61, JW 64, RA 56, RA 62, RA 65. |
| *HARPALION* | PQ 2, PQ 13, QP 3, QP 10. |
| *HARTLEBURY* | PQ 2, PQ 11, PQ 17, QP 3, QP 9. |
| *HAWKINS FUDSKE* | JW 58, JW 60, JW 64, RA 59, RA 61, RA 65. |
| *HEFFRON* | PQ 16, QP 13. |
| *HEGIRA* | PQ 14, PQ 15, QP 12, QP 13. |
| *HENRY ADAMS* | JW 61, RA 62. |
| *HENRY B BROWN* | JW 57, RA 58. |
| *HENRY BACON* | JW 56B, JW 63, RA 57, RA 64. |
| *HENRY LOMB* | JW 56B, JW 57, JW 60, JW 64, RA 58, RA 61, RA 66. |
| *HENRY VILLARD* | JW 54A, JW 58, JW 63, JW 67, RA 55A, RA 59, RA 64. |
| *HENRY WYNKOOP* | JW 56B, JW 63, JW 67, RA 57, RA 64. |
| *HERBRAND* | JW 59, RA 59A. |
| *HOLLYWOOD* | PQ 18, QP 15. |
| *HONOMU* | PQ 17. |
| *HOOSIER* | PQ 17. |
| *HOPEMOUNT* | PQ 14, RA 51. |
| *HORACE BUSHNE* | JW 65. |
| *HORACE GRAY* | JW 54B, JW 63, RA 56. |
| *HUGH WILLIAMSON* | Op FB, RA 51. |
| *HYBERT* | PQ 16, QP 13. |
| | |
| *IDEFJORD* | JW 63, JW 65, RA 64. |
| *IJORA* | PQ 9, QP 2, QP 8. |
| *ILMEN* | QP 12. |
| *INDUNA* | PQ 13. |
| *IRONCLAD* | PQ 14, PQ 17, QP 10, QP 15. |
| *ISRAEL PUTNAM* | JW 53, RA 54A. |
| *IVARAN* | JW 67. |
| | |
| *J D YEAGER* | JW 63, RA 64. |
| *J L M CURRY* | JW 51A, RA 53. |
| *JAMES A FARRELL* | JW 55A, RA 56. |
| *JAMES BOWIE* | JW 53. |
| *JAMES GORDON BENNETT* | JW 54A, RA 55B. |
| *JAMES KERNEY* | JW 63, RA 64. |
| *JAMES M GILLIS* | JW 61, JW 65, RA 62, RA 66. |
| *JAMES SMITH* | JW 54A, JW 58, RA 55A, RA 59. |
| *JAMES WOODROW* | JW 55A, RA 56. |
| *JEFFERSON DAVIS* | JW 56A (to Iceland only), JW 57, RA 58. |
| *JEFFERSON MYERS* | JW 51B, RA 53. |
| *JOHN A DONALD* | JW 57, RA 58. |
| *JOHN A QUITMAN* | JW 56A, JW 57, JW 63, RA 58, RA 64. |
| *JOHN B LENNON* | JW 58, RA 59 |

| | |
|---|---|
| *JOHN CARVER* | JW 58, RA 59. |
| *JOHN DAVENPORT* | JW 58, RA 59. |
| *JOHN FITCH* | JW 54B, RA 56. |
| *JOHN GIBBON* | JW 62, JW 66, RA 63, RA 67. |
| *JOHN H B LATROBE* | Op FB, JW 51B, JW 56B, RA 53, RA 57. |
| *JOHN IRELAND* | JW 63, JW 67, RA 64. |
| *JOHN J ABEL* | JW 55B, JW 60, JW 64, RA 56, RA 61, RA 65. |
| *JOHN LA FARGE* | JW 56B, JW 59, JW 63, RA 57, RA 60, RA 64. |
| *JOHN LANGDON* | JW 57. |
| *JOHN LAURANCE* | JW 53. |
| *JOHN McDONOGH* | JW 58, JW 65, RA 59, RA 66. |
| *JOHN PENN* | PQ 18. |
| *JOHN RANDOLPH* | PQ 16, QP 13. |
| *JOHN RUTLEDGE* | JW 57, RA 58. |
| *JOHN SHARP WILLIAMS* | JW 57, JW 61, RA 58, RA 62. |
| *JOHN STEVENSON* | JW 57, RA 58. |
| *JOHN T HOLT* | JW 58, RA 59. |
| *JOHN VINING* | JW 55B, JW 60, RA 56, RA 61. |
| *JOHN W POWELL* | JW 57, RA 58. |
| *JOHN WITHERSPOON* | PQ 17. |
| *JOHN WALKER* | Op FB, RA 51. |
| *JOHN WANAMAKER* | JW 55B, JW 64, RA 56, RA 65. |
| *JOHN WOOLMAN* | JW 57, JW 60, RA 58, RA 61. |
| *JOSE MARTI* | JW 59, JW 63, RA 60, RA 64. |
| *JOSEPH E JOHNSTON* | JW 53. |
| *JOSEPH N NICOLLET* | JW 56A, JW 63, RA 59. |
| *JOSEPHINE SHAW LOWELL* | JW 59, RA 60. |
| *JOSHUA THOMAS* | JW 58, JW 60, JW 66, RA 59, RA 61, RA 67. |
| *JOSHUA W ALEXANDER* | JW 57, JW 60, JW 66, RA 58, RA 64. |
| *JOYCE KILMER* | JW 58, JW 61, JW 64, RA 59, RA 62, RA 65 |
| *JULIEN POYDRAS* | JW 58, JW 67, RA 59. |
| *JULIUS OLSEN* | JW 60, RA 61. |
| *JUNECREST* | JW 54A, RA 55A. |
| *JUTLAND* | PQ 7B, PQ 15, QP 7. |
| | |
| *KARA* | Op FB West. |
| *KEITH PALMER* | JW 61, JW 66, RA 62, RA 67. |
| *KENTUCKY* | PQ 18. |
| *KIEV* | QP 10. |
| *KINGSWOOD* | PQ 11, QP 9. |
| *KOMILES* | PQ 5, PQ 18, QP 13, QP 15, JW 53. |
| *KOMSOMOLETS ARCTIKI* | Op FB West. |
| *KONG HAAKON VII* | JW 66. |
| *KOTLIN* | RA 51. |
| *KRASNOE ZNAMYA* | Op FB West. |
| *KRASSIN* | PQ 15. |
| *KRONPRINSEN* | JW 66, RA 67. |
| *KUZBASS* | QP 3, QP 12, QP 13, Op FB West. |
| *KUZNETZ LESOV* | QP 15. |
| | |
| *LACKLAN* | JW 58, JW 63, JW 65, RA 59A, RA 63, RA 65. |
| *LAFAYETTE* | PQ 18, QP 15. |
| *LANCASTER* | PQ 15, OP 13. |
| *LANCASTER CASTLE* | PQ 12. |
| *LANCASTRIAN PRINCE* | DERVISH, QP 1. |
| *LAPLAND* | JW 55A, JW 61, RA 59. |
| *LARRANGA* | PQ 8, QP 8. |
| *LARS KRUSE* | PQ 13 (to Iceland only). |
| *LAURELWOOD* | JW 61, JW 62, JW 66, RA 61, RA 62, RA 67. |
| *LAWRENCE J BRENGLE* | JW 61, JW 65, RA 62, RA 66. |
| *LEBARON RUSSELL BRIGGS* | JW 63, RA 64. |
| *LEO J DUSTER* | JW 59, JW 65, RA 60, RA 66. |
| *LEWIS EMERY Jr* | JW 55A, JW 60, JW 64, RA 56, RA 61, RA 65. |
| *LINN BOYD* | JW 62, JW 66, RA 63, RA 67. |
| *LLANDAFF* | PQ 12, QP 9, JW 53, RA 54B. |

| | |
|---|---|
| *LLANSTEPHAN CASTLE* | DERVISH, QP 1. |
| *LONGWOOD* | JW 62, RA 63. |
| *LORCA* | PQ 1, QP 2. |
| *LORD DELAWARE* | JW 57, JW 66, RA 58, RA 67. |
| *LOUIS D BRANDEIS* | JW 57, RA 58. |
| *LOWTHER CASTLE* | PQ 11, PQ 16, QP 9. |
| *LUCERNA* | JW 55A, JW 57, JW 60, JW 64, RA 55B, RA 58, RA 61, RA 65. |
| *LUCULUS* | JW 59, JW 62, RA 59A, RA 62. |
| | |
| *MACBETH* | PQ 18. |
| *MAKAWAO* | PQ 11, QP 9. |
| *MANA* | PQ 13, QP 10. |
| *MANO* | PQ 13 (to Iceland only). |
| *MARATHON* | JW 53, JW 61, RA 54B, RA 62. |
| *MARIE M MELONEY* | JW 57, JW 64, RA 58, RA 65. |
| *MARY LUCKENBACH* | PQ 18. |
| *MARYLYN* | PQ 11, QP 9. |
| *MASSMAR* | PQ 16, QP 13. |
| *MAUNA KEA* | PQ 16, QP 13. |
| *MEANTICUT* | PQ 18, QP 15, RA 51. |
| *MICHIGAN* | PQ 16, QP 13. |
| *MIJDRECHT* | JW 54A, JW 57, RA 55A, RA 58. |
| *MINOTAUR* | PQ 14, PQ 16, QP 10, QP 14. |
| *MIRONYCH* | Op FB West. |
| *MOBILE CITY* | JW 53, RA 54A. |
| *MONTCALM* | PQ 15. |
| *MORMACMAR* | PQ 13, QP 11. |
| *MORMACREY* | PQ 15, QP 13. |
| *MORMACRIO* | PQ 14, PQ 15, QP 10, QP 12. |
| *MORMACSUL* | PQ 16. |
| *MORRIS HILLQUIT* | JW 58, RA 59. |
| *MOSSOVET* | PQ 4, QP 1, Op FB West, RA 53. |
| *MOUNT EVANS* | PQ 6, QP 13. |
| *MSTA* | Op FB West. |
| | |
| *NACELLA* | JW 59, JW 63, RA 60, RA 64. |
| *NATHAN TOWSON* | JW 57, JW 64, RA 58, RA 65. |
| *NATHANIEL ALEXANDER* | JW 56A, JW 57, JW 60, RA 58, RA 61. |
| *NATHANIEL GREENE* | PQ 18, QP 15. |
| *NAVARINO* | PQ 12, PQ 17, QP 10. |
| *NELSON W ALDRICH* | JW 62, JW 66, RA 63, RA 67. |
| *NEMAHA* | PQ 16, QP 13. |
| *NERITINA* | JW 60, JW 64, RA 61, RA 65. |
| *NEW WESTMINSTER CITY* | DERVISH, PQ 13, QP 1. |
| *NICHOLAS BIDDLE* | JW 58, JW 61, JW 65, RA 59, RA 62, RA 66 |
| *NICHOLAS GILMAN* | JW 52, RA 53. |
| *NOREG* | PQ 9, QP 8, JW 56A, JW 58, JW 60, JW 61, RA 56, RA 59, RA 60, RA 61. |
| *NORFJELL* | JW 63. |
| *NORLYS* | JW 54A, JW 55B, RA 54B, RA 56. |
| *NORTH KING* | PQ 1, PQ 11, QP 2, QP 9. |
| | |
| *OAKLEY WOOD* | JW 59, RA 60. |
| *OB* | Op FB West. |
| *OCEAN FAITH* | PQ 18, QP 15, JW 52, RA 53. |
| *OCEAN FREEDOM* | PQ 17, QP 14, JW 53. |
| *OCEAN GYPSY* | JW 55B, RA 56. |
| *OCEAN MESSENGER* | JW 55B, RA 56. |
| *OCEAN PRIDE* | JW 55B, RA 56. |
| *OCEAN STRENGTH* | JW 54B, JW 57, RA 55A, RA 58. |
| *OCEAN VALOUR* | JW 55B, RA 56. |
| *OCEAN VANITY* | JW 54A, RA 55A. |
| *OCEAN VERITY* | JW 54A, RA 55A. |
| *OCEAN VICEROY* | JW 55B, RA 56. |
| *OCEAN VOICE* | PQ 16, QP 14. |

| | |
|---|---|
| *OKHTA* | Op FB West, RA 51. |
| *OLIGARCH* | PQ 18, QP 14, JW 51A, JW 52, RA 51, RA 53. |
| *OLIVER ELLSWORTH* | PQ 18. |
| *OLOPANA* | PQ 17. |
| *OREGONIAN* | PQ 18. |
| *OREMAR* | JW 51A, RA 53. |
| *ORIENT CITY* | PQ 2, QP 3. |
| *OSMUSSAAR* | Op FB West. |
| *OWEN WISTER* | JW 62, JW 66, RA 53, RA 67. |
| *PAN ATLANTIC* | PQ 17. |
| *PAN KRAFT* | PQ 17. |
| *PARK BENJAMIN* | JW 61, JW 66, RA 62, RA 67. |
| *PARK HOLLAND* | JW 54A, RA 55A. |
| *PATRICK HENRY* | PQ 18, QP 15. |
| *PAUL H HARWOOD* | JW 63, RA 64. |
| *PAUL HAMILTON HAYNE* | JW 56B, RA 57 |
| *PAUL LUCKENBACH* | PQ 15, QP 12. |
| *PAULUS POTTER* | PQ 17. |
| *PENELOPE BARKER* | JW 56A. |
| *PETER KERR* | PQ 17. |
| *PETROVSKI* | PQ 5, PQ 18, QP 13, QP 15, JW 53. |
| *PHILIP F THOMAS* | JW 57, JW 63, JW 67, RA 58, RA 64. |
| *PHILIP LIVINGSTON* | JW 55A, RA 56, RA 57. |
| *PIERRE S DUPONT* | JW 58, RA 59 |
| *PIETER DE HOOGH* | PQ 14, PQ 16, QP 13, JW 53, RA 54B. |
| *PONTFIELD* | JW 51B, RA 54A. |
| *PRAVDA* | QP 9. |
| *PUERTO RICAN* | JW 51B, RA 53. |
| *QUEEN CITY* | PQ 2, QP 3. |
| *R NEY McNEELY* | JW 63, RA 64. |
| *RACELAND* | PQ 13 |
| *RALPH WALDO EMERSON* | JW 51B, RA 53. |
| *RATHLIN* | PQ 17, QP 14, JW 54B, JW 58, JW 59, JW 62, JW 67, RA 55A, RA 58, RA 60, RA 62, RA 67. |
| *RAYMOND B STEVENS* | JW 60, RA 61. |
| *RENALD FERNALD* | JW 62, JW 66, RA 63, RA 67. |
| *REIGH COUNT* | PQ 7B, QP 6. |
| *REVOLUTSIONER* | PQ 9, PQ 16, QP 3, QP 8, RA 51. |
| *RICHARD BASSETT* | JW 51A, RA 53. |
| *RICHARD HENRY LEE* | PQ 16, QP 13. |
| *RICHARD BLAND* | JW 51A, RA 53. |
| *RICHARD H ALVEY* | Op FB, JW 56A, RA 51, RA 57. |
| *RICHARD M JOHNSON* | JW 57, JW 60, RA 58, RA 61. |
| *RIVER AFTON* | PQ 1, PQ 13, PQ 17, QP 2, QP 10. |
| *ROALD AMUNDSEN* | JW 67. |
| *ROBERT EDEN* | JW 57, RA 59. |
| *ROBERT J COLLIER* | JW 57, JW 67, RA 58. |
| *ROBERT LOWRY* | JW 56B, JW 62, RA 57, RA 63. |
| *RODINA* | PQ 4, QP 1, QP 13. |
| *SAHALE* | PQ 18, QP 15. |
| *SAKKO* | Op FB West |
| *SAMANNAN* | JW 59, RA 60. |
| *SAMARITAN* | JW 60, JW 63, JW 66, RA 61, RA 64, RA 67 |
| *SAMCALIA* | JW 59, RA 60. |
| *SAMCONSTANT* | JW 59, RA 60. |
| *SAMGARA* | JW 59, RA 60. |
| *SAMIDWAY* | JW 59, RA 60. |
| *SAMLOYAL* | JW 59, RA 60. |
| *SAMLYTH* | JW 59, RA 60. |
| *SAMSUVA* | JW 59, RA 60. |
| *SAMTREDY* | JW 59, RA 60. |
| *SAMUEL CHASE* | PQ 17, QP 14. |
| *SAMUEL MACINTYRE* | JW 56B, JW 67, RA 57. |

| | |
|---|---|
| *SAN ADOLFO* | JW 54B, JW 56A, RA 55A, RA 57. |
| *SAN AMBROSIO* | PQ 3, QP 4, QP 5, JW 55A, JW 57, RA 55A, RA 57. |
| *SAN CIPRIANO* | JW 51A, RA 53. |
| *SAN CIRILO* | JW 56A, RA 57. |
| *SAN VENANCIO* | JW 61, JW 65, RA 62, RA 66. |
| *SCHOHARIE* | PQ 18, QP 15. |
| *SCYTHIA* | JW 61A, RA 61A. |
| *SCOTTISH AMERICAN* | PQ 13, QP 12. |
| *SEATTLE SPIRIT* | PQ 14, PQ 15, QP 12. |
| *SEVZAPLES* | PQ 12, QP 1, QP 10. |
| *SHCHORS* | PQ 16. |
| *SHEKSNA* | Op FB West. |
| *SHELON* | QP 9. |
| *SHILKA* | Op FB West. |
| *SILAS WEIR MITCHELL* | JW 59, JW 63, RA 60, RA 64. |
| *SILVER SWORD* | PQ 17, QP 14. |
| *SKIENSFJORD* | JW 64, RA 65. |
| *SOROKA* | Op FB West. |
| *SOUTHGATE* | PQ 8, PQ 15, QP 7, QP 12. |
| *ST CLEARS* | PQ 5, QP 13. |
| *ST OLAF* | PQ 18, QP 15. |
| *STAGE DOOR CANTEEN* | JW 55A, JW 61, JW 65, RA 56, RA 62, RA 66. |
| *STALINGRAD* | PQ 18, QP 7. |
| *STANTON H KING* | JW 62, RA 63. |
| *STARY BOLSHEVIK* | PQ 8, PQ 16, QP 1, QP 7, QP 13. |
| *STEEL WORKER* | PQ 16. |
| *STEPAN KHALTURIN* | PQ 11, QP 2, QP 9. |
| *STEPHEN LEACOCK* | JW 62, RA 63. |
| *STEVENSON TAYLOR* | JW 57, JW 62, JW 66, RA 58, RA 63, RA 67. |
| *STONE STREET* | PQ 12, QP 10, QP 11. |
| *SUKHONA* | PQ 4, PQ 14, PQ 18, QP 1, QP 4. |
| *SYRIAN PRINCE* | JW 61, RA 61. |
| *SYROS* | PQ 16. |
| *TBILISI* | PQ 9, PQ 18, QP 8, QP 15, JW 53. |
| *TEMPLE ARCH* | PQ 2, PQ 12, PQ 18, QP 3, QP 10, QP 15, JW 52, RA 53. |
| *TEXAS* | PQ 15, QP 12. |
| *THISTLEDALE* | JW 55A, RA 56. |
| *THOMAS DONALDSON* | JW 59, JW 65, RA 60. |
| *THOMAS H SUMNER* | JW 59, RA 60. |
| *THOMAS HARTLEY* | JW 53, JW 57, RA 54A, RA 58. |
| *THOMAS KEARNS* | JW 54B, RA 55A, RA 55B. |
| *THOMAS SCOTT* | JW 55A, JW 63, RA 56, RA 64. |
| *THOMAS SIM LEE* | JW 54A, JW 58, JW 67, RA 55A, RA 59. |
| *THOMAS U WALTER* | JW 55B, JW 60, RA 56, RA 61. |
| *THORSTEIN VEBLEN* | JW 56A, RA 57. |
| *TOBRUK* | PQ 13, QP 14, JW 53, RA 54A. |
| *TOPA TOPA* | PQ 15, QP 12. |
| *TOWNSEND HARRIS* | JW 58, JW 64, RA 59, RA 65. |
| *TREHATA* | DERVISH, PQ 5, PQ 14, QP 1, QP 4, QP 11. |
| *TREKIEVE* | PQ 3, QP 4. |
| *TREVORIAN* | PQ 9, QP 9. |
| *TROUBADOR* | PQ 17, QP 14. |
| *TSIOLKOVSKI* | QP 11. |
| *U.S.O.* | JW 62, RA 63. |
| *URITSKI* | Op FB West. |
| *VANZETTI* | Op FB West. |
| *VERMONT* | JW 51B, RA 53. |
| *VETLUGA* | Op FB West. |
| *VILLE D'ANVERS* | PQ 1, QP 2. |
| *VIRGINIA DARE* | PQ 18, QP 15. |
| *VOLGA* | RA 51. |

| | |
|---|---|
| *W R GRACE* | JW 58, JW 62, JW 65, RA 59A, RA 63, RA 66. |
| *WACOSTA* | PQ 18. |
| *WANSTEAD* | PQ 3, QP 4. |
| *WARREN DELANO* | JW 59, JW 63, RA 60, RA 64 |
| *WASHINGTON* | PQ 17. |
| *WAZIRISTAN* | PQ 7A. |
| *WEST CHESWALD* | PQ 14, QP 11. |
| *WEST GOTOMSKA* | PQ 14, PQ 17, QP 10, JW 51A, RA 53. |
| *WEST NILUS* | PQ 16, QP 14. |
| *WEST NOHNO* | PQ 9, QP 8. |
| *WHITE CLOVER* | PQ 18, QP 15. |
| *WILL ROGERS* | JW 55B, RA 56. |
| *WILLARD HALL* | JW 56B, JW 64, RA 57, RA 66. |
| *WILLIAM CLARK* | Op FB. |
| *WILLIAM D BYRON* | JW 58, JW 66, RA 59, RA 67. |
| *WILLIAM H WEBB* | JW 57, RA 58. |
| *WILLIAM H WILMER* | JW 62, RA 63. |
| *WILLIAM HOOPER* | PQ 17. |
| *WILLIAM L MARCY* | JW 54B, RA 55A. |
| *WILLIAM MATSON* | JW 58, RA 59. |
| *WILLIAM McKINLEY* | JW 58, RA 59. |
| *WILLIAM MOULTRIE* | PQ 18, QP 15, JW 58, RA 59. |
| *WILLIAM PEPPER* | JW 58, JW 61, JW 65, RA 59, RA 62, RA 66. |
| *WILLIAM S THAYER* | JW 58, RA 59. |
| *WILLIAM TYLER PAGE* | JW 56A, JW 62, JW 66, RA 57, RA 63, RA 67. |
| *WILLIAM WHEELWRIGHT* | JW 61, JW 65, RA 62, RA 66. |
| *WILLIAM WINDOM* | JW 54A, RA 55A. |
| *WIND RUSH* | JW 51A, RA 52. |
| *WINFRED L SMITH* | JW 56B, JW 61, JW 65, RA 57, RA 62, RA 66. |
| *WINSTON-SALEM* | PQ 17, QP 14. |
| *WOODBRIDGE N FERRIS* | JW 56A, JW 62, JW 66, RA 57, RA 63, RA 67. |
| | |
| *YAKA* | PQ 14, QP 13. |
| *YELNA* | Op FB West. |
| *YORKMAR* | JW 51B, RA 53. |
| | |
| *ZAAFARAN* | PQ 17, |
| *ZAMALEK* | PQ 6, PQ 17, QP 14, JW 60, RA 60. |
| *ZEBULON B VANCE* | PQ 15, QP 12. |